TOPICS ON THE AUSTRALIAN ECONOMY
Editor: Professor J. E. ISAAC
Faculty of Economics and Politics, Monash University

TWENTIETH CENTURY ECONOMIC
DEVELOPMENT IN AUSTRALIA

TWENTIETH CENTURY ECONOMIC DEVELOPMENT IN AUSTRALIA

E. A. BOEHM

Reader in Economics
University of Melbourne

LONGMAN

Longman Australia Pty Limited
Camberwell Victoria Australia

*Associated companies, branches and representatives
throughout the world*

Copyright © Longman Australia Pty Limited 1971
First published 1971

ISBN 0 582 68405 6 *(paper)*
           68410 2 *(cased)*

*Cover illustrations by courtesy of the La Trobe Library, The Broken Hill
Proprietary Co. Ltd., and the B.H.P. Oil and Gas Division.*

*Type set by Dudley E. King Linotypers Pty Ltd
Printed in Hong Kong by Peninsula Press Ltd*

CONTENTS

Chapter	Page
1 Introducton	1
2 The Record of Economic Growth	12
3 Population	37
4 The Export Industries	66
5 Capital Accumulation	96
6 The Development of Manufacturing Industry	123
7 Institutional Developments	159
8 Living Standards	200
9 Economic Strategy	213
List of Tables	239
List of Charts	242
Index	243

EDITOR'S PREFACE

Dr Boehm's book is the second in a series aimed at providing a range of specialized and concise studies of various aspects of the Australian economy. Because of the limit on length, it is not intended that these books will be exhaustive in scope. Rather, each will attempt to deal in some depth with the more important issues affecting the economy.

These books will be concerned mainly with applied economics but, wherever necessary, the theoretical basis of applied and policy matters will be advanced to ensure that arguments are analysed with sufficient rigour.

This series is designed particularly for Australian undergraduates embarking on specialist courses after a year of studying general economic principles. The comprehensive text books normally used in these courses do not deal adequately, if at all, with the special features of Australian institutions, problems, and experiences. In focusing more directly on these matters, this series should provide a useful complement to the basic texts. While primarily designed with this object in view, happily Dr Boehm's treatment of his subject makes his book suitable for economics courses at schools and at institutes of technology.

Although these studies assume some familiarity with elementary economic terms and principles, it is hoped that they will also be comprehensible and of interest to the general reader.

March 1971   J. E. Isaac

PREFACE

My objective in this book is to provide, for students and the general reader, a critical review of the growth characteristics and performance of the Australian economy. Attention is concentrated on Australia's growth record and cyclical fluctuations, the key ingredients of growth and their interrelationships, and institutional changes. These changes have been made to help to realize the objectives of economic policy, for example achievement of the desired rate of economic growth at full employment with rising living standards. The recent growth performance of an economy, the on-going character of its development, its current and future strengths and weaknesses, and the requirements of economic policy can be much clarified when viewed in historical perspective.

A book of such limited size as this on such a vast and interesting subject may suffer from restrictions of space on any one matter. Selected references are given in some of the footnotes to sources where particular aspects are discussed more fully. Suggestions for further reading are also provided at the end of each chapter.

I am most grateful to a number of people who have assisted me in the writing of this book. I particularly wish to thank: Dr D. S. Iron-monger and Miss Daina Bremanis for assistance in computer programming; Miss Joyce Wood for her expert drawing of the charts; and Professor W. Prest, Professor G. Blainey, and Mr A. H. Boxer for reading and supplying helpful comments on parts of the book.

I must especially acknowledge the many valuable suggestions and criticisms of Mr A. Gregory on the whole draft of the book. I am much indebted to Professor J. E. Isaac for valuable advice in planning the book and very helpful criticisms on the whole manuscript. I also must thank a number of students and others in public life with whom I have had the benefit of discussing, and learning more about, some of the issues raised in this book. Finally, to my wife, Dorothy, I owe a special debt of gratitude for her continued help during the writing of this book.

June 1970   E.A.B.

Chapter 1

INTRODUCTION

1 THE WIDESPREAD INTEREST IN ECONOMIC DEVELOPMENT

The study of economic development has been at the forefront of economic thought since World War II. However, this concern with development is not new, for the modern study, for rich and poor countries alike, owes much to Adam Smith's classic, *An Inquiry into the Nature and Causes of the Wealth of Nations* (published in 1776). This has been a continuing influence on enquiries by economists into the reasons why some countries are rich and others are poor, and why countries develop at varying rates. What is largely new since World War II is the considerable attention given in practically all countries to economic development and growth as a major objective of government policy. This reflects the widespread acceptance of the view by businessmen and policy-makers, as well as by academic economists, that the government has a vital role to play in the level of economic activity and in the progress of society. Furthermore, it is now more fully recognized that growth is a joint responsibility of countries, for their economies are interdependent to some extent. Thus a major purpose of economic policy is how to achieve a desired rate of economic development and growth.

The arguments for growth were given prominence by the Vernon Committee [1]. The Committee discussed the Commonwealth Government's seven declared economic objectives of 'a high rate of economic and population growth with full employment, increasing productivity, rising standards of living, external viability and stability of costs and prices'[2] From these objectives the Committee selected economic growth as 'the central objective to which the other stated objectives should be related'[3].

The Committee summarized the national, social, and economic arguments in support of their emphasis on 'the importance of growth as a national policy objective for Australia' thus:

---

1 In Commonwealth of Australia, *Report of the Committee of Economic Enquiry*, hereafter referred to as *Vernon Report*, 1965, Vols I and II. See especially Vol. I, Chap. 2.
2 *Ibid*, p. 28.
3 *Ibid*.

'Growth provides the means of raising living standards and of promoting national security. Growth is self-generating. It stimulates enterprise, encourages innovation and provides a constant spur to technical and managerial efficiency. Moreover, a growing economy facilitates economic and social mobility; economic mobility, because changes in the pattern of industry can occur through the flow of new recruits to the work force and the flow of new investment; social mobility, because economic expansion widens the range of opportunities to enterprising and imaginative members of the community. Growth endows the community with a sense of vigour and social purpose[4].'

In this context the Committee approved Adam Smith's conclusion that

'the progressive state is in reality the cheerful and the hearty state to all the different orders of the society. The stationary is dull; the declining, melancholy[5].'

Thus the Committee asserted that growth provides benefits through non-material elements as well as through increases in goods and services. Growth 'gives man greater control over his environment and thereby increases his freedom'[6]. It also enables man to pursue cultural and scientific activities, the latter thereby increasing the potential for economic growth. At the national level an economy such as the Australian, in growing bigger and richer, benefits not only itself, but also the world economy, providing better markets, relying less on capital inflow, and contributing ultimately to the international flow of capital and the provision of aid to less developed countries. In short, both economic and non-economic arguments account for the widespread interest in the development of an economy.

2 THE MEANING AND SOURCES OF ECONOMIC DEVELOPMENT AND GROWTH

The words 'development' and 'growth' are mostly used synonymously in this study. However, in some respects, 'development' means more that what is conveyed by 'growth'. So it is helpful to begin by stating briefly the meaning and sources of economic growth.

The total production of an economy depends on the size of its labour force, its stock of capital equipment, its natural resources, and the efficiency with which these factors of production are combined. Its rate of growth is determined by the rates at which the quantity

---

4 *Ibid.*
5 *Ibid*, as quoted from Adam Smith, *The Wealth of Nations*, J. M. Dent, 1931, Vol. I, p. 72.
6 *Vernon Report*, Vol. I, p. 29, as quoted from W. A. Lewis, *The Theory of Economic Growth*, Allen & Unwin, 1955, p. 421.

and quality of these factors increase. The three main sources of increase in factor supplies are: (i) population growth which provides an increase in the amount of labour that can be productively employed; (ii) capital accumulation which the community undertakes by saving part of its income and investing it in machines, equipment, and buildings[7]; and (iii) technological progress whereby new and better techniques of production are introduced. These three sources of growth are examined in detail in this book.

The term 'development' implies not only more output, labour, capital, trade, and so on, but also changes in attitudes[8] and institutions, which accompany and in turn produce economic growth. In brief, the widespread desire for development includes many other elements besides the measurable product[9].

3 PROBLEMS OF MEASURING GROWTH

The growth of the Australian economy may be measured in various ways: (i) the aggregate of all goods and services produced, for which purpose the official estimate of gross national product at constant prices (real G.N.P.) has become the conventional indicator of the growth of the economy; (ii) real income per head of population, which provides a standard of living approach[10]; and (iii) real G.N.P. per worker, which is a productivity approach. The increase in G.N.P. per head or per worker is the main dynamic element in the process

---

7 For a fuller definition of capital, see p. 96 below.

8 The complexity of the issues in this respect was well summed up by W. A. Lewis thus: 'The most difficult problem in consistency is to explain why people hold the beliefs they do. Economic growth depends on attitudes to work, to wealth, to thrift, to having children, to invention, to strangers, to adventure, and so on, and all these attitudes flow from deep springs in the human mind. There have been attempts to explain why these attitudes vary from one community to another. One can look to differences in religion, but this is merely to restate the problem, since it raises the question why the particular religion holds these particular tenets, and why it has been accepted in this particular place and not elsewhere. Or one can look to differences in natural environment, in climate, in race, or, failing all else, in the accidents of history. The experienced sociologist knows that these questions are unanswerable, certainly in our present state of knowledge, and probably for all time. . . . We can say a fair amount about consistency between institutions and economic growth, and a fair amount about the relationship between attitudes and institutions; but when we come to explore the attitudes themselves, how they emerge, and why they change, we reach sooner or later to the limits of our understanding of human history.' Lewis, *op. cit.*, pp. 14–15.

9 For a comprehensive study of the problems of economic development within the wide setting of the various disciplines, taking into account cultural background and religious beliefs, political structures and social institutions, and demographic and economic factors, see Gunnar Myrdal, *Asian Drama: An Inquiry Into the Poverty of Nations*, Vols I, II, and III, Pantheon, 1968.

10 See p. 201 below.

of growth and in determining the way in which people work and live.

Most countries established an official system of 'social or national accounting' during or immediately after World War II, providing an integrated picture of income and expenditure flows of different sectors of the economy, and of the economy as a whole[11]. Despite practical problems of measurement[12], the quality of the official estimates of real G.N.P. of Australia used in Chart 1[13] for the years from 1948-9 to 1968-9 is very high[14]. (The same may generally be said of the official series at current prices which begins at 1938-9.)

However, the privately estimated series shown in the chart for the years up to 1938-9 are only very rough indicators of the actual level of economic activity and the rate of economic growth, and must be interpreted with caution. This applies particularly for detailed short-run (cyclical) analysis. On the other hand, for longer-term (secular) analysis, it seems that the actual underlying trend in total production up to 1938-9 is approximately indicated by the two independent estimates of real national product shown in Chart 1. The trend of both series is roughly similar and generally fits the impressions obtained from other leading statistical indicators. Thus one may reasonably assume that inaccuracies in measurement and omissions from both series do not mean any significant distortions as far as obtaining at least a broad picture of the changing pace of growth of the Australian economy.

Another problem concerns the measurement of productivity in terms of output per unit of input. The combination of the factors of production is always heterogeneous. The input of capital is especially difficult to measure. And the weather, always important in Australia's rural sector, is very difficult to assess. It is usually simpler to relate output to labour. Productivity can be measured in terms of output per man-hour or output per worker, but there are virtually no statistics of the number of man-hours worked each year in Australia. Thus we follow the common practice and measure labour productivity (or 'national productivity' as it is also called) in terms of real G.N.P. per worker.

---

11 See R. I. Downing, *National Income and Social Accounts: An Australian Study*, 12th edn, M.U.P., 1969.

12 For a detailed discussion of the statistical and conceptual difficulties, see: Commonwealth of Australia, *Supplement to the Treasury Information Bulletin: The Meaning and Measurement of Growth*, November 1964; and *Vernon Report*, Vol. II, App. A.

13 Chart 1 and Charts 2, 5, 6, 8, and 9 are presented in the form of a semi-logarithmic graph in which equal upward or downward movements signify equal percentage changes not absolute changes.

14 Problems of international comparisons are discussed on pp. 30–5 and 118–21 below.

CHART 1
ESTIMATES OF NATIONAL PRODUCT AT CURRENT AND CONSTANT(a)
PRICES, AUSTRALIA, 1900–1 TO 1968–9
(Ratio Chart)

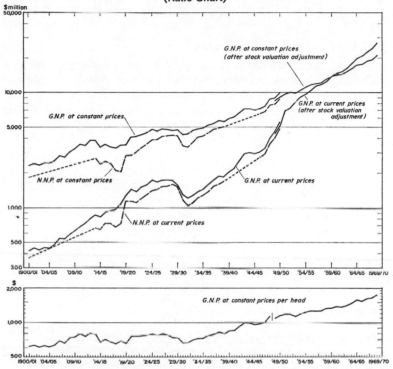

(a) At average 1959–60 prices.

Sources: N. G. Butlin, *Australian Domestic Product, Investment and Foreign Borrowing, 1861 1938/39,* C.U.P., 1962; N. G. Butlin, *Investment in Australian Economic Development 1861–1900,* C.U.P., 1964; C. Clark, *The Conditions of Economic Progress,* Macmillan, 3rd edn, 1957; Commonwealth Bureau of Census and Statistics, *Australian National Accounts,* 1967–8, pp. 28–29, *National Income and Expenditure 1968–69, Official Year Book of the Commonwealth of Australia,* No. 54, 1968, p. 1268, *Demography Bulletin* (various issues), and *Labour Report,* No. 52, 1965 and 1966, p. 35.

4 GENERAL BACKGROUND

(a) Population Growth

Australia's rate of economic development from the establishment of the British convict settlement in Sydney in 1788 is partly illustrated by her population growth, as shown in Chart 2. The population had reached about 400,000 by the mid-nineteenth century, and 3.8 million at Federation in 1901. In 1970 the population passed the 12 million mark. Throughout, the population has remained predominantly European. The subject of population is discussed in more detail in Chapter 3.

(b) The Structure of the Economy

From the beginning Australia's growth centred on the dynamic influence of leading primary exports. Land is Australia's greatest natural resource. Exploitation of land has dominated exports (initially

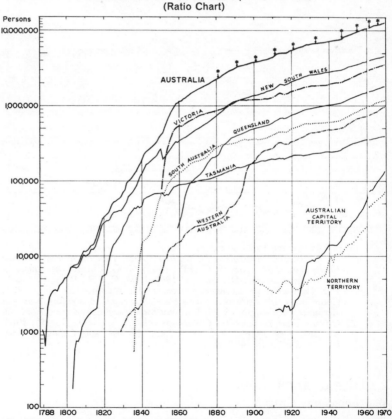

CHART 2
POPULATION OF AUSTRALIA, 1788 TO 1969
(Ratio Chart)

Sources: Commonwealth Bureau of Census and Statistics, *Official Year Book of the Commonwealth of Australia*, No. 54, 1968, p. 118 and *Monthly Review of Business Statistics*, May 1970, p. 2.

for the production of wool and, later in the nineteenth century, also for wheat, meat, and butter). Minerals have also played an important role, notably gold. In fact, after wool had been Australia's biggest export for two decades from the early 1830s, gold held this position for two decades from the early 1850s following the gold discoveries in 1851 in N.S.W. and Victoria. The gold boom during the 1850s greatly boosted immigration, and by 1860 Australia's population had reached 1·15 million, thus nearly trebling during the golden decade. Wool again became Australia's leading export in 1871, and held this position strongly at most times until the late 1960s when Australia reached a new stage of strength with mineral discoveries and their exploitation. In fact, mineral exports will probably exceed wool exports from the early 1970s by a significant and increasing margin.

The continued importance of primary production during the first half of the twentieth century is clearly shown in Table 1. It is instructive to present this table here, for it shows, for selected years from 1900-1, the changing composition and relative size of industrial groups in the Australian economy, as indicated by their contribution to G.N.P. The analysis in this book is much concerned with the changes in the combination and relative importance of the products which have comprised the growing output of the Australian economy. We are also interested in the associated shifts of labour between industries, a subject which is examined in Chapter 3.

Remember the data used to compute the figures in Table 1 for the period 1900-1 to 1938-9, as previously remarked for Chart 1, may be regarded as only very approximate and are not strictly comparable with the data for the years from 1948-9 onwards. Nevertheless, the data seem to be sufficiently reliable to indicate broadly the trends in the relative importance of each group.

Table 1 shows that primary production remained Australia's most important industry sector through to 1938-9. Meanwhile, the output of manufacturing industry had advanced considerably. Since World War II manufacturing has been the most important industry group (except briefly in 1950-1 when, with the Korean War, there was a considerable boom in the prices of strategic commodities, in particular of wool).

The importance of manufacturing since World War II marks Australia as one of the most highly industrialized countries in the world. This may be seen from Table 2, which compares the size of the manufacturing sector in Australia with that in major countries and other smaller industrialized countries. The table also shows for each country the relative contribution to G.N.P. of primary production, mining, and the tertiary industries.

TABLE 1
GROSS NATIONAL PRODUCT AT FACTOR COST BY INDUSTRY OF ORIGIN, AUSTRALIA,
SELECTED YEARS, 1900-1 TO 1967-8

Year	Primary production	Mining	Manufacturing	Public business undertakings	Construction	Private water transport	Distribution	Government services	Other services	Finance	Unallocated items	House rents	Total value
	1	2	3	4	5	6	7	8	9	10	11	12	13
	Percentage of total												$m
1900-1	19.3	10.3	12.1	4.9	7.0	1.8	15.1	3.4	13.8	1.9	0.3	10.1	382
1913-4	23.5	5.1	13.4	5.2	9.9	1.3	16.3	3.7	12.0	1.6	0.3	7.7	830
1919-20	23.5	3.0	13.5	5.3	9.8	1.3	19.2	3.8	11.6	1.8	0.3	6.7	1,161
1928-9	21.2	1.8	16.7	6.1	8.5	1.3	17.5	4.5	11.0	2.1	0.5	8.7	1,607
1938-9	19.5	3.3	18.5	5.4	6.6	0.9	18.8	4.8	10.7	2.5	0.5	8.5	1,697

Year	Primary production	Mining and quarrying	Manufacturing	Electricity, gas and water supply	Building and construction	Transport and communication	Commerce	Public administration (n.e.i.) and defence	Community and business services (incl. professional)	Finance and property	All other industries	Ownership of dwellings	
	Percentage of total												$m
1948-9	21.3	2.5	26.2	1.9	6.0	7.3	15.3	3.7	4.8	2.4	4.6	4.0	4,031
1950-1	29.0	2.1	23.7	1.5	6.3	6.3	14.7	3.2	4.2	2.2	4.0	2.7	6,583
1955-6	15.9	2.3	28.0	2.4	7.8	7.6	15.7	4.2	5.8	2.5	4.2	3.6	9,483
1960-1	13.0	1.9	28.5	3.2	7.9	8.3	14.8	3.8	6.8	3.2	4.3	4.4	13,062
1965-6	10.5	1.9	28.5	3.5	8.6	8.2	14.2	4.1	7.8	3.2	4.2	5.3	18,538
1966-7	11.4	2.0	28.0	3.4	8.3	8.1	13.9	4.3	7.8	3.3	4.2	5.3	20,384
1967-8	8.5	2.2	28.4	3.5	8.4	8.4	14.5	4.5	8.1	3.4	4.5	5.5	21,612

Sources: 1900-1 to 1938-9, computed from data in N. G. Butlin, *Australian Domestic Product, Investment and Foreign Borrowing, 1861-1938/39*, p. 11; and 1948-9 to 1967-8, computed from data in Commonwealth Bureau of Census and Statistics, *Australian National Accounts* (various issues).

TABLE 2

COMPOSITION OF G.N.P. AT FACTOR COST(a) BY INDUSTRY OF ORIGIN, SELECTED COUNTRIES, 1950 TO 1960(b)

(Per cent)

Country	Primary production	Mining and quarrying	Manufacturing	Tertiary		All industries
				Construction, utilities, transport, and communications	All other	
	1	2	3	4	5	6
(A) Major countries						
Japan	21·0	2·5	26·3	13·5	36·7	100·0
U.S.A.	5·7	1·7	30·7	13·7	48·2	100·0
Canada	10·6	4·1	27·4	17·5	40·4	100·0
West Germany(e)	9·7	5·4(d)	37·9	13·6	33·4	100·0
Italy	22·9	1·1	32·5	14·5	29·0	100·0
United Kingdom	5·1	3·3	36·8	16·7	38·1	100·0
France(c)	12·2	2·2	38·0	13·0	34·6	100·0
(B) Smaller industrialized countries						
Denmark	17·7	0·3	28·4	18·1	35·5	100·0
Australia(e)	15·2	2·0	29·4	19·2	34·2	100·0
Sweden(f)	3·0	2·0	38·0	10·0	42·0(g)	100·0
Norway	13·3	1·1	27·5	26·9	31·2	100·0
Netherlands(h)	12·5	2·2	29·8	17·7	37·8	100·0
Belgium	3·1	4·1	34·9	17·3	35·6	100·0

Notes: (a) Except for Japan and the United States, where net national product was used, and France, where gross national product at market prices was used.

(b) Average of 1950–1 and 1959–60, except where otherwise indicated.

(c) Average of 1950–1 and 1958–9.

(d) Utilities included in mining.

(e) Average 1953–4 to 1961–2.

(f) Two-year average of 1952–3 and 1954–5.

(g) Including transportation.

(h) Average of 1950–1 and 1957–8.

Source: *Vernon Report*, Vol. II, Table D.14, p. 558, reorganized into major countries and smaller industrialized countries.

(c) Climate and Geography

Geographic factors have strongly influenced Australia's economic development throughout her history. Australia is comparatively a dry, hot continent and, apart from any mineral exploitation, with present technology, much of it has limited possibilities for development. Just over a third of the continent is arid; another third is semi-arid and is unlikely to support more than a sparse population of pastoralists.

Several major factors combined from the outset to make Australia ideally suited to the large-scale production for export of a few key staples. These factors were: (i) the long distances in Australia between points of economic importance with only a sparse population in between; (ii) the relatively small domestic market; (iii) the climate and vegetation; (iv) the lack of major internal rivers; and (v) the isolation from the main world markets — in particular, from Britain and Europe — and hence the cost disadvantages in international trade.

Topographically and climatically the Australian continent has discouraged the close settlement of population other than around the coast and (with Australia's dependence on exports and imports) near the city ports. The population is concentrated predominantly in the fertile crescent of the south and east and in the south-west tip of the continent. In these regions, more favoured with climate and vegetation, intensive agricultural and pastoral development, notably wheat farming and merino sheep and beef cattle grazing, began during the 1860s and 1870s. Then during the 1870s and 1880s large areas of the relatively drier interior of N.S.W. and Queensland were opened up for extensive sheep and cattle grazing[15]. This development, aided by improved technology, was stimulated by the growing demand for wool and meat in Britain and Europe.

5 THE SUBJECT MATTER

In this book an analytical approach has been preferred to a chronological study, but the latter is used for particular aspects. The book reviews Australia's development in two ways: (i) by comparing the growth performance of the economy as a whole and of individual sectors in different periods; and (ii) by comparing leading sectors with each other during the same period. It also provides a study of the essential ingredients of growth, and of the economic institutions and policies that have provided the link from one period to another, thus contributing to growth's on-going character. Though the story

---

15 See N. G. Butlin, *Investment in Australian Economic Development*, Chap. II.

is concerned with the twentieth century, attention is given to earlier development and experiences in Australia where these assist in explaining development during the present century.

It is important for Australians to understand the growth characteristics and performance of their own economy, and helpful to know why growth has happened at the rate and in the manner it has during previous periods. This knowledge should contribute towards an understanding of the costs of economic growth[16], the efforts required to achieve continued growth, and the extent to which Australians may expect it to be steady-state growth at full employment. This study should also assist in answering the major question of how to choose the appropriate strategy for future development in order to achieve the desired balance between the required increase in material welfare and the preservation of the environment along with the improvements being sought in the quality of life.

Suggestions for further reading

Andrews, J. *Australia's Resources and Their Utilisation*, University of Sydney, revised edn, 1970;

Arndt, H. W. *A Small Rich Industrial Country: Studies in Australian Development, Aid and Trade*, Cheshire, 1968;

Blainey, G. *The Tyranny of Distance*, Sun Books, 1966;

Karmel, P. H. and Brunt, M. *The Structure of the Australian Economy*, Cheshire, 1966;

Samuelson, P. A., Hancock, K., and Wallace, R. *Economics: Australian edition*, McGraw-Hill, 1970;

Shaw, A. G. L. *The Economic Development of Australia*, Longman, 1970;

Commonwealth of Australia, *Supplement to the Treasury Information Bulletin: The Meaning and Measurement of Growth*, November 1964;

Vernon Report, Vol. I, Chaps 2 and 3, and Vol. II, Apps A, B, and D.

---

16 For a critical study of the view that there has been an 'obsessive concern with economic growth', see E. J. Mishan, *The Costs of Economic Growth*, Staples Press, 1967.

Chapter 2

THE RECORD OF ECONOMIC GROWTH

The problems of development and migration . . . are linked together inseparably. We cannot develop unless we have more population, and we cannot absorb more migrants unless we develop. (Prime Minister, Mr S. M. Bruce (later Lord) in Second Reading Speech of the 'Development and Migration Bill'. Source: Commonwealth of Australia, Parliamentary Debates, Vol. 113, 1926, p. 2464.)

The additional demand for capital caused by heavy immigration [since World War II] has been one reason why it would have been difficult for Australia to have managed without internal saving being supplemented by capital inflow . . . . This is nothing new in Australia; it is a continuation of its historical type of 'development and immigration' programme in which men and money alike have come from overseas. (Vernon Report, Vol. I, May 1965, p. 68.)

1 INTRODUCTION

There are three objectives in this chapter: first, to identify as far as possible the general growth path of the Australian economy, noting in particular the rate of economic growth, the major changes in this rate, the timing of these changes, and their connection with irregular and episodic causes (such as wars and droughts) and with systematic influences such as the trade cycle; secondly, to examine the strong historical interrelationship between the rates of economic growth, immigration, and capital inflow; and thirdly, to compare Australia's growth performance with those of other countries.

Throughout the chapter the growth of the Australian economy is viewed on a broad canvas with the aid of statistical estimates of key aggregate economic variables. This will set the stage for a more detailed study in the following chapters of the main ingredients of growth in the different sectors of the economy and of the accompanying institutional changes.

2 GENERAL OUTLINE OF AUSTRALIA'S GROWTH EXPERIENCE

Australia's growth experience can be described, at least broadly, in terms of two kinds of economic change which are themselves closely related. First, during most of the period there have been relatively short fluctuations in the level of economic activity (or national product), generally varying from 2 to 5 years' duration. In fact, this has been the main trade cycle over the last 100 years or so[1].

Secondly, this trade cycle has occurred against the background of a secular upward trend in national product. The uptrend has itself not been steady, but has fluctuated unevenly, reflecting the trade cycle as well as irregular and episodic causes. An indication of the general amplitude and duration of the major cyclical and trend fluctuations is provided by Chart 1. As previously mentioned, allowance must be made for the imperfections of the statistics.

Another way of illustrating the changing rate of economic growth is to compute the average annual rates of change in real G.N.P.[2] for selected successive sub-periods. This is done in Tables 3 and 4[3]. In choosing the successive sub-periods in both Tables, consideration was given primarily to the changes in the general trend of G.N.P. indicated in Chart 1, but also to the changes in the other variables presented in the Tables. There is thus some element of arbitrariness about the periods, but they serve the purpose of showing approximately the fluctuations in the secular uptrend. The terminal years of some periods overlap to allow for cyclical and irregular influences on the variables, in particular on G.N.P.

Inclusion of the period 1861 to 1900 in Tables 3 and 4 highlights the important historical fact that *long* periods of rapid, sustained economic growth in Australia have been periods not only of high rates of population growth through both immigration and natural increase, but also of considerable capital inflow. Two periods which are outstanding in these respects are the long upswing extending over three decades from about 1861 to 1891 and the long upswing which began about 1939, at the start of World War II, and is still continuing. Both these periods stand out from the intervening five decades when the

---

1 For a more detailed explanation of the meaning of 'trade cycle' see E. A. Boehm, 'Economic Fluctuations', in A. H. Boxer (ed.), *Aspects of the Australian Economy*, 2nd edn, M.U.P., 1969, pp. 41 and 43. 'In using the word "cycle", we are not implying that the fluctuations to which it refers occur with a definite regularity or periodicity. These are attributes of the term "cycle" in mathematics and physics. In economics it does not matter whether there is a cycle or not in the strict sense. The important thing is that economics do seem inherently to experience recurring cycles or fluctuations in the level of economic activity.' *Ibid*, p. 41.

2 The references to G.N.P. in the remainder of this chapter are to the estimates at constant prices (as used for Chart 1 and Table 3), unless otherwise indicated.

3 The average annual rates of increase which are expressed as percentages in Tables 3 and 4 have, except where otherwise indicated, been computed by fitting a straight line trend to the logarithms of the statistics for all the years in the selected period by the method of least squares.

TABLE 3

AVERAGE ANNUAL RATES OF INCREASE IN REAL G.N.P., POPULATION, EMPLOYMENT, AND PRODUCTIVITY; AND AVERAGE ANNUAL CAPITAL INFLOW AND IMPORT SURPLUS, AUSTRALIA, SELECTED PERIODS, 1861 TO 1968–9

Period	Real G.N.P. (at average 1959–60 prices) (1) %	Population — Natural increase (2) %	Population — Net migration (3) %	Population — Total (4) %	Number in work (5) %	G.N.P. per head of population (1–4) (6) %	G.N.P. per worker (1–5) (7) %	Net capital inflow (8) $m	Import surplus (9) $m
1861–70	5·2	2·7	1·2	3·9		1·3		8	9
1871–80	5·6	2·1	1·0	3·1		2·5		14	5
1881–90	4·3	2·1	1·5	3·6		0·7		34	4
1891–1900	1·4	1·7	0·1	1·8		−0·4		12	17
1900/01–1910/11	4·2	1·5[b]	0·1[b]	1·6[b]		2·6		−4	−34
1910/11–1913/14	3·7	1·7	1·3	3·0		0·7		17	−13
1913/14–1918/19	−1·8	1·5[c]	—[c]	1·5[c]	−2·0	−3·3	0·2	57	17
1919/20–1927/28	3·5	1·4[d]	0·7[d]	2·1[d]	2·9	1·4	0·6	49	−15
1928/29–1931/32	−3·1	1·0	—	1·0	−6·4	−4·1	3·3	69	−15
1932/33–1938/39	3·4	0·8	0·1	0·9	5·4	2·5	−2·0	17	−59
1939/40–1947/48	4·0	1·1	0·1	1·2	1·6	2·8	2·4	−14	−98
1948/49–1953/54	3·7	1·4	1·2	2·6	1·6	1·1	2·1	77	−41
1953/54–1962/63	4·1	1·4	0·8	2·2	1·8	1·9	2·3	307	88
1962/63–1968/69	5·1	1·1	0·8	1·9	2·6	3·2	2·5	708	341

Notes: (a) Gaps indicate that data are not available.

(b) The population figures in columns 2–4 for the periods from 1900–01 apply to the calendar years ended six months later than the period shown.

(c) 1913/14–1919/20 in order to eliminate as far as possible the effects of troop movements.

(d) 1920/21–1927/28 for reason given in previous note.

(e) Columns 1 and 5 are from trends fitted by least squares, and columns 2 to 4 from average of annual rates of change.

Sources: See p. 15.

TABLE 4
AVERAGE ANNUAL RATES OF GROWTH IN G.N.P., TOTAL POPULATION,
AND G.N.P. PER HEAD, AUSTRALIA, SELECTED PERIODS,
1861 TO 1968–9
(Per cent)

Period	Real G.N.P.	Population	G.N.P. per head
	1	2	3
1861–1891	4·9	3·4	1·5
1891–1938/9	2·3	1·7	0·6
1938/9–1968/9	4·3	2·0	2·3
1948/9–1968/9	4·4	2·2	2·2
1900/01–1928/9	2·7	1·9	0·8
1900/01–1938/9	2·2	1·8	0·4
1900/01–1968/9	3·1	1·7	1·4
1861–1968/9	3·0	2·0	1·0

Sources: As for Table 3.

rate of advance was very slow and more irregular, reflecting in particular the deep depressions in the 1890s and 1930s and the stagnation of the Australian economy during World War I. It will be convenient to compare briefly the economic experience during World Wars I and II before describing in more detail the trade cycle and the longer-run fluctuations in the upward trend.

3 CONTRASTING INCIDENCE OF WORLD WARS I AND II

During World War I G.N.P. contracted and then stagnated, while World War II ushered in a new period of rapid expansion. The fall in G.N.P. in 1914–5 was partly caused by the severe drought of that year. This greatly reduced rural output, notably wheat production, and was bad for trade in general. Dry conditions also adversely affected the harvests of 1918–9 and 1919–20. Another major factor underlying the fall in output in 1914–5 and the stagnation during the remaining years of World War I was the sharp decline in the number

Sources for Table 3: Computed from data in: N. G. Butlin, *Australian Domestic Product*, pp. 33–4; N. G. Butlin, *Investment in Australian Economic Development*, p. 453; C. Clark, *The Conditions of Economic Progress*, pp. 90–1; R. Wilson, *Capital Imports and the Terms of Trade*, M.U.P., 1931, pp. 30–1; N.S.W., *Votes and Proceedings*, 1894, 'Introduction and Withdrawal of Capital', Vol I, pp. 1041–5; T. A. Coghlan, *Seven Colonies of Australasia* (various issues); Commonwealth Bureau of Census and Statistics, *Demography Bulletin, Balance of Payments, Quarterly Summary of Australian Statistics, Australian National Accounts, Census of the Commonwealth of Australia*, and *Employment and Unemployment*, (various issues of each); Commonwealth of Australia, *National Income and Expenditure 1968–69*, p. 16; E. A. Boehm, *Prosperity and Depression in Australia 1887–1897*, O.U.P., 1971, Chap. 2; and E. A. Boehm, 'Measuring Australian Economic Growth, 1861 to 1938–39', *Economic Record*, Vol. 41, June 1965, p. 228.

in work (see Table 3, columns 1 and 5 and Chart 8[4]). Remoteness from this war limited the participation of Australia's industry. The Commonwealth Statistician reported:

'The enlistments for war service took from industry over 300,000 adult males [equivalent to about 15 per cent of the labour force and 6 per cent of the population] in the prime of life, while the dislocation of industry owing to the altered conditions arising out of the war must also have adversely affected the productivity of Australia[5].'

By contrast, considerable economic expansion occurred during World War II. G.N.P., after declining slightly in 1938-9 immediately before the war, recovered quickly and advanced rapidly during the years 1939-40 to 1942-3. This expansion involved two major, associated factors. First, the industrialization of Australia, which had been proceeding very strongly after the depression in the early 1930s, speeded up, as Australia was able to switch her manufacturing resources quite quickly to wartime production[6]. Secondly, as a consequence of the accelerated industrialization as well as the enlistments for war service, there was a sharp fall in the level of unemployment during the early part of World War II; whereas, during World War I, unemployment remained relatively high despite the enlistments for war service. By 1941 the percentage unemployed was lower than at any previous time in the twentieth century (see Chart 3). Indeed, Australia in the early 1940s rapidly approached the state of full or near-full employment which has been a feature of her economy since.

During World War II approximately 716,000 persons[7] — equal to about 25 per cent of Australia's labour force and 10 per cent of her population — were absorbed into the defence forces. But the effective reduction of the occupied civilian labour force was only about a third of the number of persons entering the defence forces, since nearly 40 per cent of the latter were drawn from a decrease in unemployment and another 25 per cent came from persons whose entry into the labour force could be attributed solely to wartime conditions[8].

---

4 P. 124.

5 Commonwealth Bureau of Census and Statistics, *Labour Report*, No. 14, 1923, p. 78.

6 The longer-run benefits which flowed from the speeding-up of Australia's industrialization during World War II are examined in more detail in Chapter 6.

7 Commonwealth Bureau of Census and Statistics, *Labour Report*, No. 35, 1945 and 1946, p. 112.

8 *Ibid.*

CHART 3
PERCENTAGE UNEMPLOYMENT, AUSTRALIA, 1906–69

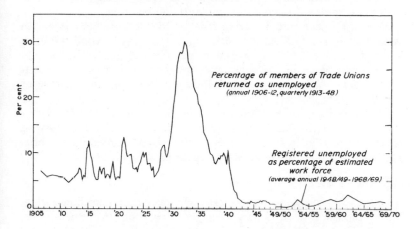

Sources: Commonwealth Bureau of Census and Statistics, *Labour Report* (various issues); *Vernon Report*, Vol. II, p. 583; and computed from data in Department of Labour and National Service, *Monthly News Release* (various issues) and the author's estimate of labour force.

4 THE TRADE CYCLE

In this section attention is concentrated on the timing and characteristics of the trade cycle, while the longer swings in the trend are examined in the next section. However, the analysis of neither kind of change can proceed far without keeping the other in view, for both kinds of change are intimately related. During the long periods of rapid, sustained growth (i.e. 1861-91 and since 1939) the recessions of the short cycle have generally been mild and relatively easy to overcome, and the economy has quickly returned to full or near-full employment. By contrast, the years of slower growth during 1891-1939 included years of protracted depression or prolonged stagnation; the recovery periods of the short cycle were often disappointing; and the economy did not return to full or near-full employment.

(a) Duration of the Trade Cycle

While it is clear that the trade cycle has generally been of short duration, the lack of sufficient, reliable short-term indicators means that the fixing of turning points may be only approximate and is still somewhat tentative[9]. Furthermore, in a detailed analysis, it would be necessary to take fully into account contrasting tendencies between leading sectors and regions of the Australian economy.

During the long upswing from 1860 to 1891 the trade cycle mostly was of 2 to 4 years' duration[10], as also during the period 1900-14, while during the 1920s it varied between about 2 to 3 years. The approximate times of the peaks and troughs in the level of economic activity for selected periods since 1900 are shown in the schedule on the opposite page.

The recessions during 1900-14 and in the 1920s prior to 1929 were relatively mild (as had been the experience during the long upswing from 1861 to 1891). These recessions generally amounted to only brief pauses in the upward trend of aggregate production.

(b) Special exceptions to relatively mild downswings

Two cyclical exceptions to the short cycle involving minor downswings during the last 100 years have been the depressions in the Australian economy in the early 1890s and the early 1930s. Both were exceptional in their severity and pervasiveness. In general, the downturn to the depression of the 1930s began in 1929. However, the 1929 peak was at about the same level of real activity (or a little below) the 1927 peak. This double-headed appearance of the cycle preceding the depression in the 1930s is similar to that before the depression in the 1890s, when peaks occurred in 1889 and 1891.

Both twin peaks must be viewed as part of the fairly regular cyclical pattern which has been a characteristic of economic activity in Australia. Identification of this pattern is complicated by divergent cyclical movements in leading regions and sectors. In retrospect it can be seen that factors which contributed to the severity of the depressions also contributed to the earlier downturns in 1889 and 1927. These factors were largely internally generated. A major difference, between the earlier relatively mild downturns and those that led to deep and protracted depressions in the 1890s and 1930s was the additional external influence of the world depressions, notably in

---

9 In this study, income indicators to which attention has been given in fixing turning points include: the quarterly figures of United Kingdom exports to each state and to Australia as a whole, the quarterly figures of recorded merchandise imports of Australia, unemployment (Chart 3) and employment (Chart 8 below), bank deposits and advances, notes held by public, and bankruptcies. Attention has also been paid to contemporary verbal evidence. For a discussion of analytical problems of using substitute income criteria for cyclical analysis, see Boehm, *Prosperity and Depression in Australia*, App. to Chap. 3.

10 For an outline of the cycle in each State of Australia during the 1880s and 1890s, see Boehm, *op. cit.*, Chap. 3.

APPROXIMATE TURNING POINTS OF TRADE CYCLE, AUSTRALIA, SELECTED PERIODS, 1900–70

Peaks	Troughs
	(A) *1900–14*[a]
Late 1900, or early 1901	Mid-1903
(Third quarter 1904)	(Second quarter 1905)
Fourth quarter 1907	Fourth quarter 1908
(Early 1911)	(Mid-1911)
Late 1912, or early 1913	Third quarter 1913
First quarter 1914	
	(B) *1920–39*[a]
Fourth quarter 1920	Fourth quarter 1921
(Fourth quarter 1922)	(Third quarter 1923)
Fourth quarter 1924	Third quarter 1925
Fourth quarter 1927	Mid-1928
Second quarter 1929	Late 1931, or early 1932
(Late 1932, or early 1933)	(Third quarter 1933)
First quarter 1938	Second quarter 1939
	(C) *1950–70*[b]
August 1951	September 1952
July 1955	July 1956
(December 1957)	(January 1959)
September 1960	July 1961
April 1965	April 1966
March–April 1970[a]	

Note: The periods between the peaks and troughs shown in brackets generally involved mild setbacks, or were periods of general stability resulting from the contrasting tendencies between leading regions and sectors of the economy.

Sources: [a] Determined by the author, as explained in the text.
[b] 1950–1968, from M. G. Bush and A. M. Cohen, *The Indicator Approach to the Identification of Business Cycles*, Reserve Bank of Australia, Occasional Paper No. 2, 1968, p. 24.

Britain, the continent of Western Europe, and the United States. The external deflationary influences were probably stronger in the 1930s, and were especially associated with the international monetary breakdown[11]. In brief, during the depressions of both the 1890s and the 1930s, increasingly strong internal and external contractionary influences produced a confluence in the determinants of aggregate economic

---

11 'The chief thing which differentiated this depression from others was the monetary breakdown; monetary guidance had failed, not merely (as it was apt to do) by a failure of policy, but by sheer impotence—the collapse of the international monetary system.' J. R. Hicks, 'A Memoir' in *Sir Dennis Robertson: Essays in Money and Interest*, Collins Fontana 1966, p. 16. See also J. R. Hicks, *A Contribution to the Theory of the Trade Cycle*, O.U.P., 1950, p. 163n.

activity that did not occur, at least on the same scale, during minor recessions. The consequent sharp and prolonged break in the early 1890s and early 1930s from the previous milder cyclical pattern then influenced appreciably the characteristics of the trade cycle in the following upswing.

(c) Recovery in the 1890s and 1900s

The recovery from the depression and stagnation of the first half of the 1890s was severely checked by the great drought which began in 1895 and lasted until 1903. During the drought Australia's sheep flock fell sharply from 100 million at the beginning of 1895 to 54 million at the beginning of 1903. However, the reduction in the sheep flock was not entirely attributable to the drought. It also reflected a long-run imbalance involving the overproduction of wool in terms of both overseas demand and carrying capacity in Australia, especially of the dry interior of N.S.W. and Queensland[12].

With the breaking of the drought in 1903 and recovery in wool production following simultaneously with improving wool prices, Australia's wool cheque doubled during the 1900s. Other export prices also rose. In fact, Australia's terms of trade improved appreciably[13].

Another major factor from which economic growth benefited in this period was the increasing returns being obtained from the unbalanced growth of the previous long upswing to 1891. The depression and then the drought were partly responsible for delaying the considerable benefits to Australia from much of the heavy capital expenditure which had been made during the long upswing. Part of the capital had been wasted or lost permanently. To an important extent it was also a matter of there having been a need for a period of absorption, of reorientation and readjustment of the economy. Furthermore, as the Australian economy grew there were reductions in unit costs resulting from the economies of scale and external economies[14] which accrued

---

12 See Boehm, *op. cit.*, Chap. 4.
13 See Chart 7, p. 81 below.
14 Alfred Marshall (*Principles of Economics*, 8th edn, Macmillan, 1920, p. 266) divided the economies arising from an increase in the scale of production of any kind of goods into 'internal' and 'external' economies. The former depend on the resources and efficiency of management of the individual firm, and occur as the firm grows larger and it benefits from the economies of large-scale production. Marshall defined external economies as 'those dependent on the general development of the [firm's] industry', other industries, and 'the aggregate volume of production in the whole civilized world'. External economies flow from the inter-dependent and complementary nature of the development process in an economy, including the accumulation of a complex of industrial skills, facilities, and services.
For a fuller discussion of the contribution to growth in Australia of internal and external economies, see *Vernon Report*, Vol. I, pp. 362–3.

from the more intensive, profitable utilization of much of the previously accumulated capital stock, including social capital. The strong restorative process of the Australian economy in the first decade of this century, from the relatively low level of its productive potential, contributed to the recession phases being relatively mild between 1900 and World War I.

(d) The Depression of 1929-32[15]

The first clear evidence of a major break from the fairly regular short cycle experienced during the uncertain prosperity of the 1920s came with the balance of payments crisis in 1929. This occurred in two ways: the drying up of the capital inflow and the sharp fall in prices of major exports.

Net capital inflow had averaged about $49 million a year during the period 1919-20 to 1927-8 (Table 3, column 8). The main borrowers had been the Australian governments, but there was also a substantial flow on private account. Since World War I public borrowing overseas had averaged just over $40 million yearly and in 1927-8 had exceeded $100 million. When this source dried up early in 1929 and private capital began to flow out instead of in, it obviously meant that Australia, which had become accustomed to this capital inflow, would have to make corresponding structural readjustments in production and expenditure. This, in part, was what the depression in the early 1930s was about. The readjustments particularly included a large decline in public and private investment and hence in real income.

Meanwhile, the fall in export prices was also contributing to the severe primary fall in income. Export prices in 1928 were just above their average level of the previous twelve years, but at their lowest point in August 1931 had tumbled to roughly half their 1928 level[16]. This was the position for prices quoted in Australian currency, which by 1931 had depreciated by 25 per cent on sterling, the currency of Australia's chief buyer.

Thus the immediate sources of the severe primary fall in the level of economic activity in Australia in 1929 were the sharp downturns

---

15 For more detailed discussions of this depression and the problems of recovery, see: L. F. Giblin, *The Growth of a Central Bank*, M.U.P., 1951, Chaps 3-7; S. J. Butlin, *Australia and New Zealand Bank*, Longmans, 1961, Chap. 15; and C. B. Schedvin, 'Origins of the Depression of the 1930's in Australia', *Economics*, Bulletin of the Economic Teachers' Association of N.S.W., October 1968.

16 See Chart 5 below. The average price per pound of greasy wool, Australia's chief export, fell from a high of 16·2 cents in 1927-8 to 13·7 cents in 1928-9, and then slumped to a trough of 7·0 cents in 1931-2. Bureau of Agricultural Economics, *Statistical Handbook of the Sheep and Wool Industry*, Canberra, 3rd edn, 1961, p. 81.

in the two most volatile determinants of income: exports and capital formation. The primary changes in both these sectors then set up the cumulative secondary changes which economists explain in terms of the multiplier. In three years, between 1928-9 and 1931-2, G.N.P. (at current prices) fell by nearly a third (see Chart 1).

The crisis in the balance of payments revealed itself in a huge deficit between merchandise exports (f.o.b.) and imports (c.i.f.) of $66 million in 1929-30. This compared with a small average annual deficit of about $4 million during the 1920s, and the deficit in 1928-9 was about this level. The capital inflow had been sufficient to meet this deficit and other net invisible items, including interest to meet borrowings. With the cessation of borrowing, the increasing deficit placed a severe strain on international reserves. In June 1928 total international reserves in gold and sterling balances were about $210 million[17], including at least $24 million required by law as backing for the note issue. 'Considerable sums were needed for working balances and it was not possible to mobilize fully the overseas funds of the trading banks, the amounts of which were known only to the individual banks. In practice, even under extreme pressure, it was not practicable to reduce reserves (excluding Note Issue Reserve) below £20 million sterling at the end of the export season, without serious embarrassment somewhere in the banking structure. Reserves came down to this figure by the middle of 1931. Breaking point was marked by Commonwealth legislation authorizing export of part of the Notes Reserve in June 1931[18].' But the chief factor which restored balance on external account was the drastic fall in merchandise imports. This was brought about principally by the collapse of the capital inflow, the heavy fall in demand, and the steep rise in unemployment, but also by the rationing of bank sterling sales to customers, import restrictions, and the progressive exchange depreciation.

In sharp contrast with the protracted depression and stagnation during most of the 1890s, the recovery from the depression in the 1930s got under way much more quickly. In terms of unemployment, the depression in the early 1930s appears to have been more severe and sharper than any previous downturn. But a solid recovery began late in 1931 or early in 1932. The recovery was essentially an internal affair, particularly with the successful implementation of the Premiers' Plan in 1931 and the support of the more rapid industrialization spurred on by protective policies (see Chapter 6). After a mild setback

17 Commonwealth Bureau of Census and Statistics, *The Australian Balance of Payments 1928-29 to 1951-52*, No. 3, p. 89.
18 Giblin, *op. cit.*, p. 63.

(or stability) during the first half of 1933, the recovery became a strong, sustained one and it was not until early in 1938 that the next general peak in G.N.P. was reached. The recession was deepening in 1939 when armament expenditure quickly turned the level of economic activity upwards again late in that year.

(e) The Trade Cycle since World War II

The earlier pattern of a fairly regular short cycle has continued since World War II with definite peaks occurring in August 1951, July 1955, September 1960, April 1965, and March or April 1970; and troughs in September 1952, July 1956, July 1961, and April 1966. These dates suggest that the duration of Australia's post-war trade cycle has been about 4 to 5 years from peak to peak or trough to trough. However, the general course of economic activity during 1957-9 is not clear. Conflicting tendencies operated, which meant that some sectors continued to contract mildly during 1955-9 while others reached a trough in 1956. In important respects the years 1957-8 were years of general stability and pause in growth. In fact, G.N.P. per head fell slightly during 1955-6 and 1957-8 (Chart 1). If we allow for a peak in December 1957 and a trough in January 1959, though these are not as clearly marked[19] as are the turning points set out above, then the duration of the post-war cycle has varied between 2 and 5 years.

Apart from the experience during the latter half of the 1950s, there has been some tendency since World War II for the cycle to be of slightly longer duration than in earlier periods. This was certainly true in the 1960s. There has also been a significant reduction in the amplitude of the fluctuations. Both these characteristics may be partly explained by the success of economic policies which have been fashioned, as far as possible, to promote rapid economic growth with economic stability. Australia's policy objectives are discussed in Chapter 9. The tendencies for a cycle of longer duration and smaller amplitude are also partly accounted for by the changing structure of the rapidly growing Australian economy, involving especially a significant decline in its dependence on exports subject to vagaries of weather and international prices. In the result, moreover, the level of economic activity since World War II has (as explained more fully in the next section) been persistently reaching and hugging the real ceiling of full employment for some time during each upswing. By contrast, a situation of full employment on this scale was not reached at any time during the first four decades of this century. Nevertheless,

---

19 Bush and Cohen, *op. cit.*, pp. 22–4.

since World War II structural maladjustments have still occurred and become sufficiently strong periodically to make necessary recession phases during which appropriate readjustments are undertaken. But the emphasis on rapid economic growth in Australia and in the countries with which Australia trades and, consequently, the strong cumulative self-reinforcing uptrend in demand have ensured (as already noted) that recessions have been short-lived with the necessary readjustments kept to a small scale and relatively easy to carry out[20].

5 LONGER-RUN CHANGES IN THE TREND RATE OF GROWTH

Attention has previously been drawn to the long wave in the trend rate of growth of the Australian economy entailing the long upswing during 1861-91, then slow advance during 1891-1939, followed by a renewed strong upswing since 1939 which is still proceeding (see Table 4). It has also been noted that the trend rate of growth itself fluctuated during these three long phases. This is illustrated in Table 3 in the alternations of periods of steeper uptrend with periods of less steep uptrend, while during 1891-1939 there were also periods of contraction.

As pointed out earlier, the selection of the sub-periods in Tables 3 and 4 was partly arbitrary. But, despite this, it does not seem appropriate to assign to the longer-run changes during each of the phases of the long wave, or to the long wave itself, any systematic influence. The fluctuations in the trend rate reflect the heterogeneous and irregular nature of the influences on the path of output, some of which need not necessarily be repeated.

Factors which contributed appreciably to the slow, irregular secular uptrend between 1891 and 1938-9 were: the sharper cyclical fluctuations (notably the exceptional depressions in the early 1890s and 1930s); the irregular, unfavourable periods of weather; and the contraction and stagnation during World War I. As previously noted, there has been a close intimate relationship between the severity of the shorter-run fluctuations and the resultant trend rate of growth of G.N.P. Furthermore, the relatively high rates of growth during most of the 1900s, 1920s, and 1930s largely reflect the recovery in output from the previous severe depression or stagnation.

The expansion from recession or depression can usefully be viewed in two stages. First, there is an increasing utilization of unemployed or underemployed resources (notably of labour and capital). This usually means that in the initial stage of recovery G.N.P. rises fairly rapidly, and faster than the longer-term trend rate. Though this stage

---

20 For further discussion of the trade cycle in Australia since World War II, see Boehm, 'Economic Fluctuations', in Boxer (ed.), *op. cit.*, Chap. 3.

was protracted in the recovery of the 1930s, the experience since World War II following the minor recessions has been for this stage to last for about a year or a little longer. The second stage, when the real ceiling of full employment has been reached, has usually been a period of longer duration when the rate of expansion is reduced to the rate of growth of capacity of the economy[21]. The rate of growth of capacity is as fast as permitted by the growth of the labour force, capital accumulation, the discovery and exploitation of natural resources, and technical progress.

The change from the comparatively slow long-term growth rate in the first four decades of the twentieth century to the sustained, rapid growth since 1939 reflects fundamental changes in the conditions and attitudes underlying Australia's economic and social development. Furthermore, the recent growth rate has not only been sustained but, since the mid-1950s, it has been increasing (see Table 3, column 1). One important factor contributing to the higher growth rate has been the faster rate of addition to the labour force (column 5). At the same time the recent rate of growth of G.N.P. per head has been the fastest, sustained rate in Australia's history (Table 3, column 6, and Table 4, column 3).

Australia's improved growth performance and the associated full employment of labour since World War II are the result of five closely related factors. First, the strong favourable influences of the growth in world demand, in particular, the rapid rates of economic growth being achieved in the countries with which Australia trades, have meant a more rapid growth in Australia's exports (see Chapter 4, section 3).

Secondly, investment demand has been high (as explained in Chapter 5). This reflects the increase in Australia's growth potential as compared with past periods and is manifested in the more rapid rates of population growth and technical progress, in the exploitation of natural resources, especially the recent mineral discoveries covering a wide range of products (including iron ore, coal, oil, natural gas, copper, nickel, uranium, beach sands, tin, and bauxite), and in the favourable changes in the organization and composition of the Australian economy. In fact, associated with the rapid increase in world demand and the high proportion of investment to G.N.P., there has been a world-wide acceleration in scientific and technological progress from which all countries are benefiting.

Thirdly, there have been important changes in the role and

---

21 For a more detailed discussion of both stages in Australia's growth-cycle during 1949–50 to 1962–3, see Boehm, 'The Australian Economy, February 1964', *Economic Record*, March 1964, Vol. 40, pp. 21–6.

techniques of economic policy, and in the relative size and nature of government activity in total activity. This has followed the Keynesian revolution in economic thought (see Chapter 9).

Fourthly, the rapid, sustained growth since 1939 has also created a productivity bonus through the elimination of the uneconomic habits and practices which developed during the inter-war period, in particular the 1930s, as a result of prolonged unemployment. The continued high demand for labour since World War II has attracted workers from safe but relatively unremunerative employment (especially in agriculture and aptly described as disguised unemployment) to more productive, remunerative jobs in secondary and tertiary industries[22]. The experience of mostly continued full employment and shortage of labour (which in turn have contributed to demand and cost inflation[23]) has stimulated technological progress leading to a more rapid increase in productivity. In short, the cumulative self-reinforcing momentum of the growth process has been especially favourable to the maintenance of strong, sustained expansion.

Finally, Australia's recent growth performance has benefited greatly from the inflow of capital and migrants. This inflow has been on a larger scale and has been maintained for longer than in any other period since the upswing of 1861-91. Furthermore, the long upswing which Australia has been experiencing since 1939 contains several significant historical parallels with the earlier long upswing.

6 HISTORICAL INTERDEPENDENCE BETWEEN THE RATES OF ECONOMIC GROWTH, IMMIGRATION, AND CAPITAL INFLOW

An important aspect, demonstrated by the data assembled in Table 3, is that the years of rapid, sustained growth of the Australian economy during 1861-91 and since 1948-9 have also been years of rapid increases in population with high immigration and capital inflow. The evidence strongly supports the proposition that additional population has always been Australia's first requirement for growth, as a source of both additions to the working population and demand for particular kinds of capital equipment.

Australia herself has not been able to provide an increase in population at a sufficient rate to achieve rapid, sustained, economic growth. For this she has relied heavily on immigration. But to entice people to leave their homes in Europe, travel the long distance to the Antipodes and start a new life, Australia has needed to offer a sufficiently attractive standard of living with favourable prospects for

---

22 For an examination of 'the impact of disguised agricultural unemployment on employment and productivity, 1950–60' in certain western countries, see A. Maddison, *Economic Growth in the West*, Allen & Unwin, 1964, pp. 59–63.

23 See pp. 192–3 and Chapter 9 below.

the future. In order to do this, a further essential requirement for Australia's growth has been capital imports to supplement domestic savings in financing the investment in capital equipment, thereby providing gainful employment for the additions to the labour force from migration as well as for Australian-born entrants. Furthermore, the larger population and labour force yield economies of scale and opportunities for specialization through the investment in bigger and more efficient capital equipment incorporating new techniques.

A central theme of this book, therefore, is the part played by, and the interrelationships between, the key economic variables of population growth (from natural increase and migration), capital formation, and capital inflow. However, the rate of population growth itself raises important questions about Australia's dependence on immigration and overseas borrowing. There is also the social question of whether Australians really desire their population to grow so big so quickly, with the associated problems of congested cities and the high proportion of savings that needs to be devoted to capital widening merely to match a growing population. These questions are discussed in more detail in later chapters[24].

No serious attention has apparently been given to finding more subtle substitutes for increasing Australia's population so quickly while still maintaining the desired rapid rate of economic growth at full employment and hence also rapid increases in productivity and material welfare. But it is doubtful if, without the considerable volume of capital widening, sufficient profitable investment opportunities would be available in Australia, at the present size of her economy, to absorb the potential savings of the fully employed Australian economy[25]. This is largely because of the long distances between points of economic importance in Australia and the relatively small scale of her industrial base. Australia's growth experience indicates that profitable investment opportunities are greater for equipping new workers than for increasing capital per worker, although there has been quite a bit of this as well. But Australia still needs to carry out a considerable spreading of her activity involving a larger population, and this in turn justifies the large inflows of migrants and capital. Thus, as Professor Downing has summed up the position: 'After more than twenty years of large-scale migration, there are some doubters but no substantial body of opinion opposes the continuance of the migration programme[26].'

---

24 For fuller discussion of capital widening in contrast with capital deepening, see pp. 96–7 below.
25 See p. 215 below for economic reasons for the emphasis on growth.
26 R. I. Downing, 'Population', in Boxer (ed.), *op. cit.*, p. 14.

A major exception to the proposition that there is a strong link between high rates of economic growth and population growth, including immigration, and of capital inflow occurred during the first decade of the twentieth century (see Table 3). In fact, during this decade net migration was very low, and there was an outflow of capital. The rapid rate of growth during this decade, as already pointed out, is explained by its being a period of full recovery from the serious setbacks of depression, stagnation, and then drought experienced in Australia during the 1890s and the early 1900s. The 1920s and 1930s were also periods when Australia's rapid growth reflected initially her quick restorative process in utilizing unused and under-used resources. Growth in the 1920s was also supported by a fairly substantial increase in population and capital inflow, but both these factors contributed much less to the economic expansion in the 1930s.

However, during the two sustained upswings in Australia's economic history (1861-91 and since 1939, or more particularly for our purposes, since the late 1940s) rapid, sustained growth has relied heavily on relatively large inflows of labour and capital. There is a close cause-effect interrelationship between these key economic variables. A high population growth itself generates profitable investment opportunities, which in Australia's experience have generally exceeded the domestic resources (savings) available. Australia has thus depended on assistance from overseas savings when the rapid increase in population has included a large inflow of migrants. However, this dependence on capital inflow has become relatively less important as the Australian economy has grown in size and become more developed, but the degree of dependence is still significant (see Chapter 5).

A striking point is that from 1891 to 1952-3 there was, on average, an export surplus — in some periods a substantial one — except for the period during World War I. An import surplus (see Table 3, column 9) is defined as the difference between exports and imports of goods and services, both net of interest and dividend receipts and payments respectively. The export surplus during most of the period from 1891 to 1952-3, was available for some debt repayment and to help meet interest and dividend payments.

There are two ways in which the act of borrowing overseas initially tends to increase the flow of imports relative to exports: first, through the direct purchases abroad of capital goods, from funds borrowed overseas; and secondly, the funds raised abroad generate income through labour (including migrants) being employed on investment projects, thereby giving rise to multiplier effects and so raising the imports of consumer goods. Furthermore, during the period of increased capital expenditure exports may grow more slowly, or even decline, as domestic-produced goods are diverted for home consumption. But Australia's capital imports financed more than an increased flow of goods and services. As already noted, these imports also assisted greatly in attracting more labour.

The real transfer of economic resources resulting from Australia's borrowing totalled about 45 per cent of the amounts borrowed during the period 1861-91 and 43 per cent from 1954-5 to 1968-9. The balance during both periods was required, in effect, to meet overseas interest and dividend payments.

The achievement of a significant import surplus since the mid-1950s goes a long way towards explaining the faster rate of growth which Australia has been able to achieve since then. Thus the historical link between development and immigration — as epitomized in the quotations at the head of this chapter — has been strongest and of greatest duration when it has been supported by a capital inflow which has been sufficiently large to provide a transfer of real resources to Australia.

In summary, in constructing a model of the Australian economy to describe the periods of rapid, sustained economic growth, it would be pertinent to specify not simply the increases in labour and capital equipment — the essential ingredients of growth in any country at any time — but also the large inflows of migrants and capital; and further to specify that these inflows have been closely interdependent with the standard of living. There is a definite circularity in the forces at work here. And while it seems that immigration to Australia has been dominated by the 'pull' of Australian economic conditions and prospects more than the 'push' of unfavourable social and economic conditions in Europe[27], it must also be recognized that countries lending to Australia, notably Britain and more recently the United States, have contributed greatly to fostering and maintaining the 'pull' by their capital exports to Australia, so supporting the high and increasing standard of living in Australia. A fundamental requirement of this process of development at any time is an adequate increase in productivity through expansion of exports and/or import replacement, not simply to pay the service debt charges, but especially to prevent a relative increase in the burden of the debt, and so avoid a balance of payments problem. Australia's performances in these respects are examined in Chapters 4 to 6.

---

27 See also p. 42 below.

7 INTERNATIONAL COMPARISONS

A country's growth performance in a particular period can be
evaluated by comparing its record in that period with its record in
other periods (as is done above), or by constructing an 'international
league table' (such as Table 5) in order to compare its growth performance with those of other countries. Growth rates of G.N.P. and
population are shown in Table 5 for two periods: in the first place
for a very long period, in most cases spanning almost the last hundred
years; and secondly, for the recent relatively short period 1955-66.
The G.N.P. (at factor cost) per head in 1966 is also shown.

It appears that Australia's growth record in terms of G.N.P. over
both the long term (column 2) and over the years 1955-66 (column
5) puts her at or near the top of the group of 'smaller industrialized
countries', or about the middle of the field of 'major countries'. There
was some shifting of the positions of other countries between the two
periods, notably in the major group. Over the long period the rates
of growth of output of Japan, the United States, and Canada were
significantly above Australia's; while over the shorter period 1955-66,
this was so again for Japan, and also for West Germany and Italy.
Several developing countries achieved a higher rate of growth of
output during 1955-66 than did Australia. These included Greece,
Malaysia, and South Africa.

Another notable aspect in Table 5 (columns 2 and 5, where the
data are available) is that only in the Argentine was the rate of growth
of G.N.P. less over the years 1955-66 than over the long term. In
fact, for most countries, including Australia, the recent growth performance has been considerably above the rate achieved over the last
century. An exception was the United States for which there was little
difference between the long term and recent growth records.

However, while an inter-country comparison is of interest and may
elucidate leading characteristics of the growth process in varying
circumstances, it can be quite misleading and must be used with
considerable caution[28]. A low or high rate of growth does not
necessarily mean either a 'bad' or 'good' economic performance
compared with that of other countries. In this context a distinction
should be made between the actual growth and the true growth-
potential relating to the maximum feasible output, given the pattern
of demand, the resources, and the most advanced technology available.
Given the optimum production relationship for the achievement of

---

28 The Vernon Committee did not favour comparisons of Australia's growth
performance with other countries. See *Vernon Report*, Vol. I, p. 32.

maximum output, there are three closely related and complex variables which, individually and in different combinations, mean different growth rates.

First, the growth rate varies according to the relative importance of the major features underlying current development. For instance, a high growth rate is likely in an economy:

(i) which is experiencing rapid technical progress;

(ii) in which the fastest growing industries are achieving a relatively high labour productivity;

(iii) where there is a transfer of labour from backward industries with a relatively low labour productivity to those with high productivity; and

(iv) where cyclical and secular fluctuations have delayed the modernization of capital equipment.

Important structural changes and the relative growth performance of leading sectors of the Australian economy are discussed in the following chapters. Here it is worth observing that each of the above features has been favourable to Australia's growth during the prosperous years since 1939. Supported by the sustained high level of demand, two fundamental factors making for the significantly higher rates of growth of output in Australia since World War II than previously are the relative shortage of labour and the era of rapid technological progress. Both factors and the associated sustained, high level of demand have also contributed greatly to the higher rates of growth achieved in other countries. The sustained, high level of demand and continued relatively full employment of labour have, in turn, stimulated rapid technical progress. This contrasts sharply with the economic conditions in the 1930s in Australia and other western countries, notably the United States, when the declining population growth rates and the existence of unemployed resources damped the incentive to adopt or seek technical improvements, including labour-saving innovations.

A *second* important variable (associated with the first) affecting growth rates is the influence of the stage of development of the country, or the actual base of G.N.P. from which growth has been proceeding. Hence on a lower base the same kind of changes produces a larger percentage increase in G.N.P. Though the growth rate in the United States during the period 1955-66 was below the rates of all other major countries except the United Kingdom, and also below the rates of 'smaller industrialized countries' (see Table 5, column 5), the United States — the richest country in the world — was operating at a level of G.N.P. per head which was nearly 50 per cent above

TABLE 5

COMPARATIVE GROWTH PERFORMANCE AND G.N.P. PER HEAD OF POPULATION IN SELECTED COUNTRIES

	Period	Long-term growth* Average annual rates of increase			Growth 1955–66† Average annual rates of increase			G.N.P. (at factor cost) per head 1966**
		Real G.N.P. %	Population %	G.N.P. per head %	Real G.N.P. %	Population %	G.N.P. per head %	$U.S. (a)
	1	2	3	4	5	6	7	8
(A) Major countries								
Japan	1879–1964	3·9	1·2	2·7	10·2	1·0	9·2	919
U.S.A.	1871–1964	3·6	1·7	1·9	3·7	1·6	2·1	3504
Canada	1870–1964	3·5	1·7	1·8	4·3	2·1	2·2	2329
U.S.S.R.	1870–1963	2·9	1·0	1·9				
Germany	1871–1964	2·8	1·0	1·8	5·5(c)	1·3(c)	4·2(c)	1740(c)
Italy	1870–1964	2·0	0·7	1·3	5·5	0·7	4·8	1040
United Kingdom	1870–1964	1·9	0·7	1·2	3·1	0·7	2·4	1644
France	1870–1964	1·7	0·2	1·5	5·0	1·2	3·8	1729
(B) Smaller industrialized countries								
Denmark	1870–1964	2·9	1·0	1·9	4·9	0·7	4·2	2246
Australia	1870–1963	2·9	2·0	0·9	4·6	2·1	2·5	1978
Sweden	1870–1964	2·8	0·7	2·1	4·3	0·6	3·7	2386
Switzerland	1890–1964	2·6	0·9	1·7	4·6	1·9	2·7	2307
Norway	1871–1964	2·6	0·8	1·8	4·2	0·8	3·4	1833
Netherlands	1870–1964	2·4	1·3	1·1	4·5	1·4	3·1	1498
Belgium	1870–1964	2·1	0·6	1·5	3·9	0·6	3·3	1667
New Zealand	1870–1964				4·5	2·1	2·4	1943

(C) Developing countries

Argentina	1902–1964	3·5	2·5	1·0	2·9	1·7	1·2	765
Mexico	1895–1963	3·3	1·7	1·6	6·0	3·4	2·6	484
India	1870–1964	1·4	0·7	0·7	3·8	2·3	1·5	81
Greece					6·4	0·7	5·7	651
Malaya a					5·5(e)	3·1(d)	2·4(d)	276
South Africa					5·0	2·4	2·6	559
Pakistan					4·6	2·1	2·5	120
Philippines					4·6	3·2	1·3	258
Ceylon					4·1(e)	2·6(e)	·5(e)	140
Indonesia					1·6(e)	2·3(e)	−0·7(e)	84

Notes: (a) In U.S. dollars of current purchasing power.
(b) Gaps indicate that data are not available.
(c) West Germany.
(d) For period 1955–55.
(e) For period 1953–56.

Sources: * A. Maddison, 'Japanese Economic Performance'; *Banca Nazionale del Lavoro Quarterly Review*, No. 75, December 1965, p. 300.
   † From trends fitted by least squares computed from data in United Nations, *Yearbook of National Accounts Statistics* (various issues) and *Demographic Yearbook 1966*, Table 4.
   ** United Nations, *Yearbook of National Accounts Statistics 1967*, pp. 828–31.

that of Sweden, the country with the next highest G.N.P. per head[29]. On the other hand Japan, with the greatest growth rate in both periods shown in Table 5, has been growing from a very much lower base, as is also the position to a greater or lesser extent of other countries. Australia, in terms of G.N.P. per head, ranked sixth among the countries shown in the Table, after the United States, Sweden, Canada, Switzerland, and Denmark. Caution must be exercised in the use of these figures of G.N.P. per head. The particular level of income of a country in the year under consideration may be distorted because of inaccuracies in measurement and through factors peculiar to the country in respect to cyclical and weather influences or other temporary disturbances[30]. Nevertheless, it seems reasonable to contend that the general impression conveyed by Table 5 is accurate. A country whose growth has previously been retarded, which is still in an early stage of technological development, and which can devote a sufficient proportion of its resources to capital formation involving technical progress has considerably greater scope for a faster rate of growth than a 'pioneer' country already employing the 'best practice' techniques. This largely explains the remarkably high rate of economic growth of Japan and has also been important for West Germany and other countries since World War II[31]. By contrast, a country such as the United States, which is already in the technical forefront throughout the country's productive units, will advance only as fast as new techniques are discovered and, also, successfully introduced[32].

29 The oil sheikdom of Kuwait, in fact, had a G.N.P. (at factor cost) per head of $US4552 in 1966. This was about 30 per cent higher than that of the United States. But Kuwait can hardly be classified a rich country, as the United States, since it presents marked contrasts between riches and poverty.

30 The United Nations, (*Year Book of the National Accounts Statistics 1967*, p. 836), in presenting the estimates of G.N.P. and G.N.P. per head for individual countries, pointed out that 'the estimates . . . should be considered as indicators of the total and per capita production of goods and services of the countries represented and not as measures of the standard of living of their inhabitants. No particular significance should be attached to small differences between the estimates of two countries because of the margin of error inherent in the method of estimation.'

31 The high growth rates of both West Germany and Japan during the latter half of the 1940s and until the early 1950s, and a little longer for Japan, reflected the considerable rebuilding programmes of their industries (incorporating the most modern technology) following the devastation and dislocation during World War II. The continued rapid growth in both countries also reflects their significant contributions to the technological frontier.

32 E. F. Denison, in an analysis of the economic growth performance of eight West European countries and the United States in the post-war years concluded (in *Why Growth Rates Differ*, Brookings Institution, 1967, pp. 342–3): 'The analysis of this book indicates that the low past and prospective standing of the United States in the "International Growth Rate League" is not an indication of poor economic performance. Rather, it has come about because the same sort of changes produce larger percentage increases in national income in Europe than they do in the United States and, in addition, there are opportunities to increase efficiency in European countries that do not exist to the same degree in the United States.'

A *third* way in which inter-country comparisons of the rate of growth of output may be misleading becomes apparent when allowance is made for the growth of population and labour force, and consideration is given to the rate of growth of G.N.P. per head and per worker. Among the major countries and smaller industrialized countries shown in Table 5, only Canada and New Zealand experienced as fast a population growth rate as Australia during the period 1955-66. The Table also shows that the rate of increase of G.N.P. per head in Australia over the long term (column 4) was the lowest among the major countries and smaller industrialized countries. But for the period 1955-66 (column 7) Australia's performance shows a considerable improvement, the rate of increase of G.N.P. per head being greater than in the United States and Canada, though still significantly less than in a number of other countries in sections A and B of the Table.

The growth rates for the period 1955-66 also indicate that the rate of increase of G.N.P. per head tended to be lower for countries with the higher population growth rates. This was so for each of the three groups of countries, but particularly for several of the developing countries, including Indonesia, Argentina, Philippines, India, and Ceylon. The poorest performance was by Indonesia, which appears to have retrogressed during the years 1958-66.

For countries experiencing a slower population growth rate in the smaller industrialized group itself, the rate of increase of G.N.P. per head has been significantly higher than Australia's. In the following chapters we examine reasons which help to explain why the rates of increase of G.N.P. per head and per worker have not been faster in Australia. One reason may be the capital-widening requirements involving assets with a relatively high capital output ratio, e.g. social capital and buildings. The rapid growth of population has meant that capital widening has absorbed a significant proportion of the resources available for capital expenditure[33].

Suggestions for further reading
Boxer, A. H. (ed.), *Aspects of the Australian Economy*, M.U.P., 2nd edn, 1969, Chaps 3, 6, and 7,
Bush, M. G. and Cohen, A. M. *The Indicator Approach to the Identification of Business Cycles*, Reserve Bank of Australia, Occasional Paper, No. 2, 1968;
Denison, E. F. *Why Growth Rates Differ: Postwar Experience in Nine Western Countries*, Brookings Institution, Washington, 1967;
Mallyon, J. S. 'Statistical Indicators of the Australian Trade Cycle',

---

33 For a fuller discussion of this reason, see pp. 120–1 below.

Australian Economic Papers, Vol. 5, June 1966, pp. 1-20;

Matthews, R. C. O. *The Trade Cycle,* C.U.P., 1959;

Samuelson, P. A. and others, *Economics: Australian edition,* especially Chaps 14 and 37-39;

Vernon Report, Vol. I, Chaps 1, 5, and 6; and Vol. II, App. D.

Chapter 3

POPULATION

We have already drawn attention to the close interrelationship between Australia's economic development and her population growth. The objective now is to review the character of this development by examining important demographic elements, in particular the distribution, growth, and structure of the population, and the occupation of the labour force.

1 GEOGRAPHIC DISTRIBUTION

The abundance of land in Australia suitable for pastoral and agricultural development and the relative scarcity of population, and hence of labour, obviously stimulated an extensive rural expansion from the beginning of Australia's settlement. Manufacturing industries (which sprang up to satisfy local needs) and commercial enterprises (which conducted the expanding overseas and internal trade) have contributed, together with Australia's economic geography, to two important demographic developments. First, there has been an increasing concentration of Australia's population in urban areas, particularly the capital city ports. Table 6 shows that by 1933 nearly half of Australia's population lived in metropolitan areas compared with just over a third at the turn of the century; and about another one-sixth resided in 'other urban' areas. The trend towards concentration in urban areas has continued. In the 1960s the proportion in metropolitan areas approached 60 per cent and in 'other urban' about 25 per cent. Thus the proportion living in rural areas has fallen from a little above 40 per cent in 1911 to about 17 per cent in the 1960s. The degree of urbanization varies considerably between the States, the highest being N.S.W. with 86·6 per cent of urban population at the 1966 Census, then Victoria 85·6 per cent, 82·2 per cent South Australia, 76·9 per cent in both Queensland and Western Australia, and 70·4 per cent in Tasmania.

The second important demographic development, which we have previously noted briefly (see Chart 2 above), and which was well established by the beginning of the twentieth century, was the concentration of the population in N.S.W. and Victoria. This is further illustrated in Table 7.

TABLE 6
POPULATION, URBAN AND RURAL, AUSTRALIA, CENSUSES 1881–1966

Census	Metropolitan	Other Urban	Rural	Total
		(a)	(a)	²000
	1	2	3	4
	———	Percentage of total	———	
1881	32·0			2,250
1891	37·1			3,178
1901	36·8			3,774
1911	38·0	19·8	42·2	4,455
1921	43·1	19·4	37·5	5,436
1933	46·9	17·1	36·0	6,630
1947	50·7	18·1	31·2	7,579
(b)				
1933	49·4			6,630
1947	54·3			7,579
1954	54·4	24·9	20·7	8,987
1961	56·3	25·9	17·8	10,508
(b)				
1966	58·3	25·1	16·6	11,550

Notes: (a) Gaps indicate that data are not available.
          (b) Breaks in the continuity of series owing to changes in the boundaries
              between metropolitan, other urban, and rural.
Source: *Census of the Commonwealth of Australia* (various issues).

TABLE 7
PERCENTAGE DISTRIBUTION OF THE AUSTRALIAN POPULATION
AMONG THE STATES AND TERRITORIES, CERTAIN CENSUSES,
1881–1966

State or Territory	Census				
	1881	1901	1921	1947	1966
N.S.W.	33·3	35·9	38·6	39·4	36·7
Victoria	38·3	31·8	28·2	27·1	27·9
Queensland	9·5	13·2	13·9	14·6	14·4
South Australia	12·3	9·5	9·1	8·5	9·5
Western Australia	1·3	4·9	6·1	6·6	7·2
Tasmania	5·1	4·6	3·9	3·4	3·2
Northern Territory	0·2	0·1	0·1	0·1	0·3
Australian Capital Territory	—	—	0·1	0·2	0·8
Australia	100·0	100·0	100·0	100·0	100·0

Source: Census of the Commonwealth of Australia (various issues).

Since the Census of 1901 there has been no change in the order of the States in terms of the size of their population. But there have been some fluctuations in the relative proportions in each State. The most significant have been: (i) the increase of 3·5 percentage points of the total population living in N.S.W. between the census years 1901 and 1947, and then the loss of 2·7 points of this gain between the censuses of 1947 and 1966; (ii) the fall of 4·7 percentage points of Victoria's share between 1901-47, and the recovery of 0·8 points since then; and (iii) the increase in Western Australia's share by 2·3 points between 1901-66 while Tasmania's share has continued the downward trend of the late nineteenth century and has fallen a further 1·4 points since 1901.

These contrasting movements reflect the complex and changing pattern of social, economic, and demographic influences operating in and between each State and occurring against the background of the increasing population. Economic factors have been the chief determinants of changes in the demand for workers, and hence in influencing the distribution of population. For instance, the considerable industrial and commercial development in Victoria has contributed to the slight recovery in the relative size of her population since 1947. For Western Australia the exploitation of mineral resources largely explains the significant gains in that State's share of Australia's population at the turn of this century and again in the 1960s; but this time the leading stimulus has not come from gold, but other minerals, particularly iron ore and nickel.

2 CHANGES IN THE RATES OF POPULATION GROWTH AND IN POPULATION STRUCTURE

(a) *The relative contributions to population growth from natural increase and immigration*

Though the overall shifts in the distribution of Australia's growing population between the States since the beginning of the twentieth century have generally been fairly small, there have been important changes in the rates of growth of total population. Up to 1860 population growth was heavily dependent on migration, which had provided about three-quarters of the total growth. Natural increase then became the main source of population formation, but migration was still important and provided about one-third of the total increase during the continued strong uptrend from the early 1860s to 1891. With birth rates considerably exceeding death rates (see Table 8), the natural increase was high. Therefore, in 1900, Australia had a relatively young population, still with a high masculinity of 111. This compared with 140 in 1860.

TABLE 8
TOTAL POPULATION, MASCULINITY, AND RATES OF INCREASE OF
POPULATION, AUSTRALIA, 1861–1968

Period	Population (end-year)		Crude rates of increase[a]— annual average rates				
	Total m.	Masculinity[b]	Births	Deaths	Natural increase	Net migration	Total increase
	1	2	3	4	5	6	7
1861–70	1·65	121	41	17	24	12	36
1881–90	3·15	116	35	15	20	14	34
1891–1900	3·77	111	30	13	17	1	18
1926–30	6·50	104	21	9	12	4	16
1931–35	6·76	103	17	9	8	—	8
1936–40	7·08	102	18	10	8	1	9
1941–45	7·43	100	20	10	10	—	11
1946–50	8·31	102	23	10	14	9	22
1956–60	10·39	102	23	9	14	8	22
1964–68	12·17	101	20	9	11	8	19

Notes: [a] Per 1,000 of mean population.
[b] Masculinity=number of males per 100 females.
Sources: Commonwealth Bureau of Census and Statistics, *Demography Bulletin* (various issues), and *Official Year Book of the Commonwealth of Australia* (various issues).

Since the early 1890s natural increase has been the predominant source of increase in Australia's population. Migration, however, has reappeared as a major factor in population growth on three occasions: during the years 1911-3 just before World War I, during the seven years 1922-8, and, most important, since World War II for what is the most prolonged period of large-scale migration since the long upswing 1861-91 (see Table 3, column 3 and Chart 4).

During the decade following World War I there were several attempts at Empire co-operation in migration settlement and development. In the early 1920s the State Governments of New South Wales, Victoria, and Western Australia jointly agreed with the Commonwealth and British Governments to assist the establishment of British migrants on the land in Australia. However, the numbers settled fell short of expectations and the cost greatly exceeded the estimates. Therefore, in 1925, the British and Commonwealth Governments agreed 'to furnish the Governments of the various States, loan moneys at a very low rate of interest, to enable suitable areas of land to be made available for settlement, or to enable such public works to be carried out as will tend to develop and expand settlement areas or

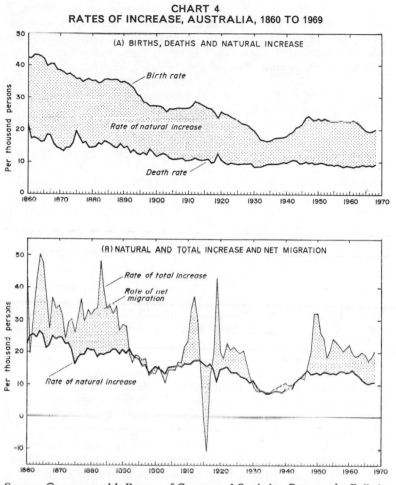

CHART 4
RATES OF INCREASE, AUSTRALIA, 1860 TO 1969

Source: Commonwealth Bureau of Census and Statistics, *Demography Bulletin* (various issues).

will enable areas already settled to carry a greater population'[1]. Britain agreed to make available loan money to a maximum amount of £34 million. Public men in Britain and Australia optimistically called for a migration target for Australia of 100,000 Britons a year. The Commonwealth Government, for its part, set up the Development and Migration Commission in 1926 to investigate (i) the condition

---

1 *Official Year Book of the Commonwealth of Australia,* No. 22, 1929, p. 929.

and development of existing industries, whether primary or secondary, and (ii) the possibility of establishing new industries that might justify loan expenditure and provide openings for additional settlers. But the Commission recommended very few projects and the number of assisted immigrants showed only a small rise from an average annual total of 25,200 during the years 1922 to 1925 to 27,900 during the years 1926 to 1928[2]. Assisted immigration practically ceased in 1929 with the onset of the depression.

Chart 4 (section B) shows that the most unstable element of population growth has been immigration. Cyclical fluctuations have contributed very largely to this instability, reflecting the predominant influence of migration to Australia for economic reasons, as compared with religious or political motives. The chief exceptions to the pull of economic forces have been the early German settlers in South Australia (from 1838 until about 1860) and the refugees immediately before and after World War II.

The effects of the minor recessions since World War II are reflected, with some lag, in the decline in net migration, especially in 1953 and the years 1961-2. However, since World War II the policy of sponsored immigration has not been abandoned at the onset of recession, as it was in the much more severe downswings of the 1890s and 1930s. The relatively mild recessions have induced only a temporary reduction of the migrant flow. The fairly quick economic recovery following each recession has meant an equally quick recovery in the demand for migrant labour.

Thus, since World War II, the rate of immigration has continued to respond sensitively to the demand for labour in Australia. But the forces making for quick recovery and the further rapid growth of the economy have soon revived the demand for migrants. Throughout the 1950s and 1960s (including during recession years), this demand considerably exceeded the non-immigrant recruits to the labour force. A major reason for this shortfall of numbers entering the labour force, relative to the great demand for labour, was the slump in birth rates in the 1930s. Fluctuations in birth rates are discussed further shortly.

(b) The Immigration Programme Since World War II

Supported by a government scheme of passage assistance, an initial target net inflow was set of at least 1 per cent of the total population. This target was reached during the years 1949-52 and in 1955; in fact, in the years 1949-50, the rate of inflow was nearly double the target. The continued active pursuit of the immigration programme as a central feature of government policies for national development

---

2 *Ibid*, p. 930.

maintained a rate of net immigration through the 1950s and 1960s close to the initial target (see Table 8, column 6).

Between the censuses of 1947 and 1966, Australia's population increased by 3·97 million. Net immigration provided just over one-third of this gain. About another one-sixth were children born to migrants. Thus approximately one-half of the national growth in population since World War II is attributable to immigration.

Passage assistance dates back to the beginning of immigration to the Australian colonies. However, what has been new since World War II has been the extension of the immigration programme and assistance to non-British immigrants. In the result, non-British (assisted and unassisted) have comprised a wide variety of nationalities. By contrast, previously the migrants were chiefly British. But during the 1950s migrants of British nationality comprised only about one-third of the total. The proportion of British recovered in the 1960s, in recent years to about one-half[3].

This great revival of immigration has dramatically changed Australia's population prospects. Forecasts as recent as the end of World War II generally concluded that Australia's population growth would be fairly slow after the effects of the post-war marriage- and baby-booms had passed. One forecast was that Australia's population might reach $9\frac{1}{2}$ million by the end of this century[4]. In fact, this total was passed in 1956. The Commonwealth Statistician, in an interim projection of the population of Australia, obtained a total population figure of nearly 23 million by 2001, which would mean a doubling of Australia's population between 1966 and 2001 (Table 9)[5]. The expectation of slow growth, in the light of Australia's spasmodic gains from immigration since the 1880s, could provide no vision of the

---

3 See R. I. Downing, 'Population', in Boxer (ed.), *Aspects of the Australian Economy*, p. 12, especially Table 11.
4 *Ibid*, p. 7.
5 See Commonwealth Bureau of Census and Statistics, *Interim Projections of the Population of Australia*, 1968 to 2001, (mimeographed, April 1969).
The Commonwealth Statistician warned: 'It is to be stressed that the projections are not to be quoted or taken in any way as official estimates or forecasts. Trends in natural increase and migration are influenced by many factors, such as economic conditions, Government policy, occurrence or fear of war and the personal reactions of individuals, both in Australia and overseas, to changing circumstances. *The forecasting of population movements is thus highly speculative and has not been attempted in these projections. . . .*
In these interim projections only one fertility assumption has been adopted, which is that the 1967 age-specific fertility rates for females will remain unchanged throughout the period covered by the projections. . . . The projected mortality experience has been based on an investigation into long-term trends in the mortality of the Australian population. . . . Net overseas migration . . . has been projected on the basis of 100,000 persons per annum.' *Ibid.*

large, continued flow of immigrants which has occurred since World War II. A further important aspect, which manifested itself in the pessimistic forecasts, was the secular decline in birth rates.

(c) Fluctuations in Birth Rates

During the latter half of the nineteenth century there was a very considerable fall in the birth rate (see Chart 4). The fall continued in the twentieth century, though more slowly. This phenomenon of a secular decline in the birth rate occurred in all Western-European-type countries. There has been much debate about the causes of this phenomenon. One cause appears to have been economic development itself. In particular, industrialization seems to have cut birth rates through urbanization and the associated decline of the proportion of people living in rural areas. Other important influences have been the increasing general standard of education (including a rise in the school-leaving age) and the continuing advances through technological progress. The process of economic development appears to have been accompanied by the growing realization on the part of people that

TABLE 9
AGE DISTRIBUTION OF POPULATION, AUSTRALIA,
CERTAIN CENSUSES 1881 TO 1966,[a] AND OF
PROJECTED POPULATION, 2001[b]

Age group	1881	1901	1933	1947	1961	1966	2001
0–4	14·2	11·5	8·6	10·0	10·6	9·9	9·9
5–9	12·8	12·1	9·5	8·0	10·0	10·1	9·3
10–14	12·0	11·5	9·4	7·1	9·7	9·4	8·9
15–19	10·7	10·0	9·3	7·7	7·7	9·1	8·6
20–29	17·6	17·8	16·9	16·0	12·9	13·8	15·6
30–39	12·0	15·0	14·4	15·3	14·3	12·6	13·5
40–49	10·1	10·0	13·0	12·7	12·7	12·6	12·6
50–59	6·3	5·7	9·0	10·9	9·8	10·3	9·8
60–64	2·0	2·2	3·5	4·3	3·8	3·8	3·4
65–74	1·8	3·0	4·7	5·4	5·7	5·5	5·0
75 and over	0·6	1·0	1·8	2·6	2·8	3·1	3·3
Total—per cent	100·0	100·0	100·0	100·0	100·0	100·0	100·0
Number (million)	2·25	3·77	6·63	7·58	10·51	11·55	22·71

Sources: [a] *Census of the Commonwealth of Australia* (various issues).
[b] Computed from data in Commonwealth Bureau of Census and Statistics, *Interim Projections of the Populations of Australia*, 1968 to 2001, mimeographed, April 1969. See p. 43, n.5.

they could provide higher standards of living for themselves and their families by limiting the size of their families. Thus the nineteenth-century family of an average size of about 6 has been replaced by one of an average of 2 to 3. Table 10 suggests that the position has stabilized. This shows that the average issue of existing marriages of wives aged 45-49 years declined from 5 in 1911 to a level of about 2½ from the mid-1950s.

Table 10 (columns 2 and 3) provides evidence of the lower birth rates of metropolitan dwellers. As the Vernon Committee reported:

Birth-rates have always varied considerably in different parts of Australia and, apart from the particularly high rates in the Northern Territory and the Australian Capital Territory, have been highest in States with the greatest proportion of rural population. . . . Tasmania, Queensland and Western Australia have the highest rates. . . . The birth rate in New South Wales is the lowest in the Commonwealth[6].

TABLE 10
AVERAGE ISSUE OF EXISTING MARRIAGES, AUSTRALIA,
CENSUSES 1911–1966

| Census | Wives aged 45–49 years | All wives | | |
		Metropolitan	Extra-metropolitan	Total
	1	2	3	4
1911	5·0	3·5[a]	4·2[a]	$\begin{cases} 3·9^{[a]} \\ 3·8^{[b]} \end{cases}$
1921	4·0	2·8	3·6	3·2
1947	2·8	2·1	2·7	2·4
1954	2·4	2·0	2·6	2·3
1961	2·5	2·1	2·7	2·3
1966	2·7	2·2	3·4	2·5

Notes: [a] All marriages.
[b] Existing marriages.
Sources: Census of the Commonwealth of Australia, 30 June 1961, Statistician's Report, pp. 372 and 381; and Commonwealth Statistician.

As well as the birth rate falling in the latter half of the nineteenth century, the death rate also experienced a secular decline, reflecting improving economic conditions and (later) advances in medical science; but since the birth rate fell faster, the rate of natural increase fell still faster. This meant that the nineteenth-century prospect of the population naturally increasing at a fairly rapid rate was also rapidly declining.

6 *Vernon Report,* Vol. II, p. 536.

TABLE 11
CRUDE BIRTH RATES AND FERTILITY RATES: AUSTRALIA,
1880–2 TO 1965–7[a]

	Average annual rates			Index Nos (Base: 1880–2=100)		
		Fertility Rates			Fertility Rates	
Period	Crude birth rate[b]	Births per 1,000 women aged 15–44 years	Nuptial births per 1,000 married women aged 15–44 years	Crude birth rate[b]	Births per 1,000 women aged 15–44 years	Nuptial births per 1,000 married women aged 15–44 years
	1	2	3	4	5	6
1880–2	35·3	170	321	100	100	100
1890–2	34·5	159	332	98	94	103
1900–2	27·2	117	235	77	69	73
1910–2	27·2	117	236	77	69	74
1920–2	25·0	107	197	71	63	61
1932–4	16·7	71	131	47	42	41
1946–8	23·6	104	160	67	61	50
1953–5	22·7	109	149	64	64	46
1960–2	22·5	112	154	64	66	48
1965–7	19·5	95	132	55	56	41

Notes: [a] Excludes particulars of full-blood Aborigines before 1965–7.
[b] Per 1,000 of mean population.
Source: Official Year Book of the Commonwealth of Australia, No. 55, 1969, p. 172.

The fall in the birth rate continued until 1934 when it reached 16·4 per 1,000 of population. The steeper decline in the birth rate in the first half of the 1930s was largely caused by the severe depression which also cut off migration. The previous severe depression in the 1890s had cut the rate of population growth. But this occurred principally through the cessation of migration. The birth rate fell in the 1890s, but its decline was only a little faster than in the previous decade.

Though the great fall in the birth rate in the first half of the 1930s now appears to have been only a temporary phenomenon, caused by the deep depression, the rate recovered quite slowly during the latter half of the 1930s as the level of economic activity improved. However, the rate rose sharply immediately after World War II during the post-war marriage- and baby-booms. There was then a small decline reflecting the slump in births in the 1930s and the consequent fall in the number of women in the 1950s in the most fertile age group of 20-29 years. Table 9 shows that 16·0 per cent of the population were in this age group in 1947, but the proportion had fallen to 12·9 per cent in 1961. Nevertheless, the birth rate remained relatively high through the prosperous 1950s.

However, after 1961, there was a further significant downward trend in the birth rate. This appears to have been largely the result of a complex of social and economic factors influencing family planning and size. Thus, in 1965, the crude birth rate fell below 20 per 1,000 of population for the first time since the late 1930s. But since 1966 the rate has risen slightly, suggesting that a new, probably fairly stable pattern is emerging.

The crude birth rate, which measures births against total population (irrespective of sex) and which is shown in Chart 1, is an imperfect measure of fertility. The principal demographic factors influencing the level of crude birth rates are the proportion of women of child-bearing age and the proportion of these women who are married. The fertility of married women may remain unchanged, yet the crude birth rate may change if the proportion of women marrying or of child-bearing age changes. Alternatively, the birth rate may remain unchanged if there are compensating changes between age composition, marriage patterns, and fertility within marriage. A more reliable indication of fertility rates is furnished by relating births to the number of women of child-bearing age, or by relating the nuptial births to the number of married women of child-bearing age, as is done in Table 11 (columns 2 and 3 respectively). This table 'shows how increasing proportions both of women of child-bearing age and of married women of child-bearing age inflate the crude birth rate. Thus, while the nuptial birth rate for married women increased by only 22 per cent over the period 1932-34 to 1946-48, the crude birth rate rose by 41 per cent owing principally to the greatly increased number of marriages during the period[7].'

Table 11 also shows that the secular decline from 1880-2 to the trough of the 1930s in births to women of child-bearing age and in nuptial births to married women of child-bearing age was generally steeper than that revealed by the crude birth rate. The former two measures reflect more fully the effects of the sociological revolution making for the reduction in family size and the slower population growth from natural increase.

Table 12 elucidates further the complex changes which have occurred in fertility. This Table indicates that the decline in fertility between 1921 and 1936 was spread over all age-groups, but it was more pronounced in the older age-groups. Then, in the following period 1936 to 1961, there was a marked rise in fertility in the younger age-groups, to new peaks in the early 1960s, reflecting the important fact of a progressive trend to earlier marriage.

TABLE 12
BIRTH RATES, BY AGE OF MOTHER,[a] AUSTRALIA,
SELECTED YEARS, 1921–68

Year of Registration	Age Group (years)						
	15–19	20–24	25–29	30–34	35–39	40–44	45–49
1921	26·6	135·9	169·0	142·5	101·9	43·6	4·3
1926	29·2	127·4	159·4	125·4	88·2	36·2	3·8
1931	27·2	110·8	130·7	104·4	67·9	27·7	3·1
1936	24·9	103·5	127·5	95·5	60·3	21·6	2·2
1941	24·3	121·0	143·5	104·9	57·8	19·6	1·7
1946	26·1	151·1	183·2	131·7	78·3	24·6	2·1
1951	38·6	177·2	185·3	123·1	65·0	21·0	1·6
1956	43·0	210·9	203·0	123·5	64·2	19·7	1·6
1961	47·4	225·8	221·2	131·1	63·4	19·2	1·4
1966	48·9	173·1	183·9	105·1	50·6	14·2	1·0
1968	48·9	173·6	190·8	103·3	46·7	12·9	1·1

Note:　(a) Number of births per 1,000 of female population in each age group. Excludes particulars of full-blood Aborigines before 1968.
Source: Commonwealth Bureau of Census and Statistics, *Births 1968*, p. 6.

But some of this rise in fertility was lost in the 1960s, as already mentioned. Meanwhile, birth rates in the older age-groups continued the decline which began earlier, but had been briefly reversed immediately after World War II. Finally, it is interesting to note the changes

---

7 *Official Year Book of the Commonwealth of Australia*, No. 55, 1969, p. 172.

in the order of importance of the leading age-groups with respect to fertility rates. In the first half of the 1920s the most fertile age-group was 25-29 years, and 30-34 years was the next. By 1926 the second most fertile group had become 20-24 years, and in 1953 this became the most fertile group, but lost the position again to the 25-29 year age-group in 1962[8].

(d) Changes in Population Structure and Age Distribution

One of the most significant demographic changes since World War II has been the greatly increased proportions of young married persons. As noted above, this influences the reproductive capacity of the population. Table 13 shows the nuptiality experience in age-groups for successive Censuses between 1891 and 1966 resulting from the influence of such factors as fluctuations in marriage rates, immigration, mortality, and previous birth rates. The pattern for individual age groups is largely independent of changes in the age distribution of the population. The Table shows that over the whole period 1891 to 1966 there have been increases in all groups except for females aged 45 and over. But during the period 1891 to 1947 there were quite marked fluctuations in most groups for both males and females. Moreover, while there was over this period as a whole an upward trend in the proportions of males 'ever married', there was a downward trend in the proportions of females 'ever married' in each individual age group during the years 1891-1933. This reflected partly the fall in masculinity with the cessation of migration. By 1947, with the additional influence of the loss of men's lives during World War II, the sexes were about equal in number (see Table 8, column 2).

Other factors which contributed to the fluctuations in 'ever married' in the first four decades of this century were the economic depression and stagnation in the 1890s; the gold rush to Western Australia in the 1890s, including the emigration of males from the eastern colonies; the influence to some extent of the Boer War; then, later on, the consequences of World War I and the depression of the early 1930s. After 1933, however, the proportions 'ever married' have (with some minor exceptions) risen steadily for males and females in all age groups, but particularly in the younger child-bearing age groups of 20-24 and 25-34.

Since the 1880s, and in particular since the 1920s, the changing age structure of the population (see Table 9) is the result of the sharp fluctuations in immigration and in the birth rate. A demographic

---

8 Commonwealth Bureau of Census and Statistics, *Births 1968*, p. 6.

TABLE 13
'EVER MARRIED' MALES AND FEMALES, PERCENTAGES OF TOTAL POPULATION OF EACH SEX, IN AGE GROUPS, AUSTRALIA, CENSUSES 1891 TO 1966

	Age last birthday—years						
	15–19	20–24	25–34	35–44	45–54	55 and over	Total aged 15 and over
	Males						
1891	0·2	11·0	48·4	70·6	75·7	79·5	47·1
1901	0·2	9·6	45·3	70·3	76·7	80·1	47·9
1911	0·4	12·2	49·7	72·1	78·6	81·4	50·3
1921	0·4	14·6	58·2	78·2	80·4	82·2	57·3
1933	0·4	12·9	55·1	81·2	85·3	83·9	58·0
1947	0·7	23·5	70·2	84·5	86·7	87·5	67·0
1954	0·8	25·5	71·9	86·8	88·3	88·7	70·2
1961	0·9	27·2	74·2	87·9	90·0	89·7	70·2
1966	1·3	30·0	77·0	88·3	90·7	90·5	69·4
	Females						
1891	4·1	34·9	73·7	89·4	93·9	95·9	62·0
1901	2·9	28·0	65·3	85·4	91·1	95·0	59·5
1911	3·8	30·0	64·9	80·7	87·2	92·6	59·8
1921	3·7	33·6	69·7	81·7	84·1	89·0	64·2
1933	3·9	31·2	69·7	83·9	85·6	86·3	65·0
1947	5·6	48·6	82·6	87·2	87·5	86·4	73·6
1954	6·9	59·0	87·7	91·1	89·2	87·1	78·5
1961	7·0	60·5	90·1	93·5	92·0	88·3	78·9
1966	8·2	59·7	90·3	94·5	93·6	89·5	78·0

Sources: 1891 to 1961, *Census of the Commonwealth of Australia, 30 June 1961, Statistician's Report,* p. 82; and 1966 computed from data in *Census of the Commonwealth of Australia, 30 June 1966, Census Bulletin No. 9.7,* pp. 5 and 7.

contrast with considerable social and economic consequences between the depressions of the 1890s on the one hand and the 1930s on the other was the more violent decline in fertility during the 1930s in a community which was exercising birth control on a greater scale than in the 1890s (Table 11). As previously noted, the cessation of immigration provided the chief source of the fall in national growth in the 1890s. Whereas migration tends to be spread more evenly over the age groups, the decline in fertility in the 1930s was of considerable significance for the future structure of the population. One major consequence was the sharp fall in the proportions in the 20-29 age group in the 1950s and early 1960s. This fall, in the environment of rapid growth, seriously aggravated the labour shortage, and gave added importance to the migration programme during the 1950s.

Another important aspect of the age distribution is the proportions in the age groups 5-19, where the expenditure on education is concentrated, and the proportion aged 65 and over, because of expenditure on aged pensions. Since World War II, with the revival of birth rates from their depression trough in 1934 and the inflow of migrant children, the greatly increasing number and proportion in the under-19 age groups have imposed a considerable strain on education resources. This has come at a time when there has been an increased awareness of the need for the labour force to be adequately educated and trained.

The proportion of the population aged 65 and over increased from 2·4 per cent in 1881 to 8·6 per cent in 1966 (Table 9). The trend towards a relatively younger population following the revival of birth rates and immigration after World War II has held the proportion of aged roughly constant at about 8·5 per cent of the population.

(e) Summary

In summary, five of the most significant changes in population growth during the twentieth century have been:

(i) the continuation from the nineteenth century of the secular decline in birth rates and the somewhat slower secular decline in death rates, and hence the sharper decline in the rates of natural increase;

(ii) the additional downward influence on birth rates associated with the depression in the 1930s;

(iii) the revival of birth rates from their depression nadir in 1934, and their continued high level in the relatively prosperous conditions which have prevailed since World War II; (Australia's demographic experience has shown that in an economy in which fertility and mortality are already subject to a significant degree of control, the main variable with changing economic and social conditions is fertility);

(iv) the trend towards earlier marriage from the mid-1940s; and

(v) the revival of immigration since World War II on a large scale.

As a result of high birth rates and immigration, Australia's population grew at the rate of 2·2 per cent a year over the period between the censuses 1947 and 1966. This has been Australia's highest sustained rate of population growth since the 1880s. The social and economic consequences of this factor alone are considerable. The sustained rapid increases in population and labour force have placed considerable demands on capital widening (as noted in the previous chapter, especially the investment in houses and other social capital, and in capital equipment to provide productive employment). The increase in the size of the Australian market and the increasing benefits from the greater economies of scale have manifested themselves in the rapid rates of growth in output and productivity. The greater momentum of Australia's economic development has also stimulated, and in turn been stimulated by, the search for, the discoveries of, and the opening up of new resources. Meanwhile major developmental projects have been undertaken by both public and private enterprises.

On purely economic grounds these developments have been raising Australia's 'optimum population' faster than the population has been growing. The concept of optimum population is meaningful only in the dynamic sense. Australia's optimum population — given her natural resources and the pool of technical knowledge awaiting exploitation through the application of scarce labour and capital — has always been above, indeed well above, her population level. According to the statistics Australia is experiencing a rate of increase of population which is close to that recently reached in some poor countries. But for Australia there is no fear of a population explosion as there is for these countries, especially countries of Asia which have a large population base and are already densely populated (e.g. India, Pakistan, and Ceylon). The population explosion in these countries has meant that their populations have not only been increasing, but increasing at a quicker rate each year with a high rate of acceleration. Nevertheless, their more rapid population growth appears now to be providing a stimulus to economic growth[9].

3 LABOUR FORCE

(a) The rate of increase

The annual increase in the labour force is determined mainly by the difference between the numbers of school leavers entering the labour force and of workers reaching retiring age, plus the net addition of migrants joining the labour force. Table 14 (column 9) shows that the rate of growth in the population of working age has fluctuated considerably during the twentieth century from a high of 2·2 per cent a year in the intercensal periods 1901 to 1911 and 1961 to 1966 to a low of only 1·1 per cent a year between 1933 and 1947. The cessation of immigration in the 1930s and, to lesser extents, the declining rate

---

9 The emergence of the population explosion in a number of developing countries appears itself to be furnishing a greater stimulus to a more rapid, sustained rate of economic development through a quicker recognition (by both governments and private individuals) of the urgency of ensuring successful 'take-off' than would probably have been so in the absence of population pressure. Thus the challenge in India, for instance, where the population growth rate has increased from just above 1 per cent a year during the early 1950s to 2·3 per cent during 1955–66, may be viewed optimistically.

TABLE 14

SIZE* AND RATES OF GROWTH†, POPULATION AND LABOUR FORCE, AUSTRALIA, CENSUSES 1901 TO 1966

Census	Total Popl.	Popl. in 15–64 age group	Labour Force			Married Females in labour force		Average Annual Compound Growth Rate from Previous Census					
			Male	Female	Total		% of Col 4	Total Popl.	Popl. in 15–64 age group	Labour Force Male	Female	Total	Married Females in labour force
	'000	'000	'000	'000	'000	'000		%	%	%	%	%	%
	1	2	3	4	5	6	7	8	9	10	11	12	13
1901	3,774	2,296	1,285	330	1,615								
1911	4,455	2,853	1,536	386	1,922			1·7	2·2	1·8	1·6	1·8	
1921	5,436	3,470	1,782	455	2,237			2·0	2·0	1·5	1·7	1·5	
1933	6,630	4,379	2,145	599	2,744	66	11·0	1·7	2·0	1·6	2·3	1·7	
1947	7,579	5,070	2,479	717	3,196	142	19·8	1·0	1·1	1·0	1·3	1·1	5·5
1954	8,987	5,677	2,857	845	3,702	290	34·3	2·5	1·6	2·0	2·4	2·1	10·7
1961	10,508	6,437	3,166	1,059	4,255	445	42·0	2·3	1·8	1·5	3·3	1·9	6·3
1966	11,550	7,172	3,398(b)	1,350(b)	4,748(b)	688(b)	51·0	1·9	2·2	1·4(b)	5·0(b)	2·4(b)	9·5(b)

Notes: (a) Gaps indicate that data are not available.
(b) A change in definition of labour force at the 1966 Census resulted in about 108,000 additional persons (−9,000 males and +117,000 females) being recorded in the labour force than would have been on the definitions used in the 1961 Census. These have been omitted here in order to provide more accurate indications of trends.

Sources: * *Census of the Commonwealth of Australia* (various issues).
† Computed from figures of the size of population and labour force shown above.

of natural increase in the 1920s (see Chart 4) and the war losses in the 1939-45 War (37,525 males and 158 females) primarily account for the sharp decline in the growth in population of working age between the Censuses of 1933 and 1947. The high rate between 1901 and 1911 reflects especially the high birth rates and immigration during the 1870s and 1880s.

Since 1947 an important feature has been the progressive increase in the rate of growth of population of working age while the rate of population growth itself (though it is still high) has steadily declined (see Table 14, column 8). The relatively high rate of increase of total population in the early post-war years was due initially to the marriage- and baby-booms and then to the very high level of immigration.

(b) Contribution from Immigration

It was the very high level of immigration that primarily explains the significantly higher rate of growth of total labour force than of population of working age during the years 1947 and 1954 (see Table 14, columns 9 and 12). In the 1950s and the first half of the 1960s immigration largely offset the low addition to the labour force accruing from natural increase following the low birth rates during the 1930s and the early years of World War II. The contribution of immigration to the labour force was most significant in the 1950s. Between the Censuses of 1947 and 1961 Australia's labour force grew from 3·20 million to 4·23 million. Immigrants who arrived in Australia between the Censuses of 1947 and 1961 provided 73 per cent of the increase of just over one million in the labour force, the share of the increase in the male labour force being 82 per cent and in the female 55 per cent. In the 1960s the contribution of immigration to the growth in the labour force, though still considerable, fell to a little below 50 per cent of the increase. The addition to the labour force from natural increase has steadily risen as those born during the post-war baby-boom have entered the labour force.

(c) Changes in the Labour-force Participation Rate

Apart from the effects of changes in the rates of natural increase and immigration upon the rates of growth of the labour force, there have been some significant changes of a social and educational character in labour-force participation rates. Table 15 reveals three important changes.

The first is the sharp decline in labour-force participation by the old-aged, in particular by males. At the 1911 Census, 91·9 per cent of males aged 65-69 years and 80·1 per cent of those 70 and over

TABLE 15
LABOUR-FORCE PARTICIPATION RATES, AUSTRALIA, CENSUSES,
1911 TO 1966
(Per cent)

Age group	1911	1921	1933	1947	1954	1961	1966
				Males			
10–14	16·1	9·9	3·1	3·3	2·8	1·5	(a)
15–19	90·7	87·1	68·8	81·1	79·7	69·6	66·2
20–24	98·9	97·7	96·0	93·7	96·6	94·9	93·8
25–29	99·6	98·8	98·1	96·7	98·4	98·2	97·2
30–34	99·6	99·2	98·1	98·0	98·5	98·6	97·7
35–39	99·6	99·2	97·1	98·0	98·3	98·5	97·6
40–44	99·5	99·2	96·7	97·7	98·0	98·0	97·1
45–49	99·5	99·1	96·2	96·7	97·4	97·5	96·3
50–54	99·3	98·8	94·7	94·2	95·7	96·0	94·7
55–59	98·9	98·1	92·1	91·3	91·5	92·7	91·2
60–64	97·3	96·6	83·3	79·9	79·8	79·6	79·5
65–69	91·9	91·7	47·8	49·6	48·8	40·1⎱	24·9
70 and over	80·1	78·1	24·0	22·8	21·6	17·8⎰	
All ages	68·7	66·8	63·2	65·3	62·8	59·6	58·8
				Females			
10–14	5·4	3·9	1·8	2·3	2·2	1·4	(a)
15–19	44·1	47·8	44·6	66·4	68·2	64·4	62·2
20–24	41·0	44·0	50·0	49·1	48·7	50·8	58·9
25–29	27·0	26·3	30·7	24·4	26·4	27·0	34·5
30–34	19·9	18·4	20·3	18·3	21·7	24·2	32·0
35–39	18·2	16·3	17·1	18·3	21·6	27·0	35·8
40–44	17·3	16·1	16·3	19·1	23·4	28·1	38·2
45–49	17·0	16·3	16·3	19·1	24·4	28·0	37·0
50–54	16·5	15·6	16·2	17·1	22·4	26·2	32·7
55–59	16·5	14·5	15·5	15·2	18·4	22·3	27·2
60–64	15·6	12·2	10·5	10·4	11·9	13·3	16·5
65–69	13·2	9·5	7·0	6·9	7·0	7·0⎱	4·9
70 and over	10·0	6·8	3·8	3·6	3·5	3·0⎰	
All ages	18·2	17·1	18·1	19·0	19·0	20·4	23·0

Note: (a) Not available.
Sources: 1911 to 1961, *Census of the Commonwealth of Australia* (various issues),
and 1966 computed from data in *Census of the Commonwealth of Australia,
30 June 1966, Census Bulletin No. 9.7*, pp. 5 and 7.

were recorded as being in the labour force. These proportions had
declined only slightly at the 1921 Census, but by the following Census
in 1933 there had been a considerable fall. The proportions then
changed little to the 1947 Census, but have fallen further and more
sharply since. The pace of this decline reflects roughly the introduction
and the progressive improvement and acceptance of the Commonwealth Government's social services in Australia which generally

commenced with the old-age pension scheme in 1908. The number who accepted the pension increased sharply with the fall in real income and employment during the depression in the early 1930s. Since World War II the increase in the range of social services and the improvements in services previously adopted, including the easing of the eligibility requirements of the pension, have contributed to the speedier decline in labour-force participation of males 65 and over.

The second major change which has occurred through the period has been the trend of young people, in particular of males, to remain longer in full-time education. The subject of education is examined in more detail later in this chapter. But there are several points worth noting here. Labour-force participation of males in the age groups 10-14 and 15-19 declined between 1911 and 1921, especially the former group. The exceptionally low participation rate at the 1933 Census was an effect of the depression in the early 1930s. However, if we view the position between 1921 and 1947, and for later Censuses, it is apparent that the earlier downward trend in male participation rates below 20 has continued since World War II. There has also been a downward trend in female participation rates below the age of 20 years, but it has been much less marked. The increasing proportion of young people continuing their education through secondary schools and at universities considerably retarded the number of new entrants to the labour force during the 1950s, and in the 1960s delayed the entry of many of the first post-war generation.

The third important change in labour-force participation (offsetting the trend to full-time education) has been the rise in the female participation rate. In 1901 the female component of the work force was 20·4 per cent[10]. By 1947 the proportion had risen to 22·4 per cent, and by 1954 to 22·8 per cent. Since then, there has been a sharper rise of the female component to 24·8 per cent at the 1961 Census and to 28·4 per cent in 1966[11]. Table 15 shows that this rise has occurred at all ages except below 20 and over 64.

The continued rise in female participation rates has contributed appreciably to the increasing rate of growth of the female labour force since 1947 (see Table 14, column 11). The increase partly offset the falling rate of growth of the male labour force between 1954 and 1961, and more than did so between 1961 and 1966. In consequence there was, during the latter period, a significant rise in the rate of growth of the total labour force, which in fact increased at the highest average annual rate for an intercensal period during this century.

---

10 Table 14, cols 4 and 5.

11 On the revised definition of the labour force at the 1966 Census the female component was 30·2 per cent. See Table 14, note (b).

Increases in the proportion of women working have occurred in many other countries, and in some, including Great Britain, the United States, Canada, West Germany, France, and Japan the proportion is higher than in Australia. It is likely that the proportion of women in Australia's labour force will continue to rise. The propensity to do so has been strong among both migrant and Australian-born women.

Another interesting development in Australia has been the strong upward trend in the proportion of the female labour force which is married. The proportion was 11·0 per cent in 1933 (Table 14, column 7). With the shortages of manpower during World War II, many married women entered the labour force, to remain after the war. The proportion thus stood at 19·8 per cent in 1947. Since then the proportion has continued to increase sharply and in February 1970 had reached 56·3 per cent[12]. Furthermore, since 1947 the increase in the female labour force has been primarily of married women. This also reflects, as noted earlier, the significantly higher proportion of married women in the population since World War II.

(d) Trends in Industrial Distribution

There is much that we can learn about the pattern of economic development of our society by studying the changes in the relative distribution of the expanding labour force between industry groups. This is the purpose of Table 16 which shows the size and percentages by industry groups of the total labour force engaged at each of the Censuses taken during this century.

These percentages contain three striking changes:

(i) The decline in the percentage of workers employed in the primary industries (which comprise mainly agricultural, pastoral, and dairying). The proportion has fallen progressively at each Census from 32·9 per cent of the total labour force in 1901 to 10·8 per cent in 1966, that is, a fall of about two thirds of the 1901 proportion. The total number engaged in primary industries has also fallen steadily since the Census peak in 1933.

(ii) The percentage of the labour force employed in manufacturing advanced from about 17 per cent to 20 per cent of the labour force during the first decade of the twentieth century. The share of the workers in manufacturing then changed little between the Censuses of 1911 and 1933. By the end of World War II the proportion had advanced to 27·6 per cent, but there has been little change since, manufacturing employment thus growing at roughly the same pace as the total labour force.

---

12 Commonwealth Bureau of Census and Statistics, *The Labour Force, February 1970.*

Twentieth Century Economic Development in Australia

TABLE 16

LABOUR FORCE CLASSIFIED BY INDUSTRY GROUPS, NUMBERS, AND

Number ('000)

Industry Group	1901[a]	1911	1921	1933	1947	1954
1 Primary Activities						
a Fishing & trapping	10	12	13	14	16	11
b Agricultural, pastoral & dairying	381	456	492	554	464	475
c Forestry	21	24	28	28	25	15
d Mining & quarrying	119	110	68	71	58	62
TOTAL PRIMARY	531	602	601	667	563	560
2 Secondary Activities	[b]	[b]	[b]			
a Manufacturing	272	394	494	519	882	1038
3 Tertiary Activities						
a Building	65	88	98	110	144	200
b Construction: roads, railways, earthworks	[c] 98	[c] 91	[c] 139	[d] 222	[e] 124	129
c Electricity, gas, water supply etc.	[b][c]	[b][c]	[b][c]	30	[e] 35	74
d Transport & communication	116	163	212	227	323	339
e Commerce & finance	212	289	336	459	517	679
f Public authority (n.e.i.) & professional	120	145	219	237	367	456
g Entertainment, sport & recreation	6	14	18	25	35	38
h Personal & domestic service	195	205	212	248	206	189
TOTAL TERTIARY	812	994	1234	1558	1751	2104
4 TOTAL LABOUR FORCE	1615	1990	2329	2744	3196	3702

Notes: [a] Includes pensioners and retired persons whose previous industry was recorded on Census Schedules.
[b] Electricity and gas included in manufacturing.
[c] Water supply etc. included in construction.

TABLE 16

PERCENTAGE DISTRIBUTION, AUSTRALIA, CENSUSES 1901 TO 1966

		Per cent							
1961	1966	1901	1911	1921	1933	1947	1954	1961	1966
8	9	0·6	0·6	0·5	0·5	0·5	0·3	0·2	0·2
444	443	23·6	22·9	21·1	20·2	14·5	12·8	10·5	9·1
17	13	1·3	1·2	1·3	1·0	0·8	0·4	0·4	0·3
56	57	7·4	5·5	2·9	2·6	1·8	1·6	1·3	1·2
525	522	32·9	30·2	25·8	24·3	17·6	15·1	12·4	10·8
		(b)	(b)	(b)					
1164	1339	16·8	19·8	21·2	19·0	27·6	28·0	27·5	27·6
240	283	4·0	4·4	4·2	4·0	4·5	5·4	5·7	5·8
		(c)	(c)	(c)	(d)	(c)			
139	155	6·1	4·6	6·0	8·1	3·9	3·5	3·3	3·2
		(b)(c)	(b)(c)	(b)(c)		(c)			
96	108				1·0	1·1	2·0	2·3	2·2
371	390	7·2	8·2	9·1	8·3	10·1	9·2	8·8	8·0
844	985	13·1	14·5	14·4	16·7	16·2	18·5	20·0	20·3
592	773	7·4	7·3	9·4	8·6	11·5	12·2	14·0	15·9
42	49	0·4	0·7	0·8	0·9	1·1	1·0	1·0	1·0
212	252	12·1	10·3	9·1	9·1	6·4	5·1	5·0	5·2
2536	2995	50·3	50·0	53·0	56·7	54·8	56·9	60·1	61·6
4225	4856	100·0	100·0	100·0	100·0	100·0	100·0	100·0	100·0

(d) Includes 165,000 labourers (6·1 per cent of persons engaged in industry) whose industry was not stated. The majority of these were unemployed or employed part-time.

Source: *Census of the Commonwealth of Australia* (various issues).

(iii) So a third prominent feature of the changing composition of the labour force has been the steady expansion of the tertiary industries, in which about 62 per cent of the total labour force is now employed, compared with about 50 per cent at the beginning of the century. Thus, in absolute terms, the greater part of the increase in the labour force is now absorbed in the tertiary industries. For instance, between the 1961 and 1966 Censuses, while the number engaged in primary industries fell by about 3,000, and those employed in manufacturing rose by 175,000, the number in the tertiary sector rose by 459,000.

These trends, involving the decline in the relative importance of employment in primary industries and the growth of manufacturing and later the dominating role of tertiary employment, are recognized characteristics of the process of development in the more highly developed countries. In Australia it means that it is now largely the white-collar industries that are absorbing the greater part of the expansion of the labour force.

There have also been some very important changes within the secondary and tertiary sectors, as may be seen more clearly from the data in Table 17. This indicates at a glance, insomuch as labour absorption is concerned, the leading growth industries, and also those that are declining or relatively slow growing in terms of employment. Among the relatively slow growing are textiles and clothing in the manufacturing sector and 'transport and storage' in the tertiary. These are also the sluggish or declining industries for employment in other relatively developed countries.

The growth industries (in terms of labour absorption) in the manufacturing and tertiary sectors may be classified as those industries whose percentage gain in employment has exceeded the percentage increase in the total labour force. The industries which stand out in this respect since World War II include the heavy manufacturing industries of founding, engineering, and metalworking, vehicles and ships, paper and printing, and chemicals; while in the tertiary group, the main growth areas have been construction and repair of buildings, communications, finance and property, commerce, and community and business services.

This analysis particularly identifies the labour-intensive growth industries, which include 'finance and property', 'commerce', and 'public authority (n.e.i.) and professional'. It also indicates industry groups which, though labour-saving or capital-intensive, are relatively new industries and/or have grown from a relatively low base, for instance, 'vehicles and ships' and 'chemicals'. But the change in the distribution of the labour force between industry groups does not

TABLE 17
PERCENTAGE CHANGES IN NUMBERS ENGAGED IN VARIOUS
INDUSTRIES, AUSTRALIA, BETWEEN CERTAIN CENSUSES,
1947 TO 1966

Industry Group	1947 to 1954	1954 to 1961	1961 to 1966
1 Primary			
Agricultural, pastoral, and dairying	2	−7	—
Mining and quarrying	7	−10	2
TOTAL PRIMARY	−1	−6	−1
2 Secondary: Manufacturing			
Cement, bricks, glass, stone	54	12	12
Founding, engineering, and metalworking	25	27	19
Vehicles and ships	104	1	25
Textiles	10	−4	8
Clothing, knitted and footwear	6	−7	5
Food, drink and tobacco	21	6	15
Paper and printing	26	23	17
Chemicals	38	28	12
TOTAL MANUFACTURING	18	12	15
3 Tertiary			
Building	39	20	18
Construction works other than building	4	8	12
Transport and storage	4	6	3
Communications	65	16	11
Finance and property	27	50	28
Commerce	42	19	14
Public authority (n.e.i.) and professional	24	30	31
Personal and domestic service	−8	12	19
TOTAL TERTIARY	20	21	18
4 TOTAL LABOUR FORCE	16	14	15

Source: Computed from data in *Census of the Commonwealth of Australia* (various issues).

adequately or necessarily indicate the relative contribution of the respective groups to the total growth in output. This is because of the variable amount of capital and land employed with labour, and hence of the varying degrees of application of labour-saving or capital-intensive techniques which have made labour redundant. Technological progress involving an increase in the capital-labour ratio has been increasing even in traditionally labour-intensive tertiary industries through, for instance, the increasing application of electronic automotive processes in finance, commerce, and public authority enterprises. The developments in this respect are discussed further in Chapter 5.

(e) The Increasing Quality of the Labour Force

During the last three decades of the nineteenth century the Australian colonies each established systems of compulsory education at the primary level. Initially school attendance was compulsory (though not always enforced) between the ages of 6 or 7 and 12 to 14 years (the variations applying between the colonies). Attendance is now compulsory throughout Australia between the ages of 6 and 15 years at least.

Australia's efforts in the field of education compare unfavourably with those of many other countries, in particular beyond the primary level. The enrolment ratios of full-time students of the age-groups 15-19 years and 20-24 years have been considerably lower in Australia than in most Western European and North American countries[13]. In 1958 the proportion of students in the 15-19 years age-group in Australia (about 20·3 per cent) was only one-third the proportion in the United States, less than one-half those in the Soviet Union and in Canada, but a little higher than the proportions in the United Kingdom, West Germany, Greece, and Italy. Australia's enrolment ratio of the 20-24 years age group (1·9 per cent) was one-sixth that in the United States and also below those in the other foregoing countries. These figures of different countries are, of course, not strictly comparable.

Australia's expenditure on education still compares unfavourably with other Western European and North American countries when the more comprehensive and common comparison is made in terms of current and capital expenditure on education as a percentage of G.N.P. In 1958 Australia's total expenditure was about 3·0 per cent (2·4 per cent current and 0·6 capital) compared with a total of 4·5 per cent in the United States, and 3·7 per cent each in Canada, the United Kingdom, and the Soviet Union. This global measure could be misleading since it conceals differences in the age structure of the population and in the structures and qualities of the educational systems. Caution must therefore be exercised in drawing conclusions from these comparisons. But it seems clear that, in comparison with the expenditure on education in other advanced countries, Australia comes well down in the field. This applies to technical education as well as to general secondary and tertiary education. The Tripartite Mission (comprising government, employer, and trade union representatives) which was appointed by the Commonwealth Government in 1968 to examine the methods of training skilled workers in a number of European countries found that Australia's position compares unfavourably in important respects simply because the resources devoted by govern-

---

13 The comparisons in this and the next paragraph are from P. H. Karmel's Buntine Oration to the Australian College of Education, Melbourne, 18 May 1962. Reprinted as Chapter 2 in R.W.T. Cowan (ed.), *Education for Australians*, Cheshire, 1964. See also *Vernon Report*, Vol. I, pp. 110–111.

ments and employers in Australia to the training of skilled workers are small compared to their counterparts in Europe[14].

Comparison with other countries becomes even more unfavourable when allowance is made for the fact that a higher proportion of Australia's population has been of school age than in most other countries. Furthermore, the increasing proportion of school age (see Table 9) partly accounts for the fact that Australia's expenditure on education as a proportion of G.N.P. has been rising since World War II. There are no official estimates of private capital expenditure on education. Estimates of public current and capital expenditure and of private current expenditure are published in the *Australian National Accounts*. If we add to these an estimate for private capital expenditure, we find that total public and private expenditure on education as a proportion of G.N.P. has risen steadily from 1·8 per cent in 1948-9 (1·6 per cent current and 0·2 per cent capital) to 4·3 per cent in 1968-9 (3·3 per cent current and 1·0 per cent capital).

TABLE 18
PERCENTAGES OF POPULATION OF CERTAIN AGE GROUPS ENGAGED IN FULL-TIME EDUCATION, AUSTRALIA, CERTAIN CENSUSES, 1911 TO 1966

Census	MALES		FEMALES	
	15–19 years	20–24 years	15–19 years	20–24 years
1911	6·5	0·7	8·6	0·5
1921	8·6	1·2	11·2	0·5
1947	12·2	4·7[a]	10·4	1·1[a]
1954	18·2	2·1	16·7	0·8
1961	20 4	3·7	24·0	1·2
1966	31·6	3·7	28·0	1·4

Note. [a] Includes Commonwealth Reconstruction Trainee Students.
Source: Census of the Commonwealth of Australia (various issues).

Though an important part of the increase in expenditure on education reflects the increase in the proportion of the population of school age, it also reflects the trend towards a higher education for an increasing proportion of young people. Evidence of the greater numbers engaged in full-time education, especially at the secondary school level, appears in Table 18. This shows that over the fifty-five years since 1911, the enrolment ratios in the age groups 15-19 years and 20-24 years have both increased about five times for males and

14 See Report of Australian Tripartite Mission, *The Training of Skilled Workers in Europe*, 1969, especially Chap. 24.

three times for females. A further interesting change is that whereas in 1911 and 1921 a higher proportion of females remained longer at secondary education (because of the lesser employment opportunities for them), since World War II the proportion of males has been higher. The higher proportion of males than females remaining at full-time education has been even more significant at the tertiary level.

We have previously noted that the trend towards a higher education during the 1950s and the first half of the 1960s significantly retarded the growth of the labour force from the natural increase in population, particularly the male labour force. By the same token, from the late 1960s there has been a substantial increase in the number in the labour force with higher educational qualifications. The number will be high both because of the increased interest in higher education and the favourable age-structure following the high birth rates in the early post-war years. Meanwhile, shortages in the supply of skilled labour in Australia have been met through the immigration programme. Proportionally more of the addition to the labour force from immigration than of the addition from natural increase has been skilled or semi-skilled.

The additional supplies of more highly educated native-born workers offers a challenge to Australian industry, and employers in particular, to take full advantage of the opportunities thus presented. It should assist Australia to keep on raising its productivity and the general standard of living, and to hold its position as a relatively highly developed country. In doing this, Australia benefits not only herself but all countries with which she trades.

Economically, the expenditure on higher education has appropriately been viewed as an investment in human capital. It is a form of investment with an especially long gestation period. But it yields high returns in the long run. It provides workers with the knowledge and skills required to meet the demand of the technological world. The increasing attention to education is not something new. For at least three centuries economists have emphasized the fundamental role of human capital. Thus it is not surprising that the revival of interest in economic growth since World War II has included increasing attention to the economics of education. This is essentially aimed at ensuring that the expenditure on education fits the requirements of the economy, thus stimulating many of the forces contributing to socio-economic progress. Education of the right quality and relevance aids the application of appropriate techniques for the discovery and successful exploitation of natural resources, and for the efficient development of industry and commerce, thereby raising productivity and living standards.

This view of education as an investment in human capital does not indicate that a purely utilitarian approach has been taken to education and the role of human life. Education is also necessary to fulfil a country's cultural, poltical, and social goals. It provides a more satisfying intellectual life as well as giving man greater freedom and control over his resources allowing a higher real income, and hence a higher standard of living. The rapid technological advance, as has occurred since World War II, gives added importance and justification to the increasing quality of Australia's labour force.

Australia has also been fortunate throughout her history in being able to bridge technological gaps in her education, training, and know-how by importing capital and labour to assist the achievement of more rapid rates of economic growth. At the same time Australia has appeared a sufficiently profitable field economically, and a stable one politically, to attract overseas investors and migrants.

Suggestions for further reading

Appleyard, R. T. 'The Effect of Unemployment on Immigration to Australia', *Economic Record*, Vol. 39, March 1963, pp. 65-80; and *British Emigration to Australia*, A.N.U., 1964;

Borrie, W. D. and Spencer, G. *Australia's Population Structure and Growth*, Committee for Economic Development of Australia, 2nd revised edn, 1965;

Boxer, A. H. (ed.), *Aspects of the Australian Economy*, Chap. 1;

Kelley, A. C. 'International Migration and Economic Growth: Australia, 1865-1935', *Journal of Economic History*, Vol. 25, September 1965, pp. 333-54;

Samuelson, P. A. and others, *Economics: Australian edition*, Chaps 2 and 29;

Vernon Report, Vol. I, Chap 4; and Vol. II, App. C;

Current Affairs Bulletin, *Immigration 20 Years After*, Vol. 13, December 1968

Chapter 4

THE EXPORT INDUSTRIES

1 THE DEVELOPMENT OF STAPLE EXPORTS

A major part of the story of Australia's economic development in the twentieth century concerns the continued expansion of the staple exports, which had been firmly established in the nineteenth century. The type of exports had been largely determined by the characteristics of the Australian economy. In particular, the smallness of Australia's domestic market made it impossible to initiate and sustain rapid growth internally. The relative scarcity of labour and capital required the development of exports which relied heavily on the intensive exploitation of the abundant natural resources of land and minerals.

(a) Staple Theory

The dynamic influence of staple exports as the leading growth sector of a new country has been discussed by economic historians in terms of the staple theory. The essence of the staple theory, for a 'colony of settlement' such as Australia, is that if it can produce and sell a product of sufficient importance to an external industrial market which is many times the size of its own market, then the product can initiate and sustain growth on a large scale.

The stimulus to growth occurs not simply through the rising income obtained from the export receipts themselves. There are fundamental spread effects of the staple on the structure of the domestic economy deriving from the production function[1] of the staple[2]. Through the production function we can make an arbitrary division between the inputs of land (or natural resources), labour, and capital, and the way in which these are combined through the level of technology in order to satisfy the diversified demand for goods and services centred on the export base.

---

1 The production function is the name economists give to the technical law relating inputs to output.

2 For a useful summary of staple theory and of the distinctive contributions by Canadian economic historians, see M. H. Watkins, 'A Staple Theory of Economic Growth', *Canadian Journal of Economic and Political Science*, Vol. 29, May 1963.

The spread effects occur in two main interrelated ways. First, there are backward and forward linkage effects. 'Backward linkage is a measure of the inducement to invest in the home-production of inputs, including capital goods, for the expanding export sector. . . . Forward linkage is a measure of the inducement to invest in industries using the output of the export industry as an input[3].' Secondly, the spread effects involve the distribution of the income which is generated directly and indirectly by the staple. The higher the average income of staple producers and the more evenly the income is distributed, the more favourable will the stimulus to domestic growth generally be. The spending of the income induces investment in other sectors. A classification of these income flows would enable staple theory to be stated in terms of the primary and induced expenditure on consumption and investment[4]. In brief, through favourable spread effects of the staple, a viable process of economic development is initiated and sustained in the domestic economy in many directions.

In Australia's early economic development several staples played a prominent part. Apparently these started with the whale and seal fisheries in the early nineteenth century[5]. This was soon replaced by wool as the leading staple, and then also gold after 1851. Wheat and minerals other than gold became important later in the nineteenth century (see Table 19[6]). In the 1890s the new exports of butter and frozen meat and the more rapid expansion of the meat by-products hides, skins, and tallow further diversified the export base[7]. The growth of the leading staples and the rise of new ones provided the most important primary basis to Australia's rapid, sustained development in the nineteenth century[8].

(b) Linkage Effects

The rise of staple exports, which entailed the exploitation of pastoral and agricultural resources and minerals, stimulated a considerable demand for labour and capital and advances in technology. The backward linkage effects in the pastoral and agricultural industries meant,

---

3 *Ibid*, p. 145.

4 This means that the staple theory can be stated in the form of 'a disaggregated multiplier-accelerator mechanism'. *Ibid.*

5 See G. Blainey, 'Technology in Australian History', *Business Archives and History*, Vol. IV, August 1964.

6 For a discussion of the treatment of gold in Table 19 (and some later tables), see E. A. Boehm, 'Measuring Australian Economic Growth, 1861 to 1938–39', *Economic Record*, Vol. 41, June 1965, pp. 222–4.

7 For a detailed account of the part played by the various exports in the 1880s and 1890s, see Boehm, *Prosperity and Depression in Australia*, Chap. 5.

8 See: J. W. McCarty, 'The Staple Approach in Australian Economic History', *Business Archives and History*, Vol. IV, February 1964; and G. Blainey, *loc. cit.*

TABLE 19
EXPORTS OF PRINCIPAL ARTICLES OF AUSTRALIAN PRODUCE AND GOLD PRODUCTION AS A PERCENTAGE OF TOTAL HOME-PRODUCED MERCHANDISE EXPORTS AND GOLD PRODUCTION, SELECTED PERIODS, 1881–1968/9

Period	Wool	Wheat	Flour	Butter	Meats	Hides and Skins	Tallow	Fruit	Sugar	Minerals (excl. gold)	Gold production	Other	Average annual of total home-produced merchandise and gold production
	1	2	3	4	5	6	7	8	9	10	11	12	13
													$m.
						Percentage of total							
1881–90	54·1	4·2	1·1	0·1	1·2	1·7	1·7	0·2	0·5	9·6	17·6	7·9	56
1891–1900	43·5	2·4	0·5	2·4	4·1	3·1	2·6	0·3	0·4	9·5	23·6	7·6	76
1901–1913	34·3	8·1	1·6	4·1	5·1	4·4	1·7	0·5	—	14·8	20·6	4·8	128
1920/21–1928/29	42·9	16·2	4·3	5·6	4·6	5·4	1·1	2·2	1·6	6·6	2·2	7·3	264
1929/30–1931/32	34·9	15·2	4·3	8·6	6·4	4·3	0·8	4·8	2·3	6·0	3·1	9·3	192
1932/33–1938/39	37·0	11·0	3·6	7·6	7·1	3·7	0·5	4·2	2·1	5·3	7·5	10·4	261
1945/46–1949/50	43·4	9·4	6·1	4·6	6·0	3·3	0·2	2·0	1·8	5·4	2·2	15·6	819
1950/51–1954/55	51·9	6·3	3·7	2·0	6·2	2·5	—	3·1	2·6	6·4	1·9	13·4	1638
1955/56–1959/60	43·9	5·5	2·0	2·9	8·2	3·0	—	3·7	3·4	7·2	1·9	18·3	1716
1960/61–1964/65	34·9	12·1	1·6	2·2	9·6	3·2	—	3·3	4·4	7·7	1·4	19·6	2255
1965/66–1968/69	25·8	10·0	0·8	1·7	9·4	2·5	—	3·3	3·4	13·8	0·7	28·6	3064

Sources: Percentages computed from data in: *Statistical Register* (various issues) of each colony for years 1881–1900, and Commonwealth Bureau of Census and Statistics, *Official Year Book of the Commonwealth of Australia* (various issues).

in particular, investment in the clearing of land and in the provision of agricultural machinery, fencing, building materials, and fertilizers. The forward linkages involved the development of the processing industries (such as, with wheat, flour milling for both local consumption and export) and the service industries handling the sale and distribution of commodities. Thus there was substantial investment in the development of financial enterprises and in road and rail transport and port facilities. The growth of base metal mining (e.g. the rich silver-lead deposits at Broken Hill) also had important linkages: backward in the demand for mining equipment and fuel, and forward in needing railways and smelting plants at or near the mine, or port of export.

Sometimes it is historically difficult or impossible to identify a particular piece of investment as resulting entirely from either backward or forward linkages. There is a close relationship between both linkages, each acting as cause and effect of the other. Thus the financial and distribution services were both supported by and aided the development associated with the backward linkages. Forward linkages of wool and wheat were the investments in extensive road and railway networks in order to provide speedy, cheap transport to ports. Backward linkages occurred when the transport systems stimulated a more intensive as well as extensive development of land. The transport systems also provided backward linkages of their own by the demand for materials, notably metal for road-making and iron, steel, and coal for the railway.

Some staples had more linkages and stronger effects than others on the growth and diversification of the economy. This reflects the different income distribution and production functions of the staples — in particular the different proportions of the factors labour and capital. The closer settlement associated with wheat and dairy farming and mining stimulated the quicker growth of country towns, with their own processing plants and manufacturing and service enterprises, in order to meet the growing demand from the staple industry and from urban dwellers. By contrast, the linkages flowing from the more land-using wool growing and cattle raising industries were less significant regionally than the linkages generated by the income obtained by both these staples. In a more detailed study of the growth of the staples it would be important to pay closer attention to the contrasting regional and national influences of different staples[9].

---

9 For emphasis on the need to study staples regionally, see McCarty, *op. cit.*, and Blainey, *op. cit.*

TABLE 20

PROPORTION OF VALUE OF EXPORTS OF AUSTRALIAN PRODUCE(a) ACCORDING TO INDUSTRIAL GROUPS, SELECTED YEARS, 1953–4 TO 1967–8

Year	Agri., Horti., and Viti-cultural	Pastoral	Dairy and Farm-yard	Mines and Quarry-ing (a)	Fisheries	Forestry	Total Primary Produce			Manu-factures	Refined Petroleum Oils	Un-classified	Total Value (a)
							Unpro-cessed	Pro-cessed	Total				$m
	1	2	3	4	5	6	7	8	9	10	11	12	13
					Percentage of Total								
1953–54	19·2	60·8	5·7	6·5	0·5	0·4	62·4	30·7	93·1	6·0	—	0·9	806
1956–57	17·1	58·8	5·0	8·2	0·6	0·4	63·7	26·4	90·1	7·7	1·0	1·2	965
1959–60	18·2	57·0	5·4	6·2	0·6	0·4	62·8	25·0	87·8	9·2	1·7	1·3	1819
1962–63	22·5	51·8	4·4	7·0	0·7	0·3	63·3	23·4	86·7	9·8	2·2	1·3	2093
1963–64	26·7	48·7	3·7	7·1	0·6	0·2	63·4	23·6	87·0	10·3	1·4	1·3	2713
1964–65	23·5	46·4	4·6	9·5	0·7	0·2	61·9	23·0	84·9	12·5	0·9	1·7	2564
1965–66	21·0	45·4	3·9	11·4	1·0	0·2	60·1	22·8	82·9	14·5	0·7	1·9	2614
1966–67	22·9	41·3	4·2	11·7	1·0	0·2	60·6	20·7	81·3	15·6	1·0	2·1	2918
1967–68	21·8	37·2	3·3	15·6	1·2	0·2	58·8	20·5	79·3	16·8	1·1	2·8	2920

Note: (a) Excluding gold.

Source: Commonwealth Bureau of Census and Statistics, *Official Year Book of the Commonwealth of Australia* (various issues).

2 MAJOR CHANGES IN THE COMPOSITION OF EXPORTS

As noted at the beginning of this chapter, the growth of Australia's export industries in the twentieth century has largely consisted of the further development of staples which were established in the previous century. One of the significant recent changes in the relative import- ance of leading exports has been the rise in the value of exports of manufactures (see Table 20). This aspect is discussed in more detail in Chapter 6.

(a) Gold Production

An outstanding change, visible in Table 19, is the sharp decline in the importance of gold production. The trend in the annual value of gold production can also be seen in the lower part of Chart 5. This shows that, except during the 1930s and the early years after World War II, gold production has moved against the trend of merchandise exports and G.N.P. Gold production generally declines during periods of rising prices and costs of production. Contrariwise, gold production has expanded when prices and costs have fallen; this was particularly so during the depressions in the 1890s and 1930s when many workers who had lost their jobs turned to gold mining[10].

(b) The Relative Importance of Exports of Wool and Minerals

At the beginning of the twentieth century wool was briefly displaced as Australia's chief export. This resulted from the combination of the peak level of gold production in 1903 and the rising exports of other minerals (mainly coal, copper, and silver-lead), while wool exports fell sharply following the effects of depression and then drought in the 1890s.

But wool regained its position as Australia's leading export by about 1905. Though wool's contribution to export receipts has fluctuated considerably, wool has strongly retained its leadership since then, as shown in Table 19. The exports of minerals (excluding gold) declined considerably in the 1920s, and remained relatively low through to the 1950s. However, the renewed rapid expansion of Australia's mineral industries since the early 1960s has meant a sharp increase in mineral exports (in particular, aluminium, copper, iron, lead, and coal). Table 20 shows that the relative importance of mineral exports (excluding gold) has risen from about 6·2 per cent in 1959-60 to 15·6 per cent in 1967-8.

---

10 See Boehm, *op. cit.*, Chap. 5 (section 3), for an explanation of why capital and labour in a gold-producing country are attracted during a depression to gold mining, and for a description of the rise in gold production in Australia in the 1890s.

CHART 5
G.N.P. AT CURRENT AND CONSTANT[a] PRICES, MERCHANDISE EXPORTS AT CURRENT AND CONSTANT[a] PRICES, VALUE OF GOLD PRODUCTION, AND EXPORT PRICE INDEX, 1901–69
(Ratio Chart)

A major reason for the rise in mineral exports was the partial relaxation in December 1960 of the embargo on the export of iron ore which had been applied in 1938. The modification of the export embargo greatly increased the exploration for, and discoveries of, iron ore. This led to a further relaxation of the restrictions on exports in 1963 when it became apparent that Australia's reserves of iron ore, especially in Western Australia, are very extensive[11].

The sharp decline in the relative importance of the value of wool exports from the early 1950s was caused principally by the falling price of wool[12] due to displacement by synthetics. As Dr Snape reported:

'in the U.K. total wool usage has not changed markedly over the last twenty years, but synthetic competitors have increased their share to roughly a quarter (by weight) of the wool-type fibres market. In Japan, on the other hand, the textile industry had grown rapidly enough to enable a doubling of wool consumption between 1956 and 1964, despite a growth of the share of wool-type synthetics from about 17 per cent to 50 per cent of the total. This displacement by synthetics can be expected to continue[13].'

In 1959-60 Japan displaced the United Kingdom as the largest buyer of Australian wool.

The outlook for Australia's mineral export trade is very bright. Mineral exports totalled $342 million in 1966-7. By 1968-9 they had reached $736 million while wool exports totalled $796·5 million. In the 1970s mineral exports will probably exceed wool exports by a significant margin. On the basis of firm contracts mineral export earnings are, on a conservative estimate by the Department of National

---

11 *Official Year Book of the Commonwealth of Australia* (various issues). For a critical discussion of Australia's export policies since World War II regarding iron ore and uranium, see G Blainey, 'The Cargo Cult in Mineral Policy', *Economic Record*, Vol. 44, December 1968, pp. 470–9.

12 The export price index for wool (base 1959–60 = 100), after being at a record peak of 235 in 1950–1, and then falling to 85 in 1958–9, in the 1960s fluctuated between a low of 92 in 1960–1 and a high of 120 in 1963–4. In 1968–9 the index stood at 99. Source: Commonwealth Bureau of Census and Statistics, *Quarterly Summary of Australian Statistics* (various issues).

13 R. H. Snape, *International Trade and the Australian Economy*, Longman, 1969, p. 49.

Chart 5
Note: (a) At average 1959–60 prices.
Sources: N. G. Butlin, *Australian Domestic Product;* N. G. Butlin, *Investment in Australian Economic Development;* R. Wilson, *Capital Imports and the Terms of Trade,* p. 89; Commonwealth Bureau of Census and Statistics, *Australian National Accounts,* 1967–8, pp. 28–9; *National Income and Expenditure 1968–69,* p. 16, and *Official Year Book of the Commonwealth of Australia* (various issues).

Development, expected to approximate $1227 million in 1970-1 and to continue to rise rapidly to about $1800 million in the mid-1970s.

(c) Wheat

The relative contribution to export receipts from wheat reached a peak in the 1920s. During the first two decades of the twentieth century, there was a strong rise in wheat exports, though sharp fluctuations from varying weather conditions occurred in some years (see Chart 6). The uptrend reflected two main elements[14]. First, there was a rise in the yield of wheat per acre. The yield had fallen from about 15 bushels in the early 1860s to between 5 and 7 bushels in the mid-1890s. The growing application of fertilizers, particularly superphosphate, from the 1890s, contributed largely to the sharp recovery in wheat yields to an average of 12 bushels between the two world wars.

The second and more important element underlying the rise in wheat exports was the increase in the area under 'wheat for grain'. The area had risen from just above 5 million acres in the early 1900s to 9·1 million in 1920-1[15]. It expanded steadily during the 1920s, reaching 12·3 million acres in 1927-8. It then accelerated to 15·0 million in 1929-30 and a peak of 18·2 million in 1930-1, which was not surpassed until 1966-7. In 1968-9 the record of 26·6 million acres was sown to 'wheat for grain'.

While the area under wheat increased strongly in the late 1920s the wheat yield declined from an average of nearly 14 bushels per acre in the first half of that decade to just under 11 bushels in the second half. The net result was the tendency for production and exports to stabilize during the 1920s. But, with the combination of favourable weather and the peak area under wheat in the early 1930s, the volume of production (and hence exports also) reached a peak level. This coincided with and contributed to the severe depression in the world price of wheat[16]. The consequent low return to wheatgrowers greatly

---

14 The sources of the statistics on wheat production in this and the following paragraphs are Commonwealth Bureau of Census and Statistics, *Production Bulletin, Rural Industries Bulletin* (various issues), and *Statistical Bulletin: The Wheat Industry, Australia*, No. 117, 1969–70 (Preliminary); and Bureau of Agricultural Economics, *The Wheat Situation*, No. 32, 1969.

15 The acreage had been higher at 12·5 million in 1915–6.

16 The export price of Australian wheat (after fluctuating during the years 1922–8 between 47 and 67 cents per bushel and averaging 57 cents) stood at 50 cents in the years 1928–30; the price tumbled by half to 25 cents in 1930–1, recovered to 30 cents the following year, but thereafter stagnated at about this level during the years 1932–5. The price recovered sharply to 53 cents in 1936–7, but fell again to 28 cents in 1938–9. For source of wheat export price and for alternative prices of wheat during the period see E. Dunsdorfs, *The Australian Wheat-growing Industry 1788–1948*, M.U.P., 1956, p. 479.

CHART 6
QUANTITY OF EXPORTS OF LEADING PRODUCTS OF AUSTRALIAN
ORIGIN, AUSTRALIA, 1900 TO 1968–9
(Ratio Chart)

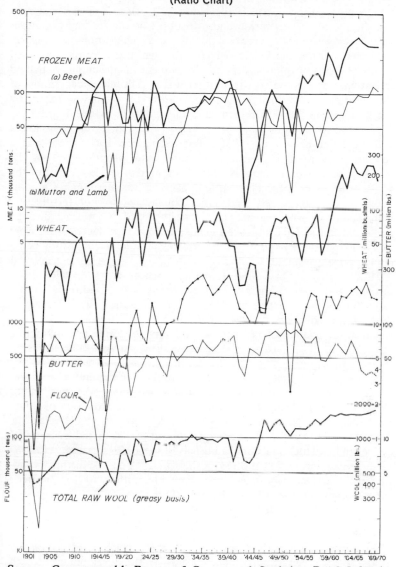

Sources: Commonwealth Bureau of Census and Statistics, *Rural Industries*
(various issues), and *Official Year Book of the Commonwealth of
Australia* (various issues).

influenced the following reduction in the area sown to wheat in Australia from the peak of 18·2 million acres in 1930-1 to 12·0 million in 1935-6 and 14·3 million in 1938-9.

The problem in the late 1920s and early 1930s was in part a significant degree of overexpansion and oversupply of wheat. The Commonwealth Government's programme of land acquisition and closer settlement during the 1920s, which had been aided by the increased inflow of British capital and public investment in communications and irrigation, contributed to the overexpansion. Ultimate recognition of this, leading to a reduction in the area sown to wheat was forced by the diminishing physical returns and the slump in prices. During the 1950s production and exports stabilized at about the level of the 1920s and the latter half of the 1930s. But during the 1960s there was a substantial increase in wheat production, and wheat's share in the rising value of exports about doubled compared to the latter half of the 1950s (see Table 19). This rapid expansion was attributable to four main, partly interrelated factors: (i) the technology of fertilization had found renewed vigour; (ii) the improved technology through better machines; (iii) improved yields; and (iv) the switch from wool to wheat induced by the relatively less favourable rate of profit being obtained from wool.

However, in 1968-9, an international wheat crisis revealed itself through high and rising exportable stocks in the traditional wheat exporting nations[17] but a shrinking volume of trade (owing largely to increasing production in Asia), and low and falling prices. The Australian wheat industry faced serious problems in storing and marketing another crop of the size of the record 1968-9 harvest. There was an estimated carryover of about 260 million bushels at the end of the 1968-9 season, compared with only 52 million at the end of the previous season. In view of the unsaleable surpluses, the two major alternatives facing the wheat industry were a price reduction or quota restrictions in order to cut production back to manageable levels. The Australian wheat industry chose quotas, and aimed to reduce national quota production to 344 million bushels in the 1969-70 season (following a production of 544 million bushels in 1968-9). A further reduction in the national wheat quota to about 318 million bushels has been agreed upon for the 1970-1 harvest. Other major wheat exporting nations have also decided to cut back production.

(d) Butter and meats

It is of interest to compare in Table 19 the experience of butter and meats, the two 'new exports' of the 1890s. In the development of both

---

17 Including Canada, U.S.A., Argentina, France, and Australia.

these staples advantage was taken of the technical advances in marine refrigeration. Both were keys to Australia's recovery from the depression of the nineties. During the first three decades of this century butter's contribution to export receipts generally rose faster than meat's. Butter's contribution reached 8·6 per cent during the depression years 1929-30 to 1931-2 while meat's provided 6·4 per cent. However, since then, butter's export earnings have declined in relative importance to a little above 2 per cent, while meat has continued to grow and at an accelerated rate since the mid-1950s.

Butter's decline in importance follows strong competition from overseas markets. Moreover, in the face of strong competition in the domestic market too from the substitute product, margarine, the total production of butter in Australia has remained fairly stable since the mid-1950s. An increase in butter production in Victoria (to about half the national total) has been compensated by falls in production in N.S.W. and Queensland (to about one-sixth each of the national total)[18]

The expansion of meat exports since the mid-1950s reflects the strong demand by the United States for Australian meat, especially beef and veal. Indeed, since 1958-9, the United States has displaced the United Kingdom as Australia's principal market for beef exports. Another important change is that whereas beef and mutton previously were shipped largely in carcass form, in recent years the quantity of boneless beef and mutton exported has exceeded that in carcass form[19].

(e) General Review

The major changes in the leading staples, as shown in Table 19, can also be seen in the industrial groups presented in Table 20: in particular, the slight rise in agricultural, horticultural, and viticultural exports since 1953-4 largely reflects the upturn in wheat exports; and the decline in the importance of pastoral and dairy produce reflects the downward trend already observed in the *receipts* for wool and butter. However, the *volume* of wool and butter exports have both risen steadily since World War II (see Chart 6). Their fall in relative importance as export earners results from falling prices and the faster rates of growth of other exports.

Export price fluctuations have been a major source of the fluctuations in total export receipts. This can be roughly seen from the

---

18 See also pp. 86–7 below.
19 See: Commonwealth Bureau of Census and Statistics, *Official Year Book of the Commonwealth of Australia,* 1968, pp. 933–6; and N.S.W. Bureau of Census and Statistics, *Official Year Book of New South Wales,* 1966, pp. 979–84.

similarity of the changes in the series of the export price index and the value of merchandise exports, which are shown in Chart 5. Outstanding parallel movements in both series are the sharp rises during World War I, the decline in both series in the latter half of the 1920s and then especially during the depression of the early 1930s, and finally the sharp inflation of prices and values in the period 1945-6 to 1950-1. The export price index has, on average, been roughly stable since the latter half of the fifties. Hence the growth of export receipts during the 1960s largely reflects growth in volume.

Though the fluctuations in export prices provide a large part of the explanation of the fluctuations in export receipts, changes in the volume of exports have also contributed. This can be seen from the estimate of merchandise exports at constant prices in Chart 5. The recorded quantities exported of wool, meat, wheat, flour, and butter are shown in Chart 6. The sharper fluctuations in the exports of meat, wheat, and butter than in wool exhibit in part the greater impact in the short run of significant weather changes, especially severe droughts of relatively short duration during the growing season. The fluctuations also reflect changes in supply which have been initiated by changes in overseas demand. Another notable point is that since World War II there has been an expansion in the export of each product except flour.

A matter of considerable importance to Australia's growth performance has been the influence on the growth process of the changes in the composition of exports and the resultant changes in the structure of the economy. It can be seen from Chart 5 that the long-term trends of the value and volume of exports have been rising, though at varying rates. So the next aspect which will be examined is the apparent relationship for Australia between the rate of growth of exports and the general growth performance of the Australian economy, in particular, to see if exports have been a leading, a lagging, or a balancing sector of the economy.

3 RELATIONSHIP BETWEEN THE GROWTH OF EXPORTS AND OF G.N.P.

So far in this chapter it has been assumed that the growth of exports has been a major element in the growth of Australia's real G.N.P. The objective of this section is to examine the available statistics to discover the nature and strength of this relationship, and the variations in it from time to time.

(a) Degree of Dependence on Export Income

Table 21 shows for the years since 1881 estimates of Australia's exports as a proportion of G.N.P. at current and constant prices. For comparison with the export ratio at current prices the investment ratio at current prices is also shown in the Table. The comparison is of special interest, since exports and investment are the two chief determinants of income.

It must be allowed that the data from which the figures in Table 21 have been computed are only rough estimates for the years before World War II. Nevertheless it is believed that the figures shown in the Table illustrate broadly two things: first, the relative importance of both exports and investment as determinants of income; and secondly, the major changes in their primary contribution to income. In particular, it is instructive to discuss further the major shorter-run changes each ratio displays between certain periods and also their longer-run trends.

TABLE 21
EXPORTS AND INVESTMENT AS PROPORTIONS OF G.N.P., AUSTRALIA, SELECTED PERIODS, 1881–1968/9

Period	Merchandise exports and gold production as percentage of G.N.P.		Gross fixed capital expenditure as percentage of G.N.P. at current prices
	At current prices	At constant (1959–60) prices	
	1	2	3
1881–90	16·5	15·3	19·0
1891–1900	22·7	23·0	12·3
1901–10	24·8	23·7	13·2
1911–13	21·6	22·7	16·6
1914/15–1919/20	19·1	19·5	14·1
1920/21–1928/29	16·9	18·4	18·3
1929/30–1931/32	14·5	21·1	12·9
1932/33–1938/39	17·0	21·1	14·3
1939/40–1944/45	12·1	15·4	8·5
1945/46–1949/50	20·5	13·6	24·0
1950/51–1954/55	19·7	12·3	23·2
1955/56–1959/60	14·5	13·7	24·0
1960/61–1964/65	13·8	14·5	25·2
1965/66–1968/69	12·4	14·9	26·7

Sources: Computed from data in: Butlin, *Australian Domestic Product*, Tables 1, 4, 7, 13, 272, and 273; Butlin, *Investment in Australian Economic Development*, Appendices I and II; Wilson, *Capital Imports and the Terms of Trade*, Tables 10 and 13; Boehm, *Prosperity and Depression in Australia*, Table 7; and Commonwealth Bureau of Census and Statistics, *Official Year Book of the Commonwealth of Australia*, No. 54, 1968, p. 1268, *Australian National Accounts*, 1968–9, Tables 10 and 11, *Balance of Payments* (various issues), *Production Bulletin* (various issues), and *Labour Report*, No. 52, 1965 and 1966, p. 35.

Looking for the moment at both export ratios, it can be seen that there have been short, divergent movements between both ratios in some periods. This was especially so in the first decade after World War II, when the average annual ratio at current prices was at its highest level since before World War II; by contrast the volume ratio for that decade was at its lowest point for the entire period covered in the Table. Major factors which contributed to the rise at current prices were the shortages of raw materials in the immediate years after World War II, followed by the stockpiling of strategic raw materials during the Korean War; hence prices of raw materials boomed until the early 1950s, wool prices being particularly high.

Another period of significant divergence between the export ratios at current and constant prices occurred during the depression of the early 1930s. On this occasion, in contrast with the decade after World War II, the volume of exports increased while export prices and receipts slumped. There have also been contrasting trends between both ratios over the whole period since the early 1950s, the ratio at current prices declining sharply from 19·7 per cent in the first half of the 1950s to 12·4 per cent recently, while the ratio at constant prices has recovered slightly from 12·3 per cent to 14·9 per cent. This contrast is undoubtedly greater because of the exceptionally high prices for raw materials in the early 1950s.

When we take a longer view of the trends in the export ratios since the beginning of the twentieth century, we see that both ratios have declined significantly in size from between one-fifth and one-quarter of G.N.P. to between one-eighth and one-seventh. Explanation of this downward trend requires attention to the influence of both episodic and long-run factors.

A long-run influence, partially accounting for the declining dependence on export income, has been the growth in relative importance of the domestic sector of the Australian economy. Falls in the export ratio and import ratio as economic growth proceeds are common experiences for countries as they become more industrialized and developed. This means that the staple theory has become more limited in the twentieth century, and especially since World War II, as an explanation of the on-going character of Australia's economic development. But the apparent long-run decline in the export ratio is partly exaggerated by the cyclical and weather fluctuations which were experienced in the 1890s and the early years of this century. These fluctuations also contributed to the inverse relationship between the export and investment ratios presented in Table 21 (columns 1 and 3).

The investment ratio indicates boom conditions in the 1880s and from the early 1950s. By contrast, the investment ratio slumped in the

CHART 7
INDEXES OF EXPORT PRICES, IMPORT PRICES, AND TERMS OF TRADE, AUSTRALIA, 1901 TO 1968–9

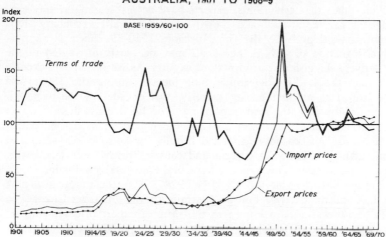

Sources: Commonwealth Bank of Australia, *Statistical Bulletin,* Reserve Bank of Australia, *Statistical Bulletin,* and Commonwealth Bureau of Census and Statistics, *Official Year Book of the Commonwealth of Australia* (various issues).

early 1890s. This contributed to, and initially reflected, the severe depression in the general level of economic activity at that time. Then the severe drought during the years 1895-1903 and the slow recovery of the economy amidst considerable excess capacity in capital equipment delayed a strong recovery in the investment ratio until just before World War I. Meanwhile, gold production had risen sharply to a peak in 1903 (see Chart 5). Moreover, with the breaking of the drought in 1903, there followed a rapid recovery in the leading staple exports of wool, wheat, and butter and, after 1908, of meat (see Chart 6). Consequently with investment recovering more slowly, the export ratio reached the exceptionally high average annual level of nearly 25 per cent for the decade 1901-10.

(b) Contribution of Exports to Growth of G.N.P.

The results of a regression analysis[20] of data on real G.N.P. growth rates and real export growth rates over the period 1953-63 in a sample of 50 countries (including Australia) indicated that real G.N.P. per head increases approximately 1 per cent for every 2½ per cent rise

20 By R. F. Emery, 'The Relation of Exports and Economic Growth', *Kyklos,* Vol. 20, 1967.

in the rate of exports. Table 22 shows that this relationship has also applied for the longer period 1950-1 to 1968-9 (see columns 4 to 6). Thus, since the early 1950s, exports have been a leading sector, supporting the rapid, sustained growth of the Australian economy. This contrasts sharply with the three decades 1910-39, when the apparent stagnation of G.N.P. per head may be partly attributed to the relatively sluggish rate of growth of exports. As we saw above, exports became the leading determinant of income during the 1890s and continued so at least during the first two decades of the twentieth century. In fact, the real export ratio declined only slightly up to 1938-9 (Table 21, column 2). But the export industries on which the Australian economy depended heavily for between one-sixth and one-fifth of G.N.P. (at current and constant prices) developed with painful slowness. This was a severe brake on total production.

Other unfavourable aspects after 1924-5 were the slump in export prices and the deterioration in Australia's terms of trade. Changes in the terms of trade, measured as the ratio of export prices to import prices, are shown in Chart 7, a deterioration in the ratio occurring when export prices fall relatively to import prices. When Australia's terms of trade worsen, this tends to mean a decline in the real income of Australians, while an improvement means an increase[21].

Two important, partly related aspects indicated by Chart 7 are: first, since import prices have been generally more stable than export prices, it has been upon the latter that the sharp fluctuations in the terms of trade have been mainly dependent; and secondly, the terms of trade improved strongly after 1921-2 until 1924-5, then lost some of the gain in 1925-6 but still remained high until the onset of the world depression in the late 1920s. During the early 1930s the terms of trade moved strongly against Australia, but quickly recovered after 1932-3. Despite the sharp fluctuations in export prices, the volume of exports rose slowly, though unevenly during the inter-war period (see Chart 5).

The sluggish performance of the old staple exports in the 1920s resulted from the exhaustion of techniques and resources that had earlier contributed towards a more rapid growth. What was also absent in the 1920s was the rise of new exports to sustain the dynamic influence of exports on economic growth in earlier years. The further development of the old staples (notably wheat) that did occur involved the opening up of less suitable areas, as already explained. Then the general slump in world trade and prices and the prevailing stagnation in most western countries contributed significantly to the

---

21 For a discussion of important qualifications to this general tendency, see Snape, *op. cit.*, pp. 50–2. See also p. 89 below.

depressed appearance of Australia's export industries in the 1930s. Chart 7 shows that the export price index remained below its 1928-9 level until after World War II, and was well below in the 1930s.

However, since World War II there has been a rapid expansion of world trade. This has, moreover, been a reflection of the more rapid economic growth in most western countries. The associated strong undercurrent of demand has significantly contributed to the more rapid growth of Australia's merchandise exports. Table 22 shows that the volume of Australia's merchandise exports has grown at the average annual rate of 5·9 per cent over the years 1950-1 to 1968-9. This compares with the slow rate of just under 2 per cent a year during the three decades 1910-39.

To summarize, the sharp, long-run decline in gold production during the period 1904-29 (Chart 5) was one reason for the poor performance of the export sector. But the main reason was that merchandise exports were a lagging sector of the economy over the period 1910-39. There was no sustained contribution to the growth of real G.N.P. as merchandise exports provided during the earlier periods 1861-90 and 1900-10, and as exports have from the early 1950s. Speaking generally, there appears to be a causal interrelationship between exports and economic growth. As R. F. Emery[22] concluded in the study previously cited, it appears that:

'this relationship is one of interdependence rather than of unilateral causation, but that it is mainly a rise in exports that stimulates an increase in aggregate economic growth rather than vice versa.'

Exports stimulate economic growth because they increase investment, productive capacity, output, incomes, and demand, and provide foreign exchange for imports.

4 TECHNOLOGICAL PROGRESS

References have been made at various points in this chapter to technical change as a significant economic variable of the production function and as a factor that it is closely associated with capital formation and labour, and their efficiency in unleashing natural resources. The objective here is to discuss the nature and general impact of important technical changes in the export industries. Though it is convenient to discuss these changes in this section, some of them have general application and wider implications for growth.

(a) The Growth of Mechanization

The development of Australia's rural industries has entailed considerable advances in mechanization. In the nineteenth century the growth

---

22 *Op. cit.*, p. 484.

TABLE 22
AVERAGE ANNUAL RATES OF GROWTH OF POPULATION, REAL EXPORTS AND G.N.P., AUSTRALIA, SELECTED PERIODS, 1861–1968/9
(Per cent)

Period	Population	Real G.N.P.	Real G.N.P. per head	Deflated merchandise exports plus gold production	Deflated merchandise exports	Column (3) × 2½
	(a) 1	(a) 2	(2−1) (b) 3	(a) 4	(a) 5	(b) 6
1861–1890	3·4	5·0	1·5	3·3	5·8	3·9
1891–1900	1·8	1·4	−0·4	1·9	0·4	−1·0
1900/01–1909/10	1·5	3·7	2·2	5·7	7·3	5·5
1909/10–1938/39	1·7	1·7	0·1	1·7	1·9	0·2
1938/39–1950/51	1·4	4·5	3·1	0·6	0·8	7·7
1950/51–1968/69	2·1	4·4	2·3	5·8	5·9	5·8
1919/20–1938/39	1·4	1·6	0·2	2·1	2·0	0·5
1900/01–1968/69	1·6	3·1	1·4	2·1	2·4	3·5
1861–1968/69	2·0	3·0	1·0	2·6	3·0	2·5

Notes: (a) Columns 1, 2, 4, and 5 are from trends fitted by least squares.
(b) Computed before rounding.

Sources: As for Table 3 above.

of mechanization essentially meant the transformation from local, non-commercial production using hand methods on small areas with low production per worker to the extensive use of machinery mostly invented for, or adapted to, Australian conditions. Notable among the inventions were the wheat stripper (1843), stump jump implements (e.g. ploughs, 1870s), and the scrub roller and mulliniser (1890s)[23]. Thus by the turn of the century, innovations had greatly increased the area that could be harvested in a season, and had extended the wheat belt into the drier mallee areas of Victoria and South Australia.

The next major change in farm machinery followed World War I, when tractor power became increasingly available in a variety of models and sizes. The Commonwealth Statistician[24] has summarized the subsequent movement towards mechanization thus:

'The increase in numbers of tractors on rural holdings and higher operating speeds led in turn to new and improved types of farm machinery drawn by tractors. These trends were interrupted by the economic depression of the 1930s. After the 1939-45 War there was a widespread expansion of labour-saving machinery and devices in all sectors of rural industry. Clearing methods were extended with the bulldozer, log, chain, and hi-ball units, and cultivation was improved by means of large disc ploughs and disc harrows, and seeding and harvesting machinery. These methods were extended to crops for which methods involving greater use of manual labour had previously been employed. Milking machines almost entirely replaced hand milking on dairy farms, and labour-saving machinery was introduced into farm and station development and maintenance operations. These operations included fencing, bulk transport of grain and fodder, pasture treatment, fodder conservation, and pasture improvement.'

(b) The Contribution of Scientific Research

Other major sources of rising productivity in Australia's staple exports have been the contributions from organized scientific research and training, such as that undertaken by the Department of Agriculture in each State and the Commonwealth Scientific and Industrial Research Organization[25]. Scientific research in Australia has led to

---

23 See *Official Year Book of the Commonwealth of Australia*, No. 53, 1967, p. 885.

24 *Ibid*, pp. 885–6.

25 This organization was established in 1926. At first it was devoted mainly to the solution of problems affecting the agricultural and pastoral industries. But in 1937 its functions were extended to assist the activities of secondary industries. It has established a number of field stations and laboratories to conduct research and to train research workers. *Official Year Book of the Commonwealth of Australia* (various issues). See also p. 137, n. 23, below.

the development of techniques which have helped to overcome local problems and resource deficiencies. The resultant advances in the productivity of agricultural and pastoral industries may be illustrated by reference to the productivity trends in the wheat, wool, and dairying industries.

Reference has previously been made to the substantial improvement in wheat yields from 5 to 7 bushels in the mid-1890s to an average of 12 bushels between the two World Wars. This followed the increasing application of fertilizers, notably superphosphate, from the 1890s. The average yield has increased further since World War II to 17 bushels in the 1950s and nearly 20 bushels in the 1960s[26]. Although the yield is influenced by the nature of the seasons, the continued improvement reflects the increasing adoption of scientific methods of cultivation, entailing the appropriate fallowing, tilling, and manuring of the land and the use of improved types of wheat.

There has also been a long-term trend towards higher average weight of wool shorn from sheep and of higher average production of milk for each cow. These gains have resulted from more skilled management in the improvement of pastures[27], fodder conservation, better breeding, and control of diseases. The average clip (from sheep and lambs) in Australia has improved from nearly 8 lbs in the 1920s to about $10\frac{1}{4}$ lbs in the 1960s[28]. The Commonwealth Statistician has summarized the improvement in milk production thus:

'The quantity of milk produced by a dairy cow can be as high as 1,000 gallons a year, and varies greatly with breed, locality and season. For all dairy cows and for all seasons for Australia prior to 1916 production averaged considerably less than 300 gallons per annum. Largely owing to an improvement in the quality of the cattle and the increased application of scientific methods the 300 gallon average has been exceeded in each year since 1924. In the

---

26 For source of yields, see footnote 14 above.
27 As the N.S.W. Bureau of Census and Statistics observed:
'Marked progress has been made since World War II in the improvement of the nutritional value of pastures by the sowing of non-native species of grasses. The grasses may be sown after cultivation and top-dressing of the soil with fertilizer (usually superphosphate), and the pasture may be further topdressed in subsequent years and renovated occasionally by further light cultivation. Some areas of improved pasture, however, have been established by sowing without cultivation, and some have been "self-sown" by the spread of non-native species from adjoining land. The sowing of pasture seed from aircraft has led in recent years to a significant extension of improved pastures in hilly areas unsuitable for cultivation.'
Official Year Book of New South Wales, No. 59, 1966, p. 878.
28 Statistics of average clip from: Bureau of Agricultural Economics, *Statistical Handbook of the Sheep and Wool Industry*, 3rd edn, 1961, p. 56; and *Official Year Book of the Commonwealth of Australia* (various issues).

last five years an average of 476 gallons per cow per annum has been obtained. In 1967-8 the average yield was 497 gallons[29].'

Despite this improvement and the fact that the manufacturing and processing sectors of Australia's dairying industry are highly organized and well-advanced technologically, a major part of the industry appears to be relatively inefficient when comparison is made with the high quality standards imposed by overseas markets. The survival of a significant part of the industry depends on the continued assistance afforded by the Commonwealth subsidies and stabilization scheme which cover the production of processed milk, butter, and cheese for home consumption and export[30]. This also means that a more efficient allocation of economic resources could be achieved in Australia by reducing the operations of the dairy industry in favour of alternatives such as meat production, by importing more dairy products, and by permitting the freer production of the substitute, margarine.

(c) Control of rabbits

Since the early 1950s rabbits have been successfully controlled. The rabbit had done 'incalculable damage to pastures since it first became a problem about 1881'[31]. It had contributed to the decline in the carrying capacity of pastures, particularly in N.S.W. and Queensland. By the late 1930s, though the rabbit had been brought under control by expenditures on fumigants and the use of extensive wire netting fences, it continued to limit carrying capacity.

However, after 1951, there was a dramatic change, as the following report of the N.S.W. Bureau of Census and Statistics indicates:

'The problem was entirely transformed . . . when the virus disease myxomatosis, introduced by the Commonwealth Scientific and Industrial Research Organization, spread rapidly down the Murray Valley, up the Darling and Lachlan Rivers, and then over the rest of the State [N.S.W.]. By mid 1953, it was estimated by the Organization that myxomatosis had destroyed four-fifths of the rabbits in eastern Australia, and that there were practically no rabbits left west of the Darling. The surviving rabbits have shown increased resistance to the disease, possibly owing to the decline in its virulence, and complete eradication is believed to depend on their destruction by other means[32]'

29 *Official Year Book of the Commonwealth of Australia*, No. 55, 1969, p. 907.
30 *Ibid*, pp. 904-6.
31 *Official Year Book of New South Wales*, No. 59, 1966, p. 985.
32 *Ibid*, p. 986.

(d) Leading Features of Technical Change Since World War II

One of the essential conditions underlying the more rapid, renewed growth in Australia's staple exports since World War II has been the stimulus to investment in these industries. The investment has embodied an increased flow of technological progress. Technical advances have also occurred through improvements in institutional and market arrangements and in managerial skills. The adoption of new techniques has involved a considerable reduction of the labour force in the primary industries (see Table 16 above) and the establishment of factor proportions that have yielded an increase in labour productivity which appears generally as good as that in other industrial groups[33]. The increasing trend since World War II to capital-using and labour-saving equipment in the primary (including extractive) industries has been stimulated by the growth of industrialization. Industrialization has meant increased competition for the scarce labour, encouraging the introduction of labour-saving equipment.

The mechanization revolution has lifted physical output in total and per worker; it has released workers from the primary industries to secondary and tertiary activities, which in turn have experienced favourable linkage effects from the primary sector. Furthermore, mechanization has made farming more congenial. It has also caused an increase in the economic size of farms, notably in the wheat[34] and dairy[35] industries, but also in the wool industry. This increase in scale has involved the grouping of small farms into larger, more efficient units which will permit the fuller utilization of machinery. Thus, to this extent, the earlier trend towards closer settlement has been reversed.

The increase in mechanization has also facilitated a greater degree of long-run flexibility in the allocation of resources to meet changing demand patterns in Australia's overseas markets. In the 1960s this involved a shift of resources towards the production of more cereals

---

33 See Table 35 below.

34 An economic survey of the wheat industry in 1967 showed 'the average size of farms growing at least 100 acres of wheat for grain was 2,503 acres; this compares with 2,085 and 2,048 recorded in the 1957 and 1962 surveys. The estimated survey average area of wheat sown for grain per farm rose from 299 acres in the 1957 survey to 469 acres in the 1967 survey'. Press Statement by the Minister for Primary Industry, 6 September 1968. See also Bureau of Agricultural Economics, *Quarterly Review of Agricultural Economics*, Vol. 24, October 1968, p. 196.

35 In Victoria where half Australia's dairy production comes from, 'dairy farming . . . is being intensified and concentrated into the more suitable environments. From 1960 to 1967 the number of licensed dairy farms dropped by more than 13 per cent but in the same period the number of milking cows rose by 16 per cent.' Source: *Victorian Year Book 1970*, No. 84, p. 348.

(notably wheat), meats, and minerals, thus taking advantage of the more favourable demand for these commodities compared with wool, dairy products, and sugar. In this way Australia has shown a way to counter the deterioration in her terms of trade which has resulted especially from the steady though uneven downward drift of prices for wool, dairy products, and sugar. The deterioration in Australia's terms of trade has not, as such, been an argument against specialization for foreign trade, but an argument for greater flexibility in resource allocation in order to meet changes in the structure of demand[36].

(e) Summary

There are three interrelated characteristics of the technological progress achieved in Australia's agricultural, pastoral, and extractive industries. First, there are the closely related phenomena of capital formation and technical progress on the one hand, and labour and the efficiency of its capital (including capacity) utilization on the other. Secondly, in order to meet the local physical requirements and the changing demand and supply conditions of the market, Australians have adapted or evolved techniques enabling them to achieve generally a high degree of efficiency in exploiting natural resources. And thirdly, Australia, with her vast natural resources awaiting exploitation with known techniques, has always been especially hungry for both labour and capital for which the export industries have competed with other sectors of the economy. It is not surprising, therefore, that the periods of most rapid economic growth in Australia have been marked by — indeed to a significant extent made possible by — relatively high levels of immigration and overseas borrowing.

5 THE CHANGING PATTERN OF AUSTRALIA'S OVERSEAS MARKET

Throughout their development, the growth in output of Australia's staples has been heavily dependent upon the existence of an adequate, growing overseas market[37]. In this, Australia has shown initiative and

---

36 For a fuller examination of the trends in Australia's terms of trade from 1948–9, see Snape, *op. cit.* See also p. 82 above.

37 This is indicated by the following figures showing the approximate proportion of Australian production that is exported:

	% Exported		% Exported
Wool	95	Butter and Cheese	40
Wheat	65 to 75	Dried Milk	45
Barley	40 to 60	Sugar	70
Beef	40	Rice	60
Mutton	20 to 30	Canning fruits	60
Lamb	8 to 10	Dried vine fruits	65 to 75

Source: *Vernon Report*, Vol. II, pp. 646–7.

adaptability in meeting, though sometimes slowly, the changing tastes and structure of overseas markets. This has been a special feature of the more rapid growth of exports since World War II.

Initially Australia was greatly aided through her strong political, social, and economic ties to the rising British market. Australia also benefited through her increasing exports to the expanding markets of Western Europe and North America: directly through her own exports to both continents and indirectly through Britain's large re-export trade. Meanwhile, the size of Australia's domestic market grew rapidly and gave increasing support to the staple linkages and diversification of domestic activity. These developments secured the high standard of living which Australians had early achieved, and which they have throughout been determined to improve upon.

Table 23 shows that during the early years of the twentieth century the share of the United Kingdom in Australian exports was nearly a half; and the share of the British Commonwealth countries as a whole was about two-thirds, while France took about 8·5 per cent, Germany 7·5 per cent, and the United States 4·5 per cent. There had already been a decline in the United Kingdom's share in Australia's exports from nearly 80 per cent in the mid-eighties. The Table indicates that the trend away from the United Kingdom has continued, and has been particularly marked since World War II. The shares of France and West Germany have also declined since the mid-1950s, while those of New Zealand, the United States, Japan, and mainland China have increased, especially in the 1960s. In fact, in 1966-7 Japan, by taking 19·4 per cent of Australian exports, became Australia's leading overseas market, displacing the United Kingdom, which took only 13·4 per cent.

Japan has a population nearly twice that of Britain and just over eight times larger than Australia's, while Japan's total area is about one-twentieth the size of Australia. Significantly for Australia's exports, Japan has a limited natural resource base. It has been the considerable growth in Japanese output of heavy capital equipment, machinery, chemicals, and motor vehicles, and her rapidly rising standard of living that have greatly increased her demand for Australian wool, iron ore, coal, copper, sugar, and mutton. Hence Japan has become one of the main centres of Australian commercial activity.

The changing spread of Australia's growing export markets in recent years away from the dominance of the United Kingdom to a more even world distribution between the United Kingdom, the continent of Europe (including the 'Common Market'), other Asian countries, and North America has strengthened significantly the basic structure of Australia's export industries. It has meant a greater share

TABLE 23

SHIFTS IN THE DIRECTIONS OF AUSTRALIAN EXPORTS(a), SELECTED YEARS, 1899-1968/9

Period	Commonwealth Countries					Other Countries							Average annual of total home-produced merchandise exports
	U.K.	Canada	New Zealand	Ceylon, India, Malaysia, Hong Kong, and Singapore	Total	China (Mainland)	France	Germany	Italy	Japan	U.S.A	Total	
	1	2	3	4	5	6	7	8	9	10	11	12	$m
					Percentage of total			(West Germany)					
1899–1913	47·2	0·2	3·1		67·0	0·4	8·5	7·5	0·4	1·1	4·5	33·0	13
1920/21–1928/29	41·3	0·4	3·6		54·5	0·5	10·3	4·9	4·2	7·2	7·3	34·4	98
1929/30–1938/39	49·5	1·3	3·6		60·8	2·3	6·4	4·2	2·6	9·4	3·3	39·2	258
													225
1947/48–1952/53	37·2	1·4	3·6		56·3		8·2	2·2	4·6	4·9	9·4	43·7	1330
1953/54–1958/59	32·3	1·5	5·4		51·3		8·2	4·1	5·1	10·9	6·8	48·7	1643
1959/60–1964/65	20·5	1·7	6·0	5·8	39·9	4·9	5·1	3·4	4·4	16·6	9·8	60·1	2210
Year													
1965/66	17·4	1·6	6·3	6·9	37·3	3·9	4·4	3·7	4·1	17·3	12·4	62·7	2721
1966/67	13·4	1·7	5·9	8·5	36·2	4·3	3·4	2·5	2·9	19·4	11·9	63·8	3024
1967/68	13·9	1·3	5·1	8·4	35·1	4·2	2·9	3·0	2·9	21·1	13·2	64·9	3045
1968/69	12·6	2·0	4·7	7·3	31·9	2·0	3·3	3·1	3·2	24·4	14·3	68·1	3374

Notes: (a) Excluding gold.
(b) Gaps indicate that data are not available.

Sources: Commonwealth Bureau of Census and Statistics, *Official Year Book of the Commonwealth of Australia* (various issues), and *Overseas Trade 1968–69*, Bulletin No. 66, pp. 1029–33.

in the big, growing markets, including countries experiencing more rapid economic growth than the United Kingdom (see Table 5)[38]. Thus the changes in the direction of Australia's exports reflect factors that have been 'trade creating' rather than 'trade diverting'[39]. The widening spread has also provided greater room for manoeuvre in trading arrangements to meet changes in supply and demand. It has contributed considerably to the renewed, dynamic, leading role which export growth has been playing in Australia's economic growth since the early 1950s. It has meant new support for the old staples: of wool, when increasing competition from synthetic fibres was making serious inroads into its traditional markets of Europe and North America; of cereals, especially through the considerable Australian wheat exports to Asia, notably mainland China; and of minerals, including not only the new exports of iron ore and non-ferrous metals (e.g. bauxite/alumina, mineral sands, and nickel), but also the older ones of coal, lead, zinc, and copper. As previously noted, the expansion of mineral exports will be considerable in the early 1970s, in particular of iron ore, coal, and bauxite, through large contracts which have been entered into during the latter half of the 1960s, mainly with Japanese industries.

6 INTERNATIONAL AGREEMENTS AND THE GOVERNMENT PROMOTION OF EXPORTS

An important feature underlying the more rapid growth of world trade since World War II has been the more positive role of national governments, including the Australian, in the negotiation of trading agreements which have reduced tariffs and other barriers to the free interchange of goods. Barriers to trade had multiplied during the depression in the 1930s when, with declining world trade, many countries attempted to protect their balance of payments and international reserves and their domestic industries against imports. By contrast, the agreements since the war have stimulated a more rapid expansion of world trade in which Australia has benefited. Australia has participated in international agreements in three main ways which are *interrelated*.

---

38 H. W. Arndt, 'The Shift in Australian Exports from the United Kingdom to Japan', *Economic Record*, Vol. 42, June 1966, concluded (p. 326) that 'about 70 per cent of the shift in the direction of Australian exports [between 1954–5 to 1963–4] was accounted for by the higher rates of growth of Japanese than of British import demand for the (major) commodities Australia exports'. The balance would be accounted for by changes in Australia's role as a supplier and in tastes in either or both the importing countries.

39 See Snape, *op. cit.*, pp. 48–9.

First, Australia is a contracting member of the General Agreement on Tariffs and Trade (G.A.T.T.). This is a multilateral trade treaty which came into force on 1 January 1948. 'At the end of January 1969 seventy-six countries, whose foreign trade represents over 80 per cent of the total volume of world trade, were full contracting parties to the Agreement[40].' As a result of the tariff negotiations carried out under the provisions of G.A.T.T., 'the tariff rates for a great many items entering into world commerce have been reduced and/or bound against increase. Australia has obtained tariff concessions from individual countries on a number of her principal or potential exports to them, as a result both of direct negotiation by Australia and of negotiation by other countries[41].'

Secondly, Australia has, within the provisions of G.A.T.T., entered into bilateral agreements with a number of countries[42], notably the United Kingdom, Japan, and New Zealand. (i) The original agreement with the United Kingdom (Ottawa Agreement) was made in 1932. Broadly speaking, this agreement secured preferences for Australia in the United Kingdom market for a wide range of Australia's commodities; in return, Australia incurred obligations through tariff levels and the grant of preference to U.K. goods. 'A new Trade Agreement designed to replace the original agreement and correct the imbalance in benefits which had emerged in the twenty-five years of its operation came into effect on 9 November 1956. Briefly, this agreement preserves security for Australian exports in the United Kingdom market, but lowers the obligatory margins of preference[43] which Australia extends to the United Kingdom.' (ii) The agreement with Japan was first made in 1957 and was renewed with amendments in 1964. It provides, together with certain specific commitments, 'that each country shall extend most-favoured-nation treatment to the other in respect of custom duties and similar charges, and import and export licensing. Japan is not entitled to claim the benefit of preferences accorded by Australia to Commonwealth countries and dependent territories.' (iii) The New Zealand-Australia Free Trade Agreement began in January 1966, and provides for free trade in certain scheduled goods. In general, there is still considerable room for the lowering of barriers for the benefit of world trade. The process also tends to be a slow one, partly because of the complexity of the negotiations between countries. However, the agreements, both multilateral

40 *Official Year Book of the Commonwealth of Australia*, No. 55, 1969, p. 308.
41 *Ibid.*
42 A full list of these countries with brief details of the agreements is set out in the *Official Year Book of the Commonwealth of Australia*, No. 55, 1969, pp. 309–10. The quotations in this paragraph are from this source.
43 See p. 154 below.

and bilateral, in which Australia has shared have, to her benefit lowered substantially the barriers to trade, and progressively contributed towards the more rapid expansion of world trade (particularly with Japan and to a lesser extent the United States), and hence towards the economic growth of the participating countries. The growth has in turn facilitated a further reduction of trade barriers.

Thirdly, Australia has participated in international commodity agreements, under the provisions of G.A.T.T., to regularize production and sales of certain primary commodities. International agreements have been made for wheat, sugar, tin, coffee, tea, and rubber. The first main international attempts at commodity agreements followed World War I, after violent fluctuations in prices in the early post-war years, and then during the depression of the 1930s. With the co-operation of the governments of the primary producing countries and the importing countries, the agreements have been designed to achieve, through orderly marketing, greater stability of prices and income for producers, and to assure adequate and appropriate expansion in supplies. Australia's main interest as a producer has been with (i) the International Wheat Agreement which commenced operation in 1949 and, after four further agreements, was superseded in 1967 by the International Grains Agreement; and (ii) the International Sugar Agreement which began in 1954 and was modelled on the earlier sugar agreement made in 1937[44].

The Australian Government has also introduced since World War II domestic policies which aim to increase exports. From 1961 the Government has provided 'a special income tax allowance for export market development expenditure . . . designed to encourage firms to incur promotion expenditure in advance of export sales and to assist exporters and potential exporters to expand sales in the existing markets and to enter new overseas markets[45]'. Earlier, in 1956, the Government established the Export Payments Insurance Corporation 'with the objective of encouraging Australian manufacturers to export by protecting their exports against risks of loss arising from the non-payment of their overseas accounts'[46]. The Government has also sent a number of trade missions abroad as part of its trade promotion programme. In these ways Australia has been assisting the more rapid growth and diversification of her export industries and markets, and thereby compensating for being a late-comer in developing exports of manufactures (see Table 20, column 10).

---

44 For details of the history and operation of both agreements see *Official Year Book of the Commonwealth of Australia* (various issues).
45 *Official Year Book of the Commonwealth of Australia*, No. 55, 1969, p. 306.
46 *Ibid*, p. 311.

Suggestions for further reading

Crawford, J. G. *Australian Trade Policy 1942-1966: A Documentary History*, A.N.U. Press, 1968;

Drysdale, P. 'Japan and Australia: The Prospect for Closer Economic Integration', *Economic Papers,* The Economic Society of Australia and New Zealand, New South Wales and Victorian Branches, No. 30, February/December 1969, pp. 12-28;

Grant, J. McB., Hagger, A. J., and Hocking, A. *Economic Institutions and Policy: An Australian Introduction,* Cheshire, 1969, Chap. 10;

McColl, G. D. *The Australian Balance of Payments: A Study of Post-War Developments,* M.U.P., 1965, Chap. 4;

Perkins, J. O. N. *Australia in the World Economy,* Sun Books, 1968, Chaps 2 and 7; and *International Policy for the World Economy,* Allen & Unwin, 1969, Chap. 4;

Samuelson, P. A. and others, *Economics: Australian edition,* Chap. 36;

Snape, R. H. *International Trade and the Australian Economy,* Longman, 1969, Chap. 3.

Vernon Report, Vol. I, Chaps 8 and 12; and Vol. II, App. K.

Chapter 5

CAPITAL ACCUMULATION

1 THE MEANING AND ROLE OF CAPITAL

(a) Definition of Capital

We have previously noted the arbitrary division which economists make between the inputs of land (or natural resources), labour and capital in analysing the factors of production. The importance of capital has long been recognized. By capital is traditionally meant the country's *stock* of produced or man-made instruments of production, comprising such items as tools, machines, equipment, factories, buildings, social overhead capital (consisting of the facilities used to provide communications, power, water, and other public services), and goods held in stock. Capital thus includes the produced tangible physical goods. Capital formation (or real investment) is the process of increasing the quantity of these goods.

This definition of capital excludes two other important aspects of economic activity for which the terms capital and investment are sometimes used: first, financial assets such as money, bank deposits, bonds, and other securities; and secondly, a kind of intangible capital which is accumulated in the knowledge and skills of the labour force. This human capital increases the efficiency of labour in co-operation with physical capital.

(b) The Contribution of Capital

There are three main ways in which capital formation contributes to economic growth.

(i) Capital widening is required merely to equip the additions to the population with physical capital of all kinds in order to maintain the productivity of workers and the standard of living[1].

(ii) If capital formation is sufficiently rapid and increases the stock of capital at a faster rate than the labour force is increasing, then there is an increase in the amount of capital per worker. This is called capital deepening, in contrast with widening, and

---

1 See pp. 26 and 35 above.

includes the use of more capital-intensive techniques of production. In this way activities formerly performed by hand or with little capital are now carried out with the aid of more mechanical devices, thus usually also increasing output per worker.

(iii) Capital formation permits technical progress. Commonly, capital widening, capital deepening, and technical progress are combined in the same piece of investment. The embodiment of technical progress is generally more likely with new investment, but it may also be embodied during replacement investment and/or when routine maintenance is carried out.

However, capital formation is not the only way in which technical progress may be introduced. Another kind of technical progress (called 'disembodied technical progress') is through better education and diffusion of skills and improvements in the organization and management of the labour force. Moreover, the appropriate education and management of the labour force are necessary to ensure that capital equipment is operated at the optimum level of efficiency.

The demand for capital widening in Australia has been particularly large since World War II because of the rapid growth of population and labour force. There has also been a considerable amount of investment of the deepening kind in most sectors of the Australian economy. As we saw in the previous chapter, the mechanization revolution in farming accelerated immediately after World War II, and has been going on ever since. This has made farming more congenial, and simultaneously lifted physical output in total and per worker. In fact, capital accumulation (embodying technical progress) has contributed to the shift of workers away from farming by making them redundant.

In tertiary industries providing personal services in which the machine plays a relatively smaller role, the opportunities are significantly fewer for improving output per worker than in industries able to substitute machinery for labour or to use capital to assist labour. Thus, as far as a number of the tertiary industries are concerned, investment in intangible capital in the form of better education and training play the main and vital roles in maintaining and increasing productivity. In these fields of activity the degree of efficiency is more closely related to the performances of the individual persons themselves. But in the primary, manufacturing, and tertiary fields of activity where capital can be employed, productivity is also dependent on the efficiency of the machine, which in many cases largely sets the pattern.

To summarize, though capital accumulation plays a key role in economic growth, it is not the only essential element. Increases in productivity are also dependent upon technical progress associated with research and innovation. Furthermore, capital, for its part, must be co-ordinated with other key requisites, including the increasing supply of labour and entrepreneurship, and the widening of the market.

2 THE SIZE AND RATE OF GROWTH OF GROSS FIXED CAPITAL EXPENDITURE

The main body of capital formation which has a direct bearing on the long-term growth rate of output is defined in the *Australian National Accounts* as 'gross fixed capital expenditure'[2]. So next we will examine the size, rate of growth, and composition of this item in order to appreciate more fully the contribution of capital to growth.

The size of gross fixed capital expenditure in relation to G.N.P. and its division between the public and private sectors are shown in Table 24 for selected years from 1948-9. The gross estimates of investment are used here rather than a net figure which allows for depreciation principally because satisfactory estimates of net investment are not available. Another reason is that the gross measures correspond with the gross estimates of national product, which are traditionally used to measure economic growth, the practice followed in this book.

A major feature of capital expenditure in Australia is the considerable role that governments have directly played, though this has been less so since World War II. During the first four decades of this century public investment was about equal in size to private investment[3] while since World War II public investment has approximated one-third of total investment. Private investment has also been growing at a significantly faster rate than public since the early 1950s, but the rate of growth of public has come closer to that of private in the 1960s, as is shown in Table 25. Another important point is the faster rate of growth of capital than of the labour force (see Table 25, columns 3 and 4 respectively). This indicates a considerable degree of capital deepening since World War II, as previously mentioned.

The increasing contribution of capital expenditure to the growth of G.N.P. itself is evident in the faster rate of growth of capital expenditure than of G.N.P. (Table 25, columns 3 and 5) and the rise in capital expenditure as a proportion of G.N.P. (the investment

---

2 This excludes increases of goods held in stock. Stocks may be excluded from the analysis here since they do not exert a direct influence on the long-term rate of growth. Increases in stocks in the long run are more the result of growth than a cause of it. See *Vernon Report*, Vol. I, p. 235, and Vol. II, p. 936.

3 See Butlin, *Australian Domestic Product, Investment and Foreign Borrowing*, pp. 16-17.

TABLE 24
SIZE OF GROSS FIXED CAPITAL EXPENDITURE AND OF G.N.P. AT
AVERAGE 1959–60 PRICES, SELECTED YEARS, AUSTRALIA,
1948–9 TO 1968–9

Year	Gross fixed capital expenditure as percentage of G.N.P.			Total gross fixed capital expenditure	G.N.P.
	Public	Private	Total		
	%	%	%	$m	$m
	1	2	3	4	5
1948–49	6·8	11·8	18·6	1,588	8,557
1954–55	9·0	15·2	24·2	2,698	11,154
1959–60	9·0	16·0	25·0	3,394	13,599
1963–64	8·8	17·1	25·9	4,201	16,232
1967–68	9·5	18·3	27·8	5,396	19,398
1968–69	9·0	18·4	27·4	5,782	21,077

Sources: Commonwealth Bureau of Census and Statistics, *Australian National Accounts*, 1967–8, pp. 28–9; and Commonwealth of Australia, *National Income and Expenditure 1968–69*, p. 16.

TABLE 25
AVERAGE ANNUAL RATES OF INCREASE OF GROSS FIXED CAPITAL
EXPENDITURE, NUMBER IN WORK, AND G.N.P., AUSTRALIA,
SELECTED PERIODS, 1948–9 TO 1968–9
(From trends fitted by least squares)
(Per cent)

Period	Gross fixed capital expenditure (at average 1959–60 prices)			Number in work	G.N.P. (at average 1959–60 prices)
	Public	Private	Total		
	(a)	(a)	(a)	(b)	(a)
	1	2	3	4	5
1948/9–1953/4	10·5	7·7	8·8	1·6	3·7
1953/4–1958/9	2·9	4·3	3·8	1·8	3·9
1958/9–1963/4	4·1	6·3	5·5	2·0	4·2
1963/4–1968/9	5·6	6·1	5·9	2·5	4·9
1948/9–1968/9	4·6	6·2	5·6	2·0	4·4
1953/4–1968/9	4·9	6·3	5·8	2·1	4·6

(a) Computed from data in Commonwealth Bureau of Census and Statistics, *Australian National Accounts*, 1967–8, pp. 28–9; and Commonwealth of Australia, *National Income and Expenditure 1968–69*, p. 16.
(b) Computed from data in Commonwealth Bureau of Census and Statistics, *Census of the Commonwealth of Australia* and *Wage and Salary Earners in Employment* (various issues in both cases); and author's estimates.

ratio) during the 1960s to a level slightly above one-quarter. Both
the public and private sectors have contributed to this higher proportion, which at the aggregate level can also be seen in Table 21
(column 3). An outstanding point evident in the latter Table is that
the investment ratio has on average been significantly higher since
World War II than at any previous time from 1881[4]. This reflects
the magnitude of the internal development programme which Australia
has been pursuing from the late 1940s with the aid of more and more
widening and deepening capital and through innovation whereby
improved technology is translated into the processes of production. At
the same time there have been greater benefits from increasing
economies of scale and from the relatively high proportion of the
capital stock which is new and incorporates improved techniques.
These factors have each been contributing to the faster rate of growth
of the Australian economy since World War II.

3 THE COMPOSITION OF FIXED INVESTMENT

Another important factor which influences the productivity of the
economy is the composition of the capital stock. We have already
noted the distribution of investment between the public and private
sectors. Both sectors largely complement each other, public investment
being concentrated in the tertiary sector in the provision of the
essential social overhead capital in order to aid the development of
industry and agriculture. Next, therefore, we will examine the main
components of both public and private investment and the changes
in them.

(a) Public Investment

Table 26 shows that at most times since World War II over two-fifths
of public investment have been devoted to the provision of transport
and communications. This group has historically taken the lion's share
of public investment, its share having been considerably greater before
World War II. The group has been dominated by three functions:
railways, post office, and roads. Significant shifts have occurred in the
relative importance of these three functions, reflecting such factors as
the state of development of the function in relation to the economy
in general, the structure of demand, and the associated technology of
each.

Initially railway development dominated government investment
activity; it comprised just over half of public investment in the first

---

4 This appears to have been so even though the estimates of private investment before World War II are, as noted earlier, probably understated.

TABLE 26

COMPONENTS OF GROSS PUBLIC INVESTMENT, AUSTRALIA, SELECTED YEARS, 1948-9 TO 1968-9

Year	Education	Public health	Development and conservation of national resources and assistance to industry	Transport and communications	Power, fuel and light	Housing	All other	Total value
	1	2	3	4	5	6	7	8
	Percentage of total							$m
1948/49	2·3	2·3	15·9	44·2	15·5	12·3	7·5	283
1954/55	4·3	3·7	16·9	38·1	23·5	8·5	5·0	849
1959/60	6·8	3·3	15·7	43·5	20·5	3·7	6·5	1219
1964/65	7·3	3·3	14·8	45·0	17·4	3·7	8·3	1843
1967/68	7·7	3·0	13·7	46·7	17·9	3·9	7·1	2367
1968/69	8·0	3·0	13·2	47·3	16·9	3·6	7·9	2553

Sources: Vernon Report, Vol. I, p. 24; and Commonwealth Bureau of Census and Statistics, *Australian National Accounts* (various issues), and Commonwealth of Australia, *National Income and Expenditure 1968–69*, p. 21.

two decades of the twentieth century[5]. During this period the miles of railway open in Australia (over 90 per cent of which was government) almost doubled from just over 13,000 miles to nearly 26,000. By this time most of Australia's railway network had been completed. Between 1920 and 1939 only a further 2,000 miles were added. This meant, of course, that investment in railways also declined, but it still comprised about 38 per cent of total gross public investment in the 1920s and 31 per cent in the 1930s.

Of the two other major components of public investment in 'transport and communication' (i.e., roads and post office), the development of roads has been next in importance, though its share in total public investment has fluctuated. It fell from about 17 per cent in the 1900s to 8 per cent in the 1910s; but then, with the development of the motor vehicle, the share rose to 11 per cent in the 1920s and to nearly 16 per cent in the 1930s. In the early 1950s capital expenditure on roads absorbed nearly 40 per cent of total public investment, and since the mid-1950s the proportion has consistently been just over half. This reflects the steep increase in the number of motor vehicles in the community[6]. The post office has also taken an increasing share. It absorbed about one-sixth in the 1950s and early 1960s, rising more recently to just over one-fifth with the increasing adoption of automatic electronic equipment. Meanwhile, the share of investment in railways has continued to decline sharply. In the early 1950s railway investment accounted for about one-quarter of public investment, but in recent years its share has been only one-eighth.

The historical importance of public investment in transport and communications reflects in part the long distances in Australia between the points of economic significance[7]. This also explains why the share of public investment in total fixed investment was higher before World War II when there was a need to build up this social capital. Australian State Governments have recognized the necessity of providing as adequate transport and communications systems as possible in order to ensure an efficient and viable pattern of economic growth. This, of course, has been the ideal. In such a vast country as Australia, with considerable known natural resources awaiting exploitation, and further important discoveries still being made, it is not difficult to find areas which appear relatively neglected partly

---

5 The source (in this and the next paragraph) for the approximate shares of the leading categories of public investment during the period 1900 to 1939 is Butlin, *op. cit.*, pp. 26–7.

6 See p. 206 below.

7 See G. Blainey, *The Tyranny of Distance.*

because of insufficient transport and communications facilities. These apparent deficiencies in social capital reflect the competition with other public functions and private investment for the scarce economic resources of capital and labour.

Table 26 shows that, after transport and communications, the two next most important public functions in terms of investment have been (i) the development and conservation of national resources, and (ii) the supply of power, fuel, and light. The major part of capital expenditure in the development of national resources (column 3) has been devoted to water supply and sewerage. Because of Australia's dryness, investment in the provision of water supplies has been increasing, necessitating capital-consuming schemes to provide adequate water to meet the rising standards of living of the rapidly growing population.

Another smaller but nevertheless very significant sphere of public investment has been in educational facilities (Table 26, column 1). This investment, as previously discussed in Chapter 3, has been increasing in relative importance since the early 1950s in recognition of the essential need to provide more adequate educational and training facilities in Australia for the growing labour force, thereby aiding the appropriate technological, structural, and social changes in the economy. Meanwhile, the share of public investment in housing (Table 26, column 6) has declined from its prominent position of the first decade after World War II when there was a need to help overcome the housing shortage resulting from the low level of dwelling construction during the war and from the large inflow of migrants.

(b) Private Investment

Table 27, column 1, shows that an outstanding feature of private investment is the decline in the relative importance of investment in primary production (mainly farming). We have previously observed the decline in the relative importance of the primary sector in terms of employment (Table 16) and the substantial fall in the relative contribution of primary production to GNP at factor cost (Table 1, column 1). At the same time investment in mining and quarrying (Table 27, column 2), though relatively small, has shown no definite trend until recently, when there has been a quickening rise in its share reflecting the increasing exploitation of minerals.

One of the most significant individual private sectors is manufacturing (Table 27, column 3). Since 1948-9 this sector has absorbed approximately one-sixth of total gross fixed capital expenditure.

The increasing share of tertiary investment evident in Table 27 reflects the traditional trend towards this sector as a country becomes

TABLE 27

GROSS FIXED CAPITAL EXPENDITURE, PERCENTAGES OF TOTAL, AUSTRALIA, SELECTED YEARS, 1948-9 TO 1966-7

Year	Private			Tertiary			Ownership of dwellings(b)		Total value
	Primary production	Mining and quarrying	Manu- facturing	Public	Commerce, finance and property Private	Other(a)	Public	Private	
	1	2	3	4	5	6	7	8	9 $m
				Percentage of total					
1948/49	16·2	1·2	15·4	31·8	6·3	6·2	4·5	18·6	788
1954/55	13·1	1·1	16·0	33·5	7·8	7·5	3·1	17·9	2352
1959/60	10·2	1·3	15·1	34·6	11·6	8·0	1·3	17·8	3395
1964/65	9·8	2·2	17·0	34·0	9·8	8·8	1·4	17·0	5236
1965/66	8·2	4·1	17·0	34·5	10·2	8·9	1·5	15·6	5679
1966/67	9·4	4·3	15·6	34·7	10·1	8·3	1·5	16·2	5957

Notes: (a) Includes 'electricity, gas and water supply', 'building and construction', 'transport and communication', 'community and business services (including professional)', and 'all other industries'.
(b) Dwellings built for sale by governments are included in private investment. The considerable activity of the government in this field is therefore greatly understated by the figures in this Table.

Source: Commonwealth Bureau of Census and Statistics, *Australian National Accounts* (various issues).

more developed, and standards of living rise. This trend was examined in Chapter 3 in terms of employment. The rise in tertiary investment has occurred mainly in the private sector, particularly in commerce, finance, and property. Other private tertiary sectors that have been increasing their share (and are included in column 6 of Table 27) are 'building and construction' and 'community and business services'.

Tertiary investment on both public and private accounts has been essential to the balanced economic growth of industry and agriculture, and has assisted the general improvement in productivity and the standard of living. By the same token the increasing demand for tertiary services has competed with the primary and secondary industries for scarce resources. So next we will examine Australia's experience regarding the sources of the funds to finance her growth.

4 RESOURCES AVAILABLE FOR CAPITAL EXPENDITURE

The process of gross fixed capital expenditure involves three inter-related aspects. One is the act of investment itself, whereby real saving (that is, current output which is not consumed) is used to increase the capital stock or to maintain or replace the existing stock. This is what has been described in the previous two sections. A second aspect concerns the financial institutions which assist the collection throughout the community of savings or claims to the community's output, and channel these savings to the use of investors. The development of financial institutions is examined in Chapter 7. A third essential step, which the second directly facilitates, is the act of making real savings to finance capital expenditure. The purpose of this section is to examine the origin and composition of the real savings which have financed Australia's capital expenditure.

(a) Domestic Savings

Fairly complete and reliable statistics of the origin and main components of savings are available for Australia since World War II. This is what is presented in Table 28. This shows that during the 1950s and 1960s domestic savings have financed on average about 90 per cent of capital expenditure in Australia. Domestic savings comprise corporate savings and personal savings. The former have financed about 66 per cent of capital expenditure, and include depreciation allowances, public authorities' surpluses, and other non-personal savings. Personal saving has provided on average nearly 25 per cent, though this proportion was higher in the first half of the 1950s. The apparent downward shift in personal savings does not mean that personal consumption in Australia is absorbing an exceptionally high proportion of resources. In fact, Australian personal consumption expenditure as a proportion of G.N.P. has been fairly moderate compared with other developed countries[8].

Since the mid-1950s depreciation allowances appear to have displaced personal savings and public authorities' surpluses as the chief source of funds for capital expenditure. However, the rise in depreciation allowances is to a large extent 'statistical', since it derives from a once-and-for-all upward shift brought about in 1957-8 by the amendment to the taxation provision for depreciation, upon which the *Australian National Accounts* are based. There has been no significant change in depreciation for taxation since 1957, its imputed contribution to capital expenditure remaining close to 29 per cent since then.

Ideally, depreciation allowances would equal the funds required to maintain a given capital stock intact. Precise information on the actual rate of depreciation is not available. In practice it is often difficult to distinguish clearly between capital expenditure which provides merely for depreciation and maintenance and capital expenditure constituting net investment. Furthermore, maintenance and replacement investment may incorporate new and better techniques, thereby increasing output without a net addition to the capital stock. For this reason it is preferable to use the gross measures of capital expenditure. Further it is probable that the amounts of depreciation based on taxation returns, and used to compute column 2 of Table 28, fall short of the actual allowances made for depreciation by Australian businesses for two reasons. First, some companies base depreciation of capital stock not on historical cost (as are taxation returns) but on their current replacement cost. In a period of creeping price inflation, as experienced since World War II, this policy would of course mean higher depreciation allowances, but it is an economic safeguard to the viability of the enterprise. Secondly, depreciation on buildings is not generally permitted for taxation purposes, but is usually provided for by businesses. These additional provisions for depreciation would be included in other non-personal savings (Table 28, column 4).

(b) Capital Inflow

Australia has continued to finance the greater part of her growing capital expenditure herself, but the continuing demand for capital for the widening and deepening processes, together with the implementation

---

8 Table 32 (col. 3) below shows that when comparison is made with the statistics of other countries for the period 1955–66, Australia's consumption expenditure as a proportion of G.N.P. ranks after Belgium, the United Kingdom, Denmark, France, and Italy in that order. As explained in Chapter 2, it must of course be allowed that these inter-country comparisons are not exact.

TABLE 28

SOURCE OF SAVINGS FOR CAPITAL EXPENDITURE, AUSTRALIA, SELECTED PERIODS, 1950–1 TO 1968–9

Yearly average	Domestic Savings					Withdrawal from (+) or additions to (−) overseas official monetary reserves	Net apparent capital inflow	Total
	Corporate Savings							
	Personal saving	Depreciation allowances	Public authorities' surpluses	Other (undistributed profits, retained income, etc.)	Total			
	1	2	3	4	5	6	7	8
								$m
	Percentage of total							
1950/51–1954/55	33·0	19·6	25·5	13·5	91·6	2·6	5·8	2214
1955/56–1959/60	22·2	28·6	26·1	14·0	90·9	−1·4	10·5	3043
1960/61–1964/65	22·1	30·9	23·2	14·8	91·0	−1·8	10·8	4495
Year								
1965/66	19·4	30·7	22·3	13·0	85·3	−1·0	15·7	5999
1966/67	23·7	31·2	19·7	15·2	89·8	1·9	8·3	6425
1967/68	15·2	32·6	20·8	14·5	83·2	−1·2	18·0	6688
1968/69	22·6	29·5	21·2	14·4	87·7	−2·0	14·2	8083

Sources: Commonwealth Bureau of Census and Statistics, *Australian National Accounts* (various issues); and Commonwealth of Australia, *National Income and Expenditure 1968–69*, F. 15.

of technical progress, have placed considerable strain on the available domestic resources and the balance of payments.

In Chapter 2 we observed that high rates of economic growth in Australia and the maintenance simultaneously of a high and rising standard of living have historically depended on significant inflows of capital and migrants. The overseas capital has been needed to supplement domestic savings and to finance the recurring deficit in the balance of payments. Thus since the early 1950s an average of about 10 per cent of total investment each year has been financed by overseas savings (see Table 29), though this proportion has fluctuated widely in some years.

There have been four outstanding features of the size, type, and source of Australia's overseas borrowing since World War II. First, the borrowing has been predominantly by private businesses, which have accounted for more than 90 per cent of the total inflow of capital (see Table 30). Compare the period 1901-39, when borrowing was mainly by Australian Governments, public borrowing totalling just over four-fifths of capital inflow. Public authorities were also slightly the heavier borrowers during the period 1861-1900.

TABLE 29
NET CAPITAL IMPORTS AS PERCENTAGE OF GROSS FIXED CAPITAL
EXPENDITURE, AUSTRALIA, SELECTED PERIODS, 1861 TO 1968-9

	Net capital imports	
Period	$m	As per cent of total gross fixed capital expenditure
1861–70	63	37·1
1871–80	97	26·8
1881–90	342	49·7
1891–1900	118	27·1
1901–1913/14	21	1·8
1919/20–1929/30	606	19·6
1930/31–1938/39	143	7·7
1950/51–1954/55	930	9·5
1955/56–1959/60	1384	9·6
1960/61–1964/65	2026	9·6
1965/66–1968/69	2667	10·5

Sources: Computed from data in: Butlin, *Australian Domestic Product*; Boehm, *Prosperity and Depression in Australia*, Table 7; Commonwealth Bureau of Census and Statistics, *Official Year Book of the Commonwealth of Australia*, No. 54, 1968, p. 1268, and *Australian National Accounts*, 1967–8, pp. 28–9; Commonwealth of Australia, *National Income and Expenditure 1968–69*, p. 16; and estimates by the author.

TABLE 30

ANNUAL INFLOW OF OVERSEAS INVESTMENT IN AUSTRALIA, PRIVATE COMPANIES AND PUBLIC, AND GROSS PRIVATE FIXED CAPITAL EXPENDITURE AS PERCENTAGE OF PRIVATE OVERSEAS INVESTMENT, SELECTED PERIODS, 1950–1 TO 1968–9

Yearly average	Overseas Investment							Gross private fixed capital expenditure	
	Private					Net Public authority	Total	$m	As % of total private overseas investment
	Direct private overseas investment in companies in Australia			Portfolio investment and institutional loans	Total				
	Undistributed profits	Other	Total						
	1	2	3	4	5	6	7	8	9
	Percentage of total						$m		
1950/51–1954/55	31·4	52·6	84·0	4·5	88·5	11·5	160	1192	11·9
1955/56–1959/60	35·5	41·4	76·8	10·2	87·1	12·9	295	1846	13·9
1960/61–1964/65	23·2	58·6	81·7	13·7	95·5	4·5	476	2709	16·8
1965/66–1968/69	22·1	35·2	57·2	34·5	91·7	8·3	851	4051	19·3

Sources: Commonwealth Bureau of Census and Statistics, *Annual Bulletin of Overseas Investment* (various issues), and *Australian National Accounts* (various issues).

Secondly, the public overseas borrowing before World War II was mainly in fixed interest securities, but the private capital inflow since the war has been largely direct investment in companies. The distribution of investment types is shown in Table 30. Each category of investment has sometimes fluctuated widely from year to year for various economic and political reasons at home and abroad. This has been particularly so of private portfolio investment, which has tended to grow proportionately since the mid-1950s. It was important during the latter half of the 1960s when the instability of sterling and political instability in countries which might otherwise have attracted the overseas investments of western countries favoured investment in Australia. This in turn became cause and effect of the strong stock market boom—especially in mining shares—in Australia during the years 1967-9.

The third important feature of Australia's capital inflow since World War II has been the growth of her borrowing from the United States and Canada, in particular the former. Previously Australia's borrowing was mainly from the United Kingdom. This has still been important. The United Kingdom has provided nearly half of Australia's overseas borrowing since 1947. The United States and Canada have provided about two-fifths, and have been the main lenders to Australia since the early 1960s[9].

The fourth is that Australia's recent dependence on overseas savings is less important in terms of the proportion of total capital expenditure financed in this way than previously. In the 1880s about half of total investment was financed by capital inflow (Table 29). In the 1920s, the next period of fairly rapid economic growth, Australia was dependent on overseas capital to the extent of only one-fifth of her fixed capital expenditure. The fact that Australia now relies much less on overseas borrowing to finance rapid economic growth than she did previously is a mark of the increasing strength of her general economic position and of her greater economic maturity.

5 FURTHER ASPECTS OF OVERSEAS BORROWING

(a) Increasing Dependence of Private Investment on Overseas Capital Since World War II

While the reliance on overseas funds has been fairly steady at about 10 per cent for total gross fixed capital expenditure, there has nevertheless been a significant upward trend in the dependence on private

---

9 See Commonwealth Bureau of Census and Statistics, *Annual Bulletin of Overseas Investment 1967–68*, Table 5; *Vernon Report*, Vol. II, p. 984; and Snape, *International Trade and the Australian Economy*, p. 99.

overseas capital. The proportion of gross private fixed capital expenditure financed by overseas savings has risen from 11·9 per cent during the first half of the 1950s to just over 19 per cent in the latter half of the 1960s (Table 30, column 9).

(b) Benefits and Costs of Overseas Capital to Growth[10]

The continued high level of new overseas investment in Australia since World War II has helped to meet a basic capital shortage in the Australian economy. In the process Australia has developed and benefited greatly in two main ways: first, as we have already seen, by increasing the resources available to the economy, thus reducing strains on domestic resources and the balance of payments; and secondly, through the overseas enterprise, technology, and know-how that have accompanied direct overseas borrowing. The benefits are, of course, very difficult to measure.

However, there are also countervailing disadvantages. One important effect of the rising proportion of overseas investment in the private sector in the 1950s and the sustained high level of borrowing in the 1960s has been the growth in the ownership and control of Australian businesses by overseas interests. The task of estimating the extent of overseas ownership and control raises considerable difficulties. Assessment has been by indirect, inevitably imperfect methods. The Vernon Committee, in reviewing this problem, reported:

> 'Our approach has been to regard the proportion of company income after tax accruing overseas as giving a rough indication of the degree of overseas ownership. If 1959-60 is taken as a starting point, this approach suggests that about one-quarter of total company assets was owned overseas, compared with roughly one-fifth in 1949-50. The degree of overseas ownership of manufacturing companies, which received most overseas investment, is undoubtedly higher, although information on which to base an estimate is lacking. Figures for direct investment income payable overseas suggest that about one-third of such companies may be directly owned overseas. The addition of overseas portfolio investment in manufacturing, for which figures are not available, would raise this proportion. . . . On the question of control, as distinct from degree of ownership, the available information suggests that something of the order of one quarter of company assets may be

---

10 For a fuller examination of important aspects of relevance in forming a judgment about the benefits and costs of overseas borrowing to Australia, see Snape, *op. cit.*, Chap. 6.

controlled overseas, but that rather more than one-third of manufacturing industry may be in this category[11].'

In 1968 the Commonwealth Statistician presented 'the results of the first of a series of studies of overseas participation in Australian industry'[12], providing estimates of the degree of overseas ownership and control of Australian mining industry. This has been followed by estimates of the size of overseas ownership and control of Australian manufacturing industry[13].

In measuring overseas ownership, the 'operations' (as expressed 'in terms of production, wages and salaries, etc.') of companies in which there is direct overseas investment were apportioned between overseas and Australian ownership according to the proportions of ordinary shares (or voting stock) of the companies held by the direct overseas investors and all other investors; the operations of companies in which there is no direct overseas investment were classified as Australian owned. This contrasts with overseas control where the operations of companies in which there is direct overseas investment were allocated wholly to overseas control; the operations of all other companies were classified as Australian controlled[14].

The study of overseas participation in Australian manufacturing industry resulted in the following percentages of manufacturing activity being apportioned to direct overseas ownership in 1962-3 and 1966-7, respectively: (1) 19·6 per cent and 22·2 per cent of the 'value of production' of manufacturing industry; (ii) 17·7 per cent and 19·5 per cent of the 'value of salaries and wages'; and (iii) 15·4 per cent and 17·5 per cent of the 'average number of persons employed over the whole year'. These statistics understate the extent of overseas ownership of Australian manufacturing industry because of the exclusion of overseas portfolio investment in the measurement of ownership. 'However, it is not considered that this understatement seriously impairs the usefulness of the statistics[15].' The estimates of overseas control gave percentages in each respect which were roughly just over one-sixth higher than for overseas ownership.

---

11 *Vernon Report*, Vol. I, p. 284.

12 Commonwealth Bureau of Census and Statistics, *Overseas Participation in Australian Mining Industry 1963 to 1965*, February 1968, p. 2.

13 See Commonwealth Bureau of Census and Statistics, *Overseas Participation in Australian Manufacturing Industry 1962–63* and *1966–67: Part I:—Overseas Ownership*, May 1969; and *Overseas Participation in Australian Manufacturing Industry 1962–63 and 1966–67: Part II:—Overseas Control*, February 1970.

14 For fuller explanations of the concepts of 'overseas ownership' and 'overseas control', see the sources in the two previous footnotes.

15 Commonwealth Bureau of Census and Statistics, *Overseas Participation in Australian Manufacturing Industry 1962–63 and 1966–67: Part I:—Overseas Ownership*, p. 2.

The above estimates of the degree of overseas ownership and control are aggregate statistical figures for manufacturing industry as a whole. These estimates conceal the important fact that the degree of ownership and control is much greater in certain major industry groups. For example, 'the motor vehicle industry is nearly 90 per cent foreign controlled. The industrial and heavy chemical industry, and the pharmaceuticals industry, are over 80 per cent foreign controlled. In the electrical and electronic industries, including in the total many small enterprises, overseas ownership is around 50 per cent. Production of alumina and aluminium is about 75 per cent owned overseas[16].'

The estimates of overseas ownership of Australian mining industry show that, in 1963 and 1967, direct overseas ownership accounted for 26·6 per cent and 40·9 per cent, respectively, of the value of production in mining, 20·9 per cent and 30·2 per cent of salaries and wages paid, and 19·6 per cent and 26·0 per cent of the average number of persons employed[17]. Overseas control was higher in each respect at 36·4 per cent and 52·9 per cent (in 1963 and 1967, respectively), 28·1 per cent and 43·1 per cent, and 26·5 per cent and 36·6 per cent, respectively. The exclusion of overseas portfolio investment from the measurement of ownership, as in the case of manufacturing industry, results in an understatement of the ownership.

The Vernon Committee 'concluded that Australian industry is much less subject to foreign ownership and control than Canadian industry'[18]. Nevertheless, the estimates of the Commonwealth Statistician show that the degree of foreign ownership and control has been increasing in recent years. This offers a challenge to Australians to display more enterprise themselves, to recognize opportunities for profitable investment, and to maintain savings as high as possible if a rapid rate of economic growth is to continue without a significant increase in the degree of overseas ownership and control.

The Commonwealth Government has enunciated broad guide-lines regarding overseas investment in Australia with the emphasis on moral persuasion and flexibility. The Prime Minister, Mr J. G. Gorton, in a Ministerial statement on the subject in September 1969, explained:

'The central aim of policy must be to provide, on terms which are

---

16 Commonwealth of Australia, *Parliamentary Debates* (House of Representatives), 5 May 1970, p. 1598, in 'Second Reading' by the Minister for Trade and Industry (Mr J. McEwen) of 'Australian Industry Development Corporation Bill 1970'.

17 The statistics in this paragraph are from Commonwealth Bureau of Census and Statistics, *Overseas Participation in Australian Mining Industry* (various issues).

18 *Vernon Report*, Vol. I, pp. 284–5.

fair as between overseas investors and the Australian people, the conditions under which investment will be attracted here. Those conditions should be such that overseas enterprises can operate securely and effectively, making the greatest contribution they can to our development at a fair return to themselves. . . . We do not believe that we can or should seek to legislate, in such a complex field. . . .

The Government has, as its general objective, the encouragement of Australian participation in and partnership with, overseas enterprises. And in speaking of partnership I place emphasis upon the offer of equity participation to Australians by overseas ventures[19].'

Guide-lines have been laid down for fixed-interest borrowings in Australia by overseas companies. The extent of such borrowings is determined partly by the share of the total equity held by Australians. The control of this borrowing is in the hands of the Reserve Bank. A takeover code has also been drawn up in which it is the policy of the government to preserve Australian ownership and control of enterprises of 'national interest', such as in banking and life assurance. For many years the government has 'opposed the entry of overseas banks into the local industry. And in the areas of television and radio broadcasting the acquisition of control by foreign interest has been excluded by statute[20].'

The Commonwealth Government is also taking steps to establish a new institution, to be known as the Australian Industry Development Corporation. The Minister for Trade and Industry (Mr J. McEwen), in introducing the Bill for the Corporation's establishment, stated that this institution 'will be fashioned and equipped especially to assist projects in export industries, and industries founded on Australia's natural resources. It will direct itself to giving assistance in ways which will help Australian companies to gain or preserve a greater Australian participation than otherwise would be the case. . . . Its role will be to assist Australian interests in marshalling financial resources, particularly from overseas . . . in non-equity form, carrying a terminating liability for income payments abroad[21].' The Corporation will be established 'with a capital of $100 million, paid up initially to $25 million. . . . The capital which the Government will be providing to the Corporation will be given not for the purpose of relending, but to give the Corporation stature and image as a borrower. The Corpora-

---

19 Commonwealth of Australia, *Parliamentary Debates* (House of Representatives), 16 September 1969, p. 1382.

20 *Ibid*, p. 1386.

21 Commonwealth of Australia, *Parliamentary Debates* (House of Representatives), 5 May 1970, pp. 1599–60.

tion will be permitted to borrow up to a limit of 5 times its capital and reserves[22].'

The creation of this Corporation was originally proposed in 1966, but it was abandoned on the establishment of the Australian Resources Development Bank. The latter's objective also is to aid the development of Australia's natural resources and the retention as far as possible of Australian equity in their ownership[23]. The proposal to establish the Corporation is supported by both the Australian Labour Party (the main Opposition party in the Commonwealth Parliament) and the Democratic Labour Party. But the proposal has come in for some criticism on the grounds that its objectives are already being met by the Resources Bank. However, this bank has relied to only a small extent on overseas borrowing, whereas it is intended that the Corporation will obtain its funds principally overseas.

(c) Servicing of the Overseas Debt

Table 31 shows the changing burden of property income payable overseas as a proportion of export income (including gold production) and of G.N.P. during the period 1861 to 1968-9. Following the relatively low level of overseas borrowing in the 1930s and the repayment of some overseas public debt in the early post-war years[24] simultaneously with a rapid rise in export income and G.N.P., the overseas debt service charge fell sharply as a proportion of exports and G.N.P. Thus, by the late 1940s property income (net) payable overseas absorbed only about 8 per cent of exports and just under 2 per cent of G.N.P., compared with proportions of 27·7 per cent and 4·6 per cent, respectively, in the latter half of the 1930s.

The repayment of overseas public debt reflected the policy of the Federal Labour Government (especially favoured by J. B. Chifley, Commonwealth Treasurer 1941-5 and Prime Minister 1945-9). A major structural weakness of the 1930s had been the heavy burden of the debt. During the depressed first half of the 1930s this burden had absorbed about 39 per cent of export income, and totalled 6 per cent of G N P In the early 1920s the servicing of the overseas debt

---

22 *Ibid*, pp. 1600–1.
23 See pp. 181–2 below.
24 Australian government securities 'domiciled overseas' declined each year between 1945–6 and 1950–1, falling overall by $236 million. Source: Commonwealth Bureau of Census and Statistics, *Balance of Payments 1968–69*, pp. 38–9. The main decline took place in the Commonwealth and State public debt 'redeemable in London'. This fell from $885·2 million at 30 June 1945 to $709·2 million at 30 June 1951, a fall of $176·0 million, or nearly 20 per cent in six years. Source: Commonwealth Bureau of Census and Statistics, *Finance 1953–54*, Bulletin No. 45, p. 49.

TABLE 31
PROPERTY INCOME PAYABLE OVERSEAS AS PERCENTAGE OF
MERCHANDISE EXPORTS[a] AND G.N.P., AUSTRALIA,
SELECTED PERIODS, 1861 TO 1968–9

	Property income (net)[b] payable overseas		
	$m (yearly average)	As percentage of	
		Merchandise exports[a]	G.N.P.
	1	2	3
1861–70	4·2	11·4	2·9
1871–80	9·6	20·2	4·2
1881–85	13·4	22·3	4·1
1886–90	25·0	33·8	5·1
1891–95	25·5	34·1	7·5
1896–1900	24·2	28·0	6·6
1901–13	29·4	22·4	5·3
1919/20–1923/24	55·6	20·3	3·9
1924/25–1928/29	72·2	25·1	4·2
1929/30–1933/34	80·2	38·8	6·0
1934/35–1938/39	76·8	27·7	4·6
1948/49–1949/50	91·5	8·1	1·9
1950/51–1954/55	137·6	8·3	1·7
1955/56–1959/60	220·6	12·6	1·9
1960/61–1964/65	269·6	11·7	1·6
1965/66–1968/69	419·2	14·2	1·8

Notes: [a] Including gold production.
　　　　[b] Property income payable overseas less property income received from overseas.
Sources: Computed from data in: Butlin, *op. cit.*; Boehm, *op. cit.*; I. W. McLean, 'The Australian Balance of Payments on Current Account, 1901 to 1964–65', *Australian Economic Papers*, June 1968, pp. 83–6; Commonwealth Bureau of Census and Statistics, *Official Year Book of the Commonwealth of Australia*, No. 54, 1968, p. 1268, *Balance of Payments*, First Half 1968–9, pp. 16–18, and *Australian National Accounts*, 1967–8, pp. 28–9; and Commonwealth of Australia, *National Income and Expenditure 1968–69*, pp. 16 and 17.

had required 20 per cent of exports and 4 per cent of G.N.P., but in the early 1930s the burden grew sharply as a result of the combined effects of the considerably increased capital inflow in the 1920s — notably through public borrowing at fixed interest rates — and the sharp fall in G.N.P. during the depression[25]. The proportion of export income required to service the largely fixed charges on the overseas

25 See pp. 21–2 above.

debt was higher in the depression of the 1930s than in the previous major depression of the first half of the 1890s, although the charges as a proportion of G.N.P. were apparently higher then than in the 1930s.

In the 1950s the renewed emphasis on a high rate of economic growth quickly leavened the official dislike of overseas borrowing. It was increasingly recognized that capital inflow was essential to ease the problems of capital shortage and the strains on domestic resources and the balance of payments. These problems resulted from the rapid increase in population and the labour force and the simultaneous desire for a rising standard of living. However, it was not public borrowing but private that expanded rapidly to supplement domestic resources. Private capital inflow has generally received official encouragement, directly through governments' facilitating the establishment and growth of overseas enterprises, and indirectly through stability of government and of policy on overseas investment.

An inevitable consequence of the increased capital inflow was some rise in (net) property income payable overseas to about 12·6 per cent of exports and 1·9 per cent of G.N.P. during the latter half of the 1950s. The deterioration in Australia's terms of trade in the 1950s (see Chart 7) contributed to the sharper rise in the proportion of exports required to finance the overseas capital. But during the 1960s the burden of overseas capital showed little change; in fact, in terms of G.N.P., it showed a slight downward trend. This reflects three main aspects: first, the general stability in the Australian economy as a whole of the proportion of capital expenditure financed by overseas borrowing from the early 1950s (and until at least the mid-1960s, as indicated in Table 29); secondly, associated with the first, the rate of return on overseas capital appears to have been little different from the rate of return on capital in general[26]; and thirdly, the greater steadiness in Australia's terms of trade since the late 1950s.

(d) Summary

The recent era of rapid growth, which has been strongly supported by overseas borrowing, provides no evidence on present trends of leading to a severe drain on the balance of payments through the

---

26 For detailed discussions of the trend in the profitability of private overseas investment in Australia, see: *Vernon Report*, Vol. II, pp. 992–3; B. L. Johns, 'Private Overseas Investment in Australia: Profitability and Motivation', *Economic Record*, Vol. 43, June 1967; and Snape, *op. cit.*, pp. 100–1. 'While there are difficulties in calculation, it appears that the average rate of return on overseas private investment in companies has fallen from about 10 or 11 per cent in the mid 1950s to about 6 per cent or less in 1965–66 and 1966–67'. *Ibid*, p. 100.

service charges on overseas capital, as occurred in the 1880s and 1920s. These were the two previous periods of rapid economic growth which were heavily supported by overseas capital. Furthermore, before World War II Australia's overseas borrowing, especially by governments, was largely through fixed interest securities, but direct borrowing has predominated since World War II. The return on direct investment has tended to fluctuate with the general profitability and state of prosperity of the Australian economy.

6 COMPARISON WITH OTHER COUNTRIES

We have previously noted that the level of investment as a percentage of G.N.P. in Australia has been higher since World War II than at any time previously in the twentieth century (see Table 21). The level of investment has also been high by comparison with other countries. This may be seen in Table 32, which shows for selected countries for the period 1955-66 the ratios of gross fixed capital expenditure and personal consumption expenditure to G.N.P. The incremental capital-output ratio, which is shown in the final column of the Table, is useful as an indicator of the rate of capital expenditure required to sustain growth in each economy.

As remarked in Chapter 2 in reference to the inter-country comparison of rates of growth of output, these comparisons are only very rough. Though considerable uniformity in the measurement of G.N.P. has been achieved between countries, there are still differences of definition, and hence of measurement, arising from historical or legal provisions peculiar to a country. In connection with capital accumulation this applies to depreciation allowances which are used for statistical purposes. Important variations also occur in the provision of social capital, such as roads and schools. The relative adequacy and efficiency of social capital may have an important bearing on the productivity of agriculture and industry, but its services are excluded from G.N.P. as measured[27]. These differences and exclusions are more significant in international than in intertemporal comparisons. Nevertheless, inter-country comparisons do help to clarify some of the leading factors which account for the variations in the growth experiences of different countries.

Table 32 (column 1) shows that for the period 1955-66 the proportion of resources devoted to gross fixed capital expenditure in Australia was the fourth highest among the fifteen countries listed, Australia in order of rank coming after Japan, Norway, and Switzerland, with West Germany and the Netherlands close behind.

---

27 See *Vernon Report*, Vol. II, p. 556.

TABLE 32

SIZE OF CAPITAL AND CONSUMPTION EXPENDITURE, AND GROWTH INDICATORS, SELECTED COUNTRIES, AVERAGE 1955 TO 1966

	Gross fixed capital expenditure		Personal consumption expenditure		Growth(a)		Incremental capital-output ratio
	% of G.N.P.	Rank	% of G.N.P.	Rank	Real G.N.P. %	Popu-lation %	(col. 1) divided by (col. 5)
	1	2	3	4	5	6	7
(A) Major countries							
Japan	30·8	1	56·1	15	10·2	1·0	3·0
U.S.A.	17·1	14	63·3	7	3·7	1·6	4·6
Canada	23·3	7	62·1	9	4·3	2·1	5·4
West Germany	24·5	5	57·5	13	5·5	1·3	4·5
Italy	21·2	10	64·2	5	5·5	0·7	3·9
United Kingdom	16·5	15	66·2	2	3·1	0·7	5·3
France	20·1	11	64·7	4	5·0	1·2	4·0
(B) Smaller industrialized countries							
Denmark	19·8	12	65·2	3	4·9	0·7	4·0
Australia	24·8	4	63·6	6	4·6	2·1	5·4
Sweden	22·1	9	58·8	11	4·3	0·6	5·1
Switzerland	25·5	3	62·1	10	4·6	1·9	5·5
Norway	29·1	2	56·6	14	4·2	0·8	6·9
Netherlands	24·5	6	58·7	12	4·5	1·4	5·4
Belgium	19·6	13	67·8	1	3·9	0·6	5·0
New Zealand	22·5	8	62·8	8	4·5	2·1	5·0

Note: (a) From trends fitted by least squares.
Sources: United Nations, *Yearbook of National Accounts Statistics* (various issues) and *Demographic Yearbook 1966*, Table 4.

Comparison in Table 32 of the ratio of capital expenditure to G.N.P. is made in order to see to what extent the evidence supports the widely held view that one of the key causes of differences in growth rates between countries is variations in the ratio of investment to G.N.P. This relationship, of course, also applies in reverse, in that a country that is efficient in the use of its capital and achieves a high growth rate will have further capital accumulation. This brings out the circularity in the economic system involving the close interrelationship between key economic variables. It gives meaning to the saying that 'success breeds success'.

Some evidence supporting a correlation between the investment ratio and the growth rate is contained in Table 32 in respect to the similarity of Australia's position with that of Canada, the Netherlands, and Switzerland. However, there are also important exceptions. For instance, West Germany achieved a similar investment ratio to Australia but a significantly higher growth rate. On the other hand, other countries have been investing lower proportions of G.N.P. than Australia, but have been achieving similar or higher growth rates, notably France, Italy, Denmark, and Sweden. The poorer growth performance of Australia does not appear to be attributable to the expenditure of an abnormally high proportion of G.N.P. on personal consumption. As noted earlier, the proportion of G.N.P. devoted to personal consumption, has been relatively moderate. Japan, as Table 32 shows, has been the exception in this regard with the highest investment ratio, the lowest consumption ratio, and the highest rate of economic growth. Though Japan devotes a higher proportion of her current resources to investment than Australia, her significantly faster growth rate shows that the inputs of new capital required to secure growth in output are significantly less than for Australia. Australia's incremental capital-output ratio was 80 per cent higher than for Japan during the period 1955 to 1966. Norway makes the situation and international comparisons appear even more perverse with relatively high investment and consumption ratios but a relatively low growth rate of real G.N.P.

These contrasts between countries show that a country's growth performance depends on other factors as well as the rate of investment. Also important are the stage of development of the country, the size and age of the capital stock, the capital mix, and the economies of scale achieved. Where an industrialized country is achieving a high investment ratio, and its stock of capital is both relatively large and new and incorporates modern techniques, then labour productivity tends to be high. The capital mix is also determined by the proportion of investment which is required to equip and house a growing population and labour force. Some of the differences between countries and the exceptions observed in Table 32 may be explained by the requirements of the more rapid rate of growth of populations in these countries for widening capital[28]. This is one reason why Canada, the Netherlands, the United States, Switzerland, and Australia have undertaken relatively large capital expenditure for comparatively small gains in productivity. This is reflected in the relatively high incremental capital-output ratios in these countries.

Australia's population growth rate has been one of the highest among industrialized countries. The high population growth rate and the consequent high proportion of widening investment have made it more difficult for Australia to increase appreciably capital per worker in the more productive fields of capital. This may have provided a brake on the potential rise in productivity, at least in the short run. From a longer-run point of view, the rapid increase of the population — together with the improving standards of education and training as explained in Chapter 3 — could mean bigger increases in productivity. In particular, the larger, rapidly growing domestic market is slowly compensating for the drag on productivity arising from 'the tyranny of distance', and is making possible a more viable pattern of growth and greater economies of scale in production than have been available previously. This applies especially to the manufacturing industries, to which we now turn our attention.

Suggestions for further reading

Brash, D. T. *American Investment in Australian Industry*, A.N.U. Press, 1966;

Hunter, A. (ed.), *The Economics of Australian Industry: Studies in Environment and Structure*, M.U.P., Chap. 5;

Johns, B. L. 'Private Overseas Investment in Australia: Profitability and Motivation', *Economic Record*, Vol. 43, June 1967, pp. 233-61;

Nevile, J. W. 'How Productive is Australian Capital?', *Economic Record*, Vol. 43, September 1967, pp. 405-11;

---

28 See *Vernon Report*, Vol. II, pp. 556-7, for an examination of the relative importance of dwelling expenditure and public authority expenditure, capital and current, in selected countries for the period 1950–60 and for the conclusion that the evidence 'presents an inconclusive picture'. However, the Vernon Committee did not take into account the full range of widening capital required by a growing population, though dwellings and public authority capital expenditure comprise a significant part. The data to examine completely the size of widening capital expenditure are not available. Furthermore, not all dwellings and public authority capital expenditure would be widening investment.

Perkins, J. O. N. *Australia in the World Economy*, Chap. 5; and
'Some Fallacies About Overseas Borrowing', *Australian Quarterly*,
June 1960, pp. 74-88; reprinted in Drohan, N. T. and Day, J. H.
(eds), *Readings in Australian Economics*, Cassell, 1965, Chap. 16;
Snape, R. H. *International Trade and the Australian Economy*, Chap.
6;
Commonwealth of Australia, *Supplement to the Treasury Information
Bulletin: Private Overseas Investment in Australia*, May 1965;
Vernon Report, Vol. I, Chaps 9 and 11; and Vol. II, Apps H. and J.

Chapter 6

THE DEVELOPMENT OF MANUFACTURING INDUSTRY

1 THE RELATIVE IMPORTANCE OF MANUFACTURING

The study of manufacturing industry presents formidable difficulties owing to its complexity, the great variety of its products, the wide range of its operations, and the fragmentation of the industry and its market — because of geography and federal history — between six States. The task is made easier by the detailed statistical information published by the Commonwealth Statistician. One aspect of the growth of manufacturing industry which was observed in Chapter 3, and which is examined further in this chapter is the considerable rise during the twentieth century in the proportion of Australia's total labour force engaged in manufacturing. The proportion rose from about 17 per cent in 1901 to between 19 and 21 per cent during the period 1911-33. In the 1930s following the depression, when ideas of industrial diversification began to be more strongly held and employment became a major objective of national policy, the proportion engaged in manufacturing rose further. By the early 1940s it had reached nearly 28 per cent. The proportion has been steady at about this level since then (see Table 16).

The relative importance and growth of manufacturing employment can also be seen in Chart 8 through both the official series of manufacturing employment and Keating's revised series. The latter is larger than the official series, particularly in the earlier years, because it includes estimates for employment in factories employing less than four people and not using power, and for certain sales, managerial, and clerical staff[1].

The growth of manufacturing employment has not occurred steadily. There have, in fact, been six periods of rapid advance in manufacturing employment. These were: (i) the decade before World War I (reflecting largely the full recovery from the deep depression in the first half of the 1890s and then severe drought in the remainder of that decade and the early 1900s); (ii) about 1919 to 1927; (iii) 1934 to 1938 after the recovery in manufacturing employment (during 1932

---

1 M. Keating, 'Australian Work Force and Employment, 1910–11 to 1960–61', *Australian Economic History Review*, Vol. VII, September 1967, p. 153.

CHART 8
AUSTRALIAN LABOUR FORCE AND EMPLOYMENT, MANUFACTURING
AND TOTAL, 1904 TO 1968–9
(Ratio Chart)

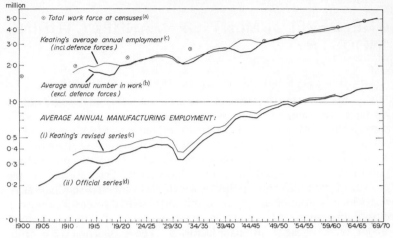

Sources: (a) Table 16.
     (b) 1913–4 to 1952–3 from C. Clark, *The Conditions of Economic Progress*, pp. 90–1; 1953–4 to 1968–9, author's estimates from *Census of the Commonwealth of Australia* and Commonwealth Bureau of Census and Statistics, *Employment and Unemployment* (various issues), and *The Labour Force* (various issues).
     (c) Keating, 'Australian Work Force and Employment, 1910–11 to 1960–61', Table 4.
     (d) *Official Year Book of the Commonwealth of Australia* (various issues).

to 1934) from the depression of the early 1930s; (iv) the renewed speedy advance during World War II after a pause in 1938-9; (v) the rapid expansion from 1946 to 1951 following the structural adjustments immediately after the war; and (vi) following a recession during 1951-53 (in manufacturing employment), the period of sustained rapid advance which is still continuing with only minor fluctuations. During periods (i), (iii), and (iv), manufacturing employment grew significantly faster than the total number in work, while in other periods manufacturing employment grew (and is currently growing) approximately *pari passu* with total employment.

We have previously observed that manufacturing industry is the source of about 28 per cent of G.N.P. (Table 1), and accounts for approximately 17 per cent of gross fixed capital expenditure (Table 27). Industrialization in terms of the development of heavy, complex, and diversified manufacturing began in Australia during World War

I. Thus Australia was a comparatively late entrant into the age of heavy industrialization. Nevertheless, despite the small size of the Australian economy, in terms of population, it has become one of the most highly industrialized economies in the world. Manufacturing industry's share in the Australian economy of 27 to 28 per cent for employment and 28 per cent of G.N.P. compares with about 24 per cent and 28 per cent, respectively, in the United States, 37 per cent and 35 per cent in the United Kingdom, and 24 per cent and 26 per cent in Canada for the period 1960-4[2].

The considerable importance of manufacturing industry in the Australian economy stems not only from its size, but also from the central role it plays between the primary and tertiary industries: the inputs of manufacturing industry comprise raw materials supplied by Australian primary industry together with imports; and its output comprises goods which are transported, stored, advertised, distributed, insured, and financed by tertiary industry. Thus the economic growth of manufacturing industry has been a mainspring of Australian economic growth in general, and must continue so.

2 GROWTH AND STRUCTURE

(a) Before Federation in 1901

During the nineteenth century the Australian market for manufactured goods—spread through six autonomous colonies—was too small for cheap production. The pre-federation market was strongly divided by tariff barriers through the protectionist policies of Victoria, South Australia, and Tasmania while New South Wales was solidly free trade. The market was also hampered by inadequate, expensive transport over the long distances between the colonies. Furthermore, it was isolated from the world's main industrial centres and the demand in Europe and North America.

The smallness and fragmentation of the Australian market contributed to a tendency for techniques and capital equipment in Australia to be simple and primitive. Manufacturing was largely restricted to production for domestic requirements of goods using basic local or imported materials. The conditions specially favoured the light industries which were naturally protected from the competition of imports, including textiles, clothing, footwear, foundry and general

---

2 These percentages were derived from data in: United Nations, *Yearbook of National Income Statistics 1967;* United States Department of Commerce, *Statistical Abstract of the United States 1965*, p. 220; London and Cambridge Economic Service, *The British Economy Key Statistics 1900–1964*, Table C; and Dominion Bureau of Statistics, *Canada Year Book 1968*, p. 759.

engineering. In the strongly protectionist colony of Victoria, manufacturing industry tended to be biased to labour-intensive techniques, for instance textiles and clothing[3].

However, the natural shelter which resulted from the local peculiarities of demand and isolation from the world's main suppliers of industrial imports was generally a more important influence on manufacturing development than was the artificial protection granted through tariffs[4]. Thus manufacturing activity was concentrated in the production of the following industrial groups: food and drink from local products, the manufacture of clothing and textiles (mainly from imported materials), bricks, printing, the preliminary treating of agricultural and pastoral products (such as wool scouring and washing and flour milling), and metal works and machinery (especially for repairs and maintenance).

(b) 1901-1939

After Federation, the expansion of manufacturing industry in Australia was assisted by the elimination of customs barriers between the States. This, of course, was a major purpose of Federation, which improved the allocation of economic resources between the States. An early effect of the enlarged common market in Australia was to favour specialization and the more rapid growth and concentration of manufacturing industry in the two dominant States of N.S.W. and Victoria. Each held about one-third of Australia's population. This gave their industries greater relative benefits from economies of scale, and hence enabled the industries to compete more favourably for the market in the smaller States. Consequently manufacturing industry in the smaller States generally grew comparatively slowly[5].

Table 33, which presents the broad industry classification provided by the Commonwealth Statistician, shows that nearly two-thirds of manufacturing activity, as measured by employment and value of production, was concentrated in three industrial groups: (i) metal works

---

3 In Victoria 7·6 per cent and 7·3 per cent of the labour force were engaged in textiles at the 1891 and 1901 Censuses, respectively, compared with 5·2 per cent and 5·5 per cent in N.S.W. See Boehm, *Prosperity and Depression in Australia*, Table 35.

4 See W. A. Sinclair, 'The Tariff and Manufacturing Employment in Victoria, 1860–1900', *Economic Record*, Vol. 31, May 1955.

5 Between the Censuses of 1901 and 1921 the proportion of the labour force classified as 'industrial' (predominantly manufacturing and excluding construction and building) grew from 18·9 per cent to 25 per cent in New South Wales and from 21·8 per cent to 28·5 per cent in Victoria, compared with a slower growth in Queensland from 18·8 per cent to 21·0 per cent, in South Australia 21·4 per cent to 23·9 per cent, and in Western Australia 15·7 per cent to 17·1 per cent. In Tasmania the proportion fell from 20·1 per cent to 19·3 per cent. Source: *Census of the Commonwealth of Australia, 1921*, pp. 1220–5.

and machinery; (ii) food and drink; and (iii) clothing and textile fabrics. The first group of metal works and machinery grew steadily over the four decades, 1901-39, and was emerging as the leading group.

TABLE 33
MANUFACTURING: AVERAGE EMPLOYMENT AND TOTAL VALUE OF PRODUCTION BY MAJOR INDUSTRY GROUPS, AUSTRALIA, SELECTED YEARS, 1903 TO 1967-8

Section A

Year	Metal works and machinery	Food and drink	Clothing and textiles	Books, paper, printing	Working in wood	Other	Total
	1	2	3	4	5	6	7
			Average employment				
			Percentage of total				'000
1903	18·5	16·5	27·6	8·9	8·6	19·9	192
1907	19·3	16·5	28·1	8·5	8·0	19·6	243
1913	21·0	15·2	25·7	7·9	9·7	20·5	328
1920–1	21·5	15·4	23·6	7·4	8·5	23·6	374
1928–9	22·4	15·3	24·9	7·7	5·9	23·8	438
			Value of production				
			Percentage of total				$m
1913	24·7	23·8	13·7	8·2	8·9	20·7	122
1920–1	21·5	21·8	16·3	8·0	8·3	24·1	208
1928–9	22·7	23·0	15·6	7·9	5·5	25·3	314

Section B

Year	Industrial metals, machines, conveyances	Food, drink and tobacco	Clothing (except knitted)	Textile and textile goods	Chemicals, dyes, explosives, paints, oils, grease	Other	Total
			Average employment				
			Percentage of total				'000
1928–9	29·6	15·6	18·6	6·4	3·2	26·6	440
1938–9	32·0	15·1	15·5	8·3	3·6	25·5	556
1948–9	38·0	13·5	13·5	7·4	3·8	23·8	877
1958–9	43·8	11·7	9·9	6·3	4·5	23·8	1071
1967–8	47·6	11·0	8·5	5·6	4·2	23·1	1315
			Value of production				
			Percentage of total				$m
1928–9	29·1	23·2	11·0	4·6	5·2	26·9	316
1938–9	32·5	21·7	8·6	5·7	6·5	25·0	384
1948–9	38·1	16·2	9·4	6·5	6·1	23·7	1106
1958–9	41·7	13·3	6·3	5·4	9·1	24·2	3532
1967–8	44·3	13·1	5·0	4·4	9·6	23·6	7132

Sources: Commonwealth Bureau of Census and Statistics, *Production Bulletin* (various issues) and *A Summary of Principal Statistics of Factories* (various issues).

During the period 1901-39 two important external disturbances greatly influenced the growth and structure of Australia's manufacturing industry: (i) World War I, and (ii), the world-wide economic depression during the late twenties and early thirties. The immediate effect of the war on Australia's manufacturing industries appeared small. Employment in manufacturing actually declined slightly during the years 1913 to 1915, and then recovered slowly (Chart 8). It was not until 1918-9 that the 1913 level was exceeded. Australia was too remote from the war scene, and her industries were insufficiently developed, to assist greatly in meeting the demands of the war. The curtailment of imports of manufactured goods from Australia's traditional sources of the U.K. and the continent of Western Europe was partly met by increased imports from Japan and the United States[6]. The curtailment did also stimulate the rise of various new industries in Australia to meet demands that could not be satisfied by imports under the wartime conditions.

One of the most significant developments during the war was the opening of the steelworks at Newcastle in 1915. This marked in many ways the commencement of the diversification of Australia's manufacturing industry, though iron and steelworks had been earlier established elsewhere in N.S.W., notably at Lithgow in the mid-1870s[7]. The planning of the steelworks at Newcastle had been undertaken before the war; the construction of the plant began early in 1913. The war gave added stimulus and importance to its establishment and the growth of related, subsidiary industries. The war also emphasized the strategic weakness of Australia's heavy reliance on manufactured imports. The Commonwealth Government aimed at overcoming this weakness as far as possible and assisting the various new industries which arose during the war by granting them tariff protection. A further important development in the 1920s was the commencement of motor body assembly by Ford at Geelong in 1925 and by General Motors at Adelaide the following year.

During the 1920s protection in Australia grew substantially, and was increased sharply in 1930 as the economic depression deepened. The tariff and other aspects of protection to manufacturing industry are discussed in more detail in Section 5 of this chapter. Here it is worth noting that the rise in manufacturing employment after about 1931-2 apparently led the general recovery of the total number in work in Australia. Furthermore, the growth of manufacturing

---

6 The effects of these changes on aggregate imports may be seen in Table 39 below.

7 H. Hughes, *The Australian Iron and Steel Industry 1848–1962*, M.U.P., 1964.

employment was the major dynamic element behind the growth of total employment throughout the 1930s. Between 1932-3 and 1938-9 the number of workers engaged in manufacturing increased by just over half while the total number in work increased by one-third.

To summarize the leading trends over the period 1901 to 1939, there were three periods of marked industrial growth which contributed appreciably to the development of the Australian economy. The *first* occurred during the decade before World War I. After some decline and stagnation during the war, the *second* period followed in the 1920s with the renewed expansion in manufacturing activity providing a major source of real advance in general economic activity. This expansion was checked by the world depression which in turn, however, contributed to the introduction of further protective policies and provided the environment which led to the *third* period, when Australia began a more extensive and intensive development of her industrial base. This was supported by the growing domestic demand in which an ever present policy objective was the achievement of a rising standard of living, (though this has been more explicit in official policy since World War II). At the same time the Australian labour force was growing in size and acquiring the skills and know-how needed for the increasingly more sophisticated techniques of industrial production. In this process Australia was fortunate in receiving considerable assistance from the establishment in Australia of the branch factories or subsidiaries of overseas enterprises, mostly from the U.K. and the U.S.

The derivative character of manufacture has been a significant aspect from the beginning of Australia's industrialization[8]. This was only natural in view of Australia's close economic and social ties with the U.K., Europe, and the U.S. As we have previously seen, Australia's economic development, especially when rapid, has been greatly assisted by the import of capital and techniques. This has also been supported by immigrants bringing with them the training and new skills required for manufacturing industry.

When World War II began in 1939 the stage was firmly set for Australia to play a more dominant, positive role industrially than she could in World War I. In particular, Australian manufacturing industry was sufficiently diversified and developed for it to be adapted quite quickly to supplying war material and equipment. Leading manufacturing activity included iron and steel, some non-ferrous metals, machinery and engineering, electrical and electronic equipment, motor vehicle assembly and parts, chemicals and fertilizers, food

---

8 See A. Hunter (ed.), *The Economics of Australian Industry*, M.U.P., 1963, pp. 2-6.

processing, textiles and clothing, wood products, and printing and publishing.

(c) Since 1939

The war provided a considerable stimulus to the growth of Australia's manufacturing industries. The stimulus occurred in three main ways: first, the interruption to imports meant a switch in demand to home-produced goods; secondly, the increasing expenditure associated with the war raised the level of real income and demand as unemployed resources were absorbed; and thirdly, Australia became a major source of supply for British countries east of Suez[9]. Hence key existing industries expanded and new ones developed rapidly to produce all classes of munitions, ships, aircraft, new kinds of equipment and machinery, chemicals, textiles, and so on. The resultant expansion in productive capacity, the acquisition of new skills, the development of new strategies and techniques, the greater diversification of scientific and technical knowledge, and the confidence and experience thereby attained during this period of forced expansion established a firm basis for rapid post-war industrial growth[10].

Table 33 (Section B) shows the relative importance of the five major industrial groups in terms of employment and value of production in the manufacturing industry as a whole. The outstanding change has been the considerable increase in the relative importance of the 'industrial metals, machines, conveyances' class. The composition of this class is further subdivided in Table 34, again presenting the percentages in terms of manufacturing industries as a whole. Table 34 shows that three sectors — iron and steel, motor vehicles (including parts and repairs), and electrical and electronic equipment — largely account for the rapid advance in the relative importance of the total of 'industrial metals, machines, conveyances'. Another notable change displayed in Table 34 is the significant decline in the relative importance of 'other' transport equipment.

Table 35 presents further evidence of the recent growth record of the leading industrial classes in manufacturing in comparison with the records of primary and tertiary industries. The Table indicates that in manufacturing the fastest growing class in providing employment has been 'industrial metals, machines, conveyances', the number in work in this class having risen at the average annual rate of 3·3 per cent during 1949-50 to 1967-8 compared with a rate of 2·0 per cent for the number in work in the whole economy. Two other industrial classes which grew faster in terms of output and productivity

---

9 *Official Year Book of the Commonwealth of Australia*, No. 51, 1965, p. 144.
10 *Vernon Report*, Vol. I, pp. 200–1.

TABLE 34

CLASSIFICATION OF THE MAJOR INDUSTRY GROUP 'INDUSTRIAL METALS, MACHINES, CONVEYANCES', AUSTRALIA, SELECTED YEARS, 1948-9 TO 1967-8

| Year | Iron and steel | Transport equipment | | Plant, machinery and engineering | Electrical and electronic equipment | Processing and refining of other metals | Total of industry group (cols 1–6) | Total manufacturing industries |
		Motor vehicles, parts and repairs	Other(a)					
	1	2	3	4	5	6	7	8
				Average employment Percentage of col. 8				'000
1948–9	3·5	7·1	7·8	9·6	4·5	5·5	38·0	877
1953–4	3·8	9·2	7·8	10·2	4·8	5·1	40·8	974
1958–9	5·0	10·6	6·4	10·3	6·2	5·3	43·8	1071
1963–4	5·4	12·0	5·4	11·3	6·4	5·7	46·3	1194
1967–8	5·3	12·3	5·2	12·0	6·8	5·9	47·6	1315
				Value of Production Percentage of col. 8				$ m.
1948–9	4·4	6·2	6·5	9·5	4·1	7·5	38·1	1106
1953–4	4·5	8·5	6·0	10·0	4·7	5·9	39·6	2386
1958–9	6·8	9·1	4·6	9·8	5·7	5·6	41·7	3532
1963–4	7·0	9·8	3·7	10·6	5·7	6·3	43·1	5042
1967–8	6·6	9·9	3·3	11·1	5·7	7·2	44·3	7132

Note: (a) Comprises tramcars and railway rolling stock, horse-drawn vehicles, aircraft, cycles, and ship and boat building and repairing.

Source: Commonwealth Bureau of Census and Statistics, *A Summary of Principal Statistics of Factories* (various issues).

were 'chemicals, dyes, explosives, paints, oils, grease', and 'paper, stationery, printing'. The former, which has provided the fastest growth class in output and productivity, has advanced its rank among the groups shown in Table 33 from fifth largest in terms of value of production in 1948-9 to third in 1967-8. But it is still fifth in terms of employment. This manifests the capital-intensive growth of this class, which, in turn, has been a major element underlying its speedy productivity advance. The rapid rates of growth of output and productivity achieved in the 'paper, stationery, printing' class is also largely attributable to capital-intensive expansion.

Capital-intensive development has occurred in other manufacturing classes as well, notably within the class 'industrial metals, machines, conveyances' (in iron and steel, non-ferrous metals, and motor vehicle manufacture), and in the tertiary group in 'heat, light and power'. In short, as we have previously seen, it is the industries absorbing large volumes of capital incorporating technological progress that have experienced the fastest increases in labour productivity.

On the other hand, the older industries of 'clothing', 'food, drink, and tobacco', and 'sawmills, joinery, boxes, etc.' have (among the manufacturing classes) experienced the slowest increases in output, employment, and productivity since 1949-50. As Table 33 shows for the former two industries, there has been a significant fall in the relative importance of both industries in the economy. The number in work in the clothing industry has, in fact, declined slowly. An exception to slow growth among the older industries has been 'textiles and textile goods'. Though employment in this industry class has been growing quite slowly, productivity has been advancing a little faster even than the rapidly growing industrial metals class, reflecting the considerable technical advances (including the use of automatic machines) that have been introduced in textile production[11].

It is only since the mid-1950s that serious attempts have been made to measure the contribution of technical progress to the increase in productivity in any economy. Several Australian economists have attempted to measure technical progress in Australian manufacturing. A recent estimate by Professor H. F. Lydall[12] for the 1950s shows

---

11 See *Vernon Report*, Vol. II, pp. 762-3 and 768-9.
12 In 'Technical Progress in Australian Manufacturing', *Economic Journal*, Vol. 78, December 1968. See also: H. R. Edwards and N. T. Drane, 'The Australian Economy, July 1963', *Economic Record*, Vol. 39, September 1963, pp. 266-81; and the three articles in the *Economic Record*, Vol. 40, June 1964, by: J. W. Nevile, 'Technical Change in Australian Manufacturing'; H. R. Edwards and N. T. Drane, 'Notes on Technical Change in Australian Manufacturing'; and J. W. Nevile, 'A Reply'.

that technical progress[13] contributed on the average 1·66 per cent a year[14]. He concluded that economies of scale contributed a small part to technical progress while a larger part accrued from technical progress which is independent of scale ('disembodied technical progress')[15]. The latter would include managerial and/or organization changes and the efficiency of labour and capital inputs. Lydall also found that productivity in manufacturing had increased by nearly 4 per cent which compares with 4·1 per cent shown in Table 35 for the longer period 1949-50 to 1967-8. His estimates mean that technical progress accounted for about $41\frac{1}{2}$ per cent of the increase in productivity during the 1950s and the remaining $58\frac{1}{2}$ per cent was attributable to an increase in capital per worker (capital deepening).

Table 35 also shows the contrast in the growth rates since 1949-50 of the industrial divisions of primary, manufacturing, and tertiary. The estimates for the tertiary industry other than 'heat, light, and power' have been computed as the residual in the economy as a whole and hence are only very approximate.

If we define a leading growth sector as one in which the average annual rate of growth is greater than the national average, then the leading growth sectors vary depending upon whether we take as the criterion output, number in work, or productivity. Of the three criteria, manufacturing as a whole is outstanding, since it grew significantly faster than the national averages in terms of output and productivity, and at about the same rate with respect to employment. The improvement in productivity in manufacturing in Australia compares favourably with movements in productivity in other countries. The Vernon Committee concluded that 'this has not only been vital for Australia's economic growth, but it has also prevented the much more marked upward pressure on tariff levels which might have otherwise occurred[16]'.

A major reason why productivity has risen faster in manufacturing industry, as also in primary industry, than the average for the whole economy is the much greater application of capital equipment (incorporating innovations) in these industries than in certain of the tertiary industries. As we noted in the previous chapter, in some

13 From a sample of 54 manufacturing industries which 'accounted in 1953–54 for about half of total employment in manufacturing, and for more than half of gross output'. Lydall, *op. cit.*, p. 814.

14 This 'figure is very similar to the estimates obtained by Solow for the United States private non-farm sector, 1909–49, of 1·5 per cent; Aukrust for the Norwegian economy, 1900–55, of 1·8 per cent; and Niitamo for Finnish manufacturing, 1922–52, of 1·5 per cent'. *Ibid*, pp. 818–9.

15 See p. 97 above.

16 *Vernon Report*, Vol. I, p. 353.

TABLE 35
AVERAGE ANNUAL RATES OF GROWTH OF OUTPUT, EMPLOYMENT, AND PRODUCTIVITY IN MAJOR INDUSTRIAL DIVISIONS, AUSTRALIA, 1949–50 TO 1967–8
(Per cent)

		Output (at average 1959–60 prices)	Number in work	Productivity (2–3)
		(a)	(a)	
	1	2	3	4
1 Primary:				
(a) Farming		3·3	−0·4[b]	3·7
(b) Mining		5·7[c]	−0·1[b]	5·8
	Proportion of total value added in all manufacturing classes in 1959–60			
2 Manufacturing: Major classes				
(a) Industrial metals, machines, conveyances	42·6	7·1	3·3	3·8
(b) Food, drink and tobacco	13·0	3·5	0·9	2·6
(c) Chemicals, dyes, explosives, paints, oils, grease	8·9	9·9	2·5	7·4
(d) Paper, stationery, printing, etc.	7·5	7·7	3·2	4·5
(e) Clothing (except knitted)	5·9	2·9	−0·3	3·2
(f) Textiles and textile goods (not dress)	5·4	5·1	0·8	4·3
(g) Sawmills, joinery, boxes, etc.	4·9	3·1	0·3	2·8
Total—all classes	100·0	6·1	2·0	4·1
3 Tertiary:				
(a) Heat, light and power		7·7	0·6	7·1
(b) Other		3·4[d]	2·6[d]	0·8
4 Total		4·3	2·0	2·3

Notes: [a] The rates in columns 2 and 3 for (i) each class of manufacturing, (ii) heat, light, and power, and (iii) total (row 4), and in column 2 for farming and mining are from trends fitted by least squares.

[b] The rates of decline of the number of work in farming and mining are the compound rates between Censuses 1947 and 1966.

[c] Calendar years 1950–68.

[d] Computed as the residual balance of items 1 to 4 in the table, using the weights for national product and employment of each sector as indicated approximately in Tables 1 and 16 respectively.

tertiary industries providing personal services, capital plays a relatively minor role. Hence the opportunities are considerably less for improving output per worker as quickly, or to the same extent as in those industries able to substitute machinery for labour on a significant scale. It is true that some tertiary industries have achieved notable advances in productivity, as has also occurred in heat, light, and power. There is a lack of sufficient statistical evidence to measure this change. But again it has tended to be concentrated where mechanical office equipment has been employed.

In brief, as previously noted[17], in much of tertiary industry the degree of efficiency is a function more fully of the performances of the individual persons themselves, whereas in the primary and manufacturing industries productivity is also greatly dependent on the efficiency of the machine, which in many cases largely sets the pattern. We should also note here that the measure of productivity which we have been using, namely physical output per worker, is not entirely satisfactory for purposes of economic planning for the most desirable and efficient allocation of resources, or for making inter industry comparisons. More ideally, for these purposes, what we require is a measure of output per unit of capital employed as well as per worker. But this information is not available.

3 CONCENTRATION AND COMPETITION

The degree of concentration and competition within industry is a reflection of the economic and institutional forces that have been fashioning the industrial pattern. It is generally recognized that ownership of manufacturing industry in Australia is highly concentrated. High concentration exists when the bulk of the market in a sector is supplied by industries which are oligopolized by a very few dominant firms in terms of market share, is duopolized (two dominant firms), or is monopolized (one dominant firm).

Professor Brunt[18], using 1957-8 data, covering 142 Australian manufacturing industries employing 89 per cent of the manufacturing labour force, found that 'highly concentrated' industries employed 37 per cent of the labour force and 'highly' plus 'fairly concentrated' 51 per cent of the labour force. A highly concentrated industry

---

17 See pp. 60–1 and 97 above.
18 In P. H. Karmel and M. Brunt, *The Structure of the Australian Economy*, Chap. 3.

Sources for Table 35: Commonwealth Bureau of Census and Statistics, *Indexes of Factory Production 1949–50 to 1967–68*, pp. 10–11, and *Official Year Book of the Commonwealth of Australia* (various issues); Bureau of Mineral Resources, *Australian Mineral Industry Review* (various issues); and Table 16.

was defined as one in which the largest four firms account for 50 per cent of the employment in the industry, and 'fairly concentrated' where the largest eight account for 50 per cent of employment. Thirty-one large highly concentrated industries were identified, mostly manufacturing producer goods. The industries range from basic steel, mineral oils, motor vehicles, electric light and power, chemicals, rubber goods, newspapers, tobacco, glass, soap, to newsprint and tin cans. Further evidence of high concentration is that in 1957-8 fourteen firms were 'large national monopolies' or virtual monopolies, the largest including Broken Hill Proprietary Co. Ltd (for basic steel), John Lysaght (Aust.) Limited (steel sheets), Colonial Sugar Refining Co. Ltd (refined sugar), Australian Consolidated Industries Ltd (glass and glass products), Imperial Chemical Industries of Australia and New Zealand (explosives), Broken Hill Associated Smelters Pty Ltd (extracting and refining of lead), Australian Newsprint Mills Ltd (newsprint), Australian Paper Manufacturers Ltd (heavy paper and paper board), and Associated Pulp and Paper Mills Ltd (fine and special papers).

Kyoko Sheridan[19] pointed out that the choice of a 50 per cent share of employment to determine concentration conceals many examples of monopolistic, duopolistic, or strongly oligopolistic industry structures. To meet this weakness she determined concentration on the basis of the number of the largest firms required to account for at least 80 per cent of gross output or employment. She examined 104 industries which employed 60 per cent of the manufacturing labour force, using data for 1961-2. The firm was 'defined as the aggregate of establishments under single ownership and under the same trading name'[20]. Sheridan found that (i) six single-firm monopolies and six two-firm duopolies together represented 7 per cent of employment in the 104 industries; and (ii) that 52·8 per cent of the labour force in her sample was employed in monopolistic, duopolistic, or oligopolistic industries.

Though international comparisons of concentration in manufacturing industry involve considerable difficulties, it is clear that the industry in Australia shows a higher degree of monopoly and oligopoly than most countries, including the U.K. and the U.S. It is the relatively small size of the Australian market on the one hand and the need to take advantage of economies of scale as far as possible on the other, in particular in capital-intensive industries, that explain why concentration is generally greater in Australia. It accounts for

19 'An Estimate of the Business Concentration of Australian Manufacturing Industries', *Economic Record*, Vol. 44, March 1968.
20 *Ibid*, p. 28.

the high concentration in the heavy industries of iron and steel, zinc and lead, chemicals, and paper. Concentration should mean lower unit costs than would apply if the industries were less concentrated. In this respect the high concentration that characterizes much of manufacturing industry in Australia appears economically desirable, and will probably continue to be so for many years[21].

This leads to the question of whether high concentration may damp incentives to change and innovation, and may facilitate the taking of unreasonable profits. A number of economic policies are available to counter any unfavourable influences. In particular, appropriate changes in fiscal policy may be made, including heavier taxes on unreasonable profits and special taxation allowances on new investment. Protective policies may also be relaxed to provide more effective competition from imports. Action to stimulate enterprise and compensate for high concentration which is inhibiting progress may also now be taken through restraints on restrictive practices, that is, on agreements or arrangements to restrict competition. Such action is provided for through the *Trade Practices Act* 1965-9 which is entitled 'an Act to preserve competition in Australian trade and commerce to the extent required by the public interest[22]'.

One of the best safeguards encouraging a progressive, competitive society is a rapid rate of economic growth, as Australia has been experiencing since World War II. In particular, the rapid growth in the manufacturing sector has meant the entry of a considerable number of new industries producing new products for the first time in Australia. Though many industries have not competed directly with other industries, they have experienced the effects of insidious competition through substitutes provided by innovation; for instance, plastics for glass, and aluminium for steel. A rapidly growing economy by providing greater opportunities for new entrants and the expansion of existing firms also increases the fear of competition. This stimulates innovation, and encourages industries to remain abreast of technological developments. These progressive, competitive elements have been contributing to the recent rapid growth in productivity in Australia and other industrial countries. They have also emphasized the importance of fundamental research[23], and of education and training. By contrast, when economic growth proceeds slowly, and particularly

---

21 *Vernon Report*, Vol. I, p. 213.
22 Quoted in Commonwealth of Australia, *Commissioner of Trade Practices First Annual Report Year Ended 30th June 1968*, p. 3.
23 Australia's research effort has been small by the standards of other industrial countries. See the figures of expenditure on research and development in: P. Stubbs, *Innovation and Research: A Study in Australian Industry*, Cheshire, 1968, p. 26; and *Vernon Report*, Vol. I, p. 421.

when there is a tendency to stagnation at relatively low levels of activity (as was the experience in western industrial countries, including Australia, in the 1930s), the incentive to innovate and to seek new and better ways of doing things is low. In short, a slow rate of growth is self-generating.

The rapid rate of economic growth and the entry of overseas companies into Australian manufacturing industry since World War II have meant a considerable number of new entrants with a consequent reduction in concentration and increase in competition in some industries. However, this has not always resulted in an efficient allocation of resources. The reduction in concentration has included some undesirable fragmentation and over-capitalization, as the Vernon Committee[24] and the Tariff Board[25] have observed. This has retarded the future rate of increase in output and material welfare.

To some extent the process of deconcentration has been reversed by mergers[26]. Mergers have occurred in several sectors of manufacturing industry. Allowance for the merger movement complicates the picture of the changing degree of concentration and competition. Some mergers have increased the competitive position of small firms, while others have made for a higher degree of oligopolized concentration.

Lest the above sound too idealistic, it should be allowed that the apparent inefficient allocation of resources (which one obviously can recognize more easily and clearly with hindsight) resulting from such elements as undesirable fragmentation and over-capitalization is one of the prices of a rapid rate of economic growth in any dynamic society. Knowledge and foresight are imperfect, and economic situations inevitably change with growth, including the discovery of new resources and techniques. The unfavourable effects which may accompany a reduction in concentration reflect the apparently perennial problems resulting from the limited size of the Australian market. The influence of size on Australia's rate of industrialization is examined further in Section 7 below in connection with the benefits of expanding manufactured exports. The size of the market has also influenced the location of industry.

---

24 *Vernon Report*, Vol. I, p. 213.
25 'The Board again found in the course of its enquiries that the Australian market for some products has been or was being fragmented among more manufacturers than the market could economically sustain, and this fragmentation has tended to accentuate the difficulties arising from the scale of production. The Board is hesitant to recommend protective duties at a level which could sustain uneconomic fragmentation of the market. Significant cost savings could follow a decrease in the number of manufacturers in some industries'. Source: Tariff Board, *Annual Report for Year 1963–64*, p. 15. See also *Annual Report for Year 1964–65*, pp. 11–12.
26 See J. A. Bushnell, *Australian Company Mergers 1946–1959*, M.U.P., 1961; and Karmel and Brunt, *op. cit.*

4 LOCATION

The location of manufacturing industry is generally a compromise between the availability of labour, markets, raw materials, capital, power, transport, and ancillary services[27]. A major feature of Australia's economic development has been the concentration of labour and markets in the metropolitan areas. Moreover, the factors working for this concentration have been cumulative and self-reinforcing, and have provided little scope for decentralization on economic grounds, except where special advantages have applied to the processing of raw materials at their source[28].

The early development of the Australian economy with its dependence on imports and exports, and its geography, favoured the development of a limited number of city ports. The construction of inland communications was centred on these ports. This was further justified by the extensive character of rural expansion: a sparse population requires only small centres for services. These centres offered little scope for manufacturing (or tertiary) employment. Furthermore, as seen in the previous section, the smallness of each State's market itself meant that, in order to secure economies of scale, manufacturing industry has to a considerable extent been concentrated in one or a few factories in metropolitan areas at the source of markets and labour supply.

The net result of the dynamic and geographic factors which have determined the location of manufacturing industry in Australia is shown in two ways in Tables 36 and 37, respectively. Table 36 demonstrates that factory employment in relation to population has been most intensive in N.S.W. and Victoria and least in Queensland and Western Australia. Table 37 indicates the high degree of centralization of manufacturing industry in the capital cities. In fact, factory employment is even more highly concentrated than population in each metropolitan area except Hobart[29].

Some exception to the pull of the metropolitan areas (with especially their markets and labour supply, but also with their sea ports and centres for inland transport), has been provided by the peculiarities of certain raw materials. Materials are, of course, used in every factory. But they have influenced location, and provided some decentralization of industry only where it is economic to process at the source of supply, particularly where resources are either perishable (e.g. dairy products) or lose weight in processing (e.g. timber).

---

27 See G. J. R. Linge, 'The Location of Manufacturing Industry in Australia', in Hunter (ed.), *op. cit.*, Chap. 2.
28 *Vernon Report*, Vol. 1, p. 215.
29 See also p. 37 above.

TABLE 36
RELATIVE DISTRIBUTION OF POPULATION AND FACTORY
EMPLOYMENT, BY STATES, 1967–8

State	Population as percentage of total[a]	Factory employment as percentage of total[a]	Col. 2 divided by col. 1
	1	2	3
New South Wales	37·0	40·1	1·08
Victoria	28·1	33·9	1·21
Queensland	14·6	9·1	0·62
South Australia	9·5	9·2	0·97
Western Australia	7·6	5·1	0·67
Tasmania	3·2	2·7	0·84
All States	100·0	100·0	1·00

[a] Computed from data in Commonwealth Bureau of Census and Statistics, *Quarterly Summary of Australian Statistics*, June 1969, pp. 2 and 33.

TABLE 37
PROPORTION OF POPULATION AND FACTORY EMPLOYMENT IN
METROPOLITAN AREAS, BY STATES, 30 JUNE 1961

City	Percentage of State population in metropolitan area	Percentage of State factory employment in metropolitan area	Col. 2 divided by col. 1
	1	2	3
Sydney	55·7	73·7	1·32
Melbourne	65·1	80·2	1·23
Brisbane	40·8	53·2	1·30
Adelaide	60·7	80·5	1·32
Perth	57·0	68·9	1·21
Hobart	33·1	32·7	0·99

Source: Vernon Report, Vol. I, p. 214.

With technical progress and the discovery and exploitation of new resources, the economics of production may change and justify a different location. A notable example is the location and subsequent development of the Australian steel industry. When the Broken Hill Proprietary Co. Ltd established its Newcastle steelworks in the mid-1910s, 'it took approximately one and a half tons of ore and three tons of coal to make a ton of finished steel. Obviously, the economics were in the direction of taking the ore to the coal'[30]. Newcastle, apart

---

30 Essington Lewis, *The Importance of the Iron and Steel Industry to Australia*, Joseph Fisher Lecture in Commerce, University of Adelaide, Hassell Press, 1948, p. 32.

from cheap, easy access to coal, was also favoured as a sea-port to receive the iron ore from Whyalla in South Australia. The location of steelworks at Port Kembla (which began operation in 1928 under the ownership of Australian Iron and Steel Ltd) was made especially on account of it being adjacent to adequate supplies of good coking coal and also having good potential for development as a port. In 1935 the steel plants at Newcastle and Port Kembla were brought into close association when the B.H.P. Co. acquired all the ordinary shares of Australian Iron and Steel. By the latter half of the 1930s, significant improvements had been made in fuel conservation, so that it became economic to carry coal to the ore under some circumstances. Thus, for this reason, and also strategic reasons, B.H.P. erected a blast furnace at Whyalla in 1941, followed by the opening of an integrated steelworks there in 1965. B.H.P. also started building ships at Whyalla in 1940[31].

Apart from population distribution, two other institutional features influential in industrial location have been differences in (i) transport facilities, and (ii) State legislation and influence in providing assistance, advice, and encouragement through the various State instrumentalities. The great distances between the centralized markets on the periphery of each State have meant that the cost, delays, and difficulties of interstate transport have discouraged the development of a national market. The lack of uniform railway gauge between Sydney and Brisbane until 1930 and between Sydney and Melbourne until 1962 further handicapped the transport of goods. In respect to State legislation one of the major differences occurred through different rates of income taxation, Victoria having the lowest rates before the introduction of uniform taxation in July 1942 (see Chapter 7, Section 2 (b)).

Continuing improvements in transport between the States (such as double-deck railway transporters, especially favourable for the motor industry) and the greater importance of national economic policies in an environment of rapid economic growth have stimulated a more speedy spread of the activities of an increasing number of firms from supplying only one or two States to a more national approach. The *Trade Practices Act* has also provided a spur to increasing enterprise and the greater opening up of the Australian market on a national scale. Previously many firms have been slow to pursue business outside their native State. Many more have shown still less enterprise in exploring prospects of widening their market beyond Australia.

However, as discussed further in Section 7 below, a widening of the market to include export of manufactures is essential if Australian

---

31 *Ibid* and Hughes, *op. cit.*

manufacturers are to be able to achieve and justify the increasing size of factories. Greater size is essential (for instance, in automation, electronics, and nuclear power development) to take advantage of technological progress, and thereby to achieve economies of scale, which will enable Australian products to remain competitive with imports without requiring increasing protection.

5 THE TARIFF

(a) Extent of Dependence on Protection

It is difficult to summarize in a dozen pages all that needs to be said about the protective tariff in stimulating Australia's industrial development.

Throughout most of the twentieth century a large part of Australian manufacturing industry has in some degree been dependent on the tariff. In recent years this protection has applied to approximately two-thirds of Australian manufacturing industry, measured by employment and by value of production[32]. Industries which rely in part on the tariff include especially those producing plant and machinery, motor vehicles, electrical equipment, chemicals, clothing, textiles, and paper. Some part of these industries would, of course, undoubtedly survive if there were no tariff. The main manufacturing industries which are not competing with imports, or where import competition would not be significant, are food and drink processing, motor vehicle repairs, and newspaper printing.

The Vernon Committee showed that the proportion of Australia's imports bearing protective rates as a percentage of all imports has varied between 15 and 20 per cent since World War II, and that in 1938-9 the proportion was much higher at 39·8 per cent[33]. The Committee also showed that this decline was matched by a fall in 'dutiable imports as a percentage of all imports' from 54·4 per cent in 1938-9 to 43·8 per cent in 1962-3. This proportion had fallen further to 42·0 per cent in 1967-8[34].

The decline in the proportion of imports bearing protective rates does not indicate a fall in the degree of protection in Australia. It

---

32 See *Vernon Report*, Vol. I, p. 354.

33 *Ibid*, p. 352. In this calculation the Committee excluded imports bearing low rates of duty and specifically revenue duties, as well as imports bearing no duty. The Committee defined 'imports bearing protective rates' as: 'imports bearing (i) ad valorem rates above $12\frac{1}{2}$ per cent, and (ii) specific rates, except for revenue items such as tobacco, spirits, petrol, etc., and except, in the years other than 1938–39, for specific rate items with a low ad valorem equivalent. Low ad valorem equivalent items are those specific-rate duties grouped around the equivalent of 5 per cent ad valorem.' *Ibid*.

34 *Official Year Book of the Commonwealth of Australia*, No. 55, 1969, p. 351.

reflects fundamental changes in the pattern of imports resulting largely from industrialization in Australia. Industrialization, *per se,* has been stimulated in part by the protective tariff, which in turn has contributed to the general rapid growth of the Australian economy by supporting more rapid population growth and capital formation incorporating technological progress. The changing pattern of imports has occurred in two main interrelated ways: (i) import replacement; and (ii) a shift in the composition of imports from finished or near-finished consumer goods to capital equipment, while the proportion of producers' materials has changed little[35]. 'Many of these producer goods pay little or no duty. They enter predominantly under by-law items, which provide free entry or low rates for goods not produced in Australia or not produced in sufficient quantities[36].' Though the protective tariff has contributed cumulatively to import replacement and the changing pattern of imports, these changes have arisen in part independently of tariff protection, occurring also as the result of economic growth itself. Import replacement and changes in the pattern of imports are examined in more detail in Section 6 of this chapter.

(b) Stages in the Development of the Tariff[37]

(i) 1908-1920

Since Federation there have been four main periods during which the tariff has been used to protect certain Australian industries from competition with imports in the domestic market. The first occurred with the 'Lyne tariff' in 1908 when the Commonwealth of Australia's protectionist policies were laid. Previously the Commonwealth tariff (since 1901) had been used primarily for revenue purposes.

(ii) 1920s

The second and more significant period began with the 'Greene tariff' in 1921 when the Commonwealth decided to provide protection from competition with imports to industries which had developed during World War I. This objective led to the Commonwealths' creation in 1921 of an independent advisory authority — the Tariff Board[38].

---

35 See Table 38 below.

36 *Vernon Report*, Vol. I, p. 354.

37 See W. M. Corden, 'The Tariff', in Hunter (ed.), *op. cit.*, especially pp. 184–97.

38 The *Tariff Board Act* 1921–1966 provides for the appointment of a Tariff Board consisting of eight members.

The Board examines proposals for tariff changes referred to it by the Department of Trade and Industry. Most of the Board's recommendations are accepted, the changes in tariff rates being the responsibility of Parliament. The actual administration of the tariff is undertaken by the Department of Customs and Excise.

Australia's industrialization acquired a more solid base for future growth and diversification during World War I and the 1920s with the establishment of the iron and steel industry and motor body assembly. During the 1920s, under the guidance of the Tariff Board, further substantial increases were made in the protective tariff to compensate for the fall in costs overseas when the post-war boom ended. Earlier there had been protests from primary producers who claimed that the burden of the higher cost structure imposed on the Australian economy through the protection granted to manufacturers was ultimately borne by the farmer. These protests were being met — with the approval of the Country Party — by providing 'protection all round' through guaranteed price schemes for certain farm products (notably a scheme for the stabilization of prices of butter and cheese introduced in 1926).

(iii) 1930s

Opposition in Australia to protection was also disappearing for strategic and employment reasons. Support on employment grounds in manufacturing industries strengthened greatly as the world-wide depression began in 1929, and unemployment in Australia rose sharply. And so the third phase of considerably increased protection to manufacturing industries against competition from imports occurred in 1930. This included especially the 'Scullin tariff', which was imposed without reference to the Tariff Board and provided for a large, widespread increase in ordinary tariff rates. Some imports were prohibited, and primage duties for revenue were imposed on almost all imports. Further protection was provided in 1931 by the devaluation of the Australian pound from parity with sterling to £A125 to £stg100.

From 1933 on, following recommendations of the Tariff Board, the tariffs imposed by the Government during the depression were lowered and modified. The reductions included a special adjustment to allow for the exchange devaluation in 1931. Australia found it necessary to adopt a more conciliatory approach to other countries which were markets for Australian primary products, and which might have retaliated if their own manufactured goods were not permitted to sell in Australia. Thus, in the course of the 1930s, Australia negotiated a number of Trade Pacts to improve her trading relationships.

The most important to which Australia was a party was the Ottawa Agreement in 1932. Through this Australia agreed to grant considerable preferential treatment to imports from Britain. Britain agreed to continue to permit free entry into Britain of a number of primary products from all Empire countries and not to increase existing duties[39].

Though the Tariff Board modified the tariffs imposed by the Government during the depression, with the competitive advantage also provided by devaluation most industries continued to be adequately protected against overseas competition. This was manifested in the fact that Australia's protective policy in the 1930s attracted many more overseas firms to come in 'behind the tariff wall' and to establish branch factories or subsidiaries in Australia.

One industry that has been a major growth industry since World War II, and that received a strong fillip from the protective policies in the 1930s, is the Australian motor industry. 'The Scullin tariff of 1930 stimulated the local component industry, and in 1937 the Tariff Board reckoned local content[40] in locally made cars between 43 and 50 per cent, including such items as tyres, shock absorbers, spark plugs, batteries, gears, piston rings, and valves — manufacture of which had grown up under the tariff protection[41].'

However, from 1939 until the Japanese Trade Treaty in 1957, and the commencement of the easing of import restrictions in 1958, the tariff was relatively unimportant as a means of protection. Manufacturing industries, including many infants, received effective protection against any adverse trend in Australia's competitive position in four main ways: first, by World War II; secondly, by the supply shortages in overseas markets during the early post-war years; thirdly, by the 1949 devaluation with sterling, of the Australian pound against the dollar; and fourthly, by the dollar import licensing, and general import licensing (the latter from 1952 on). These import restrictions were almost completely lifted in 1960.

(iv) 1960s

It was during the latter half of the 1950s, and especially from 1960, that the Commonwealth's protective tariff again became important as a major element influencing resource allocation[42]. The Vernon Committee showed that the average duty on imports bearing protective rates

39 For details of the Ottawa Agreement, see *Official Year Book of the Commonwealth of Australia*, No. 27, 1934, pp. 226-7 and 236-7.

40 'i.e., percentage of Australian labour and material in the factory cost of complete cars manufactured in Australia.' Source: P. Stubbs, *The Australian Motor Industry*, reprint series No. 6 of University of Melbourne Institute of Applied Economic Research, 1965, p. 130; originally published as *Current Affairs Bulletin*, Vol. 35, No. 9, 15 March 1965.

41 *Ibid.*

42 For a critical review of Australian trading patterns and protectionist policies (of imports and exports since World War II), see Snape, *International Trade and the Australian Economy*, Chap. 3.

had risen from nearly 26 per cent in 1948-9 to almost 32 per cent in 1962-3, but was still slightly below the average in 1938-9[43]. The Committee considered that

'since the mid-1950s, the general cost disability of Australian industry as indicated by the relative movements in price indexes in Australia and overseas, has not risen appreciably. This cost disability is, in our view, somewhat less than the average of protective tariffs, which we have set at about 30 per cent. . . . This apparent constancy in cost disability is due in part to the increase in productivity of manufacturing in Australia during the past decade, compared wtih movements in productivity in other countries[44].'

The indications are that Australia's comparative disability has not increased significantly since the Vernon Committee reported in 1965. The continued rapid advance of productivity in Australia's manufacturing industry has been a major element in this relatively favourable position. It means that the upward pressure on the protective tariff rates has been less than it might have been otherwise.

(c) The Case for the Tariff

The Vernon Committee devoted two chapters to a critical analysis of the protective tariff, considering (in Chapter 13) 'the impact of protection', in particular the question of whether Australia has benefited from the tariff. They concluded moderately in favour of the tariff, and then discussed (in Chapter 14) 'policy elements' regarding the desirable pattern and size of the tariff.

Looking back we can see more confidently several grounds on which Australia's protective tariff can be shown to have largely vindicated its early supporters. There are both economic and non-economic arguments to be taken into account. The most powerful economic justification for tariffs is that it provided aid to economic growth through industrialization. The 'infant industry' or 'infant economy' argument for protection is particularly relevant here. This argument, recognized by the English classical economists (in fact, J. S. Mill in the late 1860s made special reference to the Australian case[45]), holds that protection from competition with imports is justified during the transitional phase while new industries are being established, and the industrial sector is becoming self-sustaining. When this occurs, and the infants have 'grown up', the tariffs are removed. The removal, of course, may occur in stages.

---

43 *Vernon Report*, Vol. I, Table 13.2, p. 352.
44 *Ibid*, p. 353.
45 See A. J. Reitsma, *Trade Protection in Australia*, University of Queensland Press, 1960, Chap. VII.

The problems of achieving a self-supporting industrial sector, and the time required to do so, tend to be considerable, as Australia's experience clearly shows[46]. The magnitude of these problems and the long time often involved before tariffs can be removed may be inevitable features of industrialization in a country, such as Australia, which has a relatively small domestic market and is a later starter in industrialization. Furthermore, it is important to recognize that Australia's industrialization is occurring in a dynamic international setting involving continuous rapid industrial growth in the already more highly developed industrial countries, whose products provide the main competition with Australian manufactures.

Nevertheless, this does not detract from the positive gains which have been accruing to Australia from the industrialization which has already been promoted by tariff protection. One of the main reasons linked with the infant industry argument for protection is that economies of large-scale production and external economies are not available in the early stages of development. Some industries experience significant reductions in unit costs as their output expands. This may result from the introduction of larger, more efficient capital equipment and from general economies of production and distribution as industries gain in size and experience. The Vernon Committee concluded: 'in our view, the case for tariff protection or other assistance in the early stages of industries which are likely to benefit from large-scale production is strong[47].'

The case for protection to foster internal economies is considerably strengthened and, indeed, logically justified by external economies which are created by manufacturing industries and the increasing diversification of the economy. These external economies which lead to lower unit costs in the economy, accrue from the greater spread of scientific and technical knowledge, the greater efficiency in industrial production and management, and the creation of a greater market, which in turn stimulates further capital formation and

---

46 One notable exception of a protected infant industry which grew up quite quickly in Australia was the steel industry. The Broken Hill Proprietary Co. Ltd began its operations with the protection of World War I and then the Greene tariff. The tariff was increased during the 1920s and in the depression. Devaluation in 1931 also aided the industry. During the 1930s the industry's competitive position changed significantly and by the eve of World War II most types of steel were being sold in Australia at prices lower than those ruling overseas. See Hughes, *op .cit.*

For case studies, illustrating historically the structure and complexity of the tariff in connection with the main protected industries in Australia, see Corden, 'The Tariff' in Hunter (ed.), *op. cit.*, pp. 207–13.

47 *Vernon Report*, Vol. I, p. 362. For a critical review of the Vernon Committee's discussion of 'infant industry protection' see W. M. Corden, 'Protection', *Economic Record*, Vol. 42, March 1966, pp. 140–3.

economic growth, with favourable linkages throughout the economy, including more efficient tertiary industries.

The argument to assist manufacturing industries during their formative years has strengthened with the higher demand for, and hence higher prices of, manufactured products relative to primary products. Australia's experience during the past forty years or so has clarified and supported strongly the conclusion of the Brigden Committee[48] in 1929 that the primary industries could not have expanded at a rate sufficient to have absorbed the population increase at that time[49].

As previously noted, the primary industries have continued to expand: Table 35 shows that the average annual rate of increase of farming productivity over the period 1949-50 to 1967-8 is not far below that in manufacturing as a whole. However, the rural expansion could not have supported Australia's rapidly increasing population and labour force since World War II. The increasing output and labour productivity in primary industry have largely resulted from increasing capital intensity[50]. In fact, employment in primary industry since the war has fallen below the level reached in the 1920s and 1930s (see Table 16).

The stimulus to industrialization by the protective tariff has contributed to and justified the rapid expansion of population. It is important to recognize the circular relationship between industrialization and population growth since World War II. The favourable stimulus to economic development has occurred thus: rapid industrialization has made Australia attractive for migrants and overseas capital, hence contributing to a more rapid economic growth and realization of economies of scale and benefits from external economies with the larger market. Overseas capital has been attracted by the strongly favourable profit expectations. The attraction for migrants has been provided on the one hand by the wider range of employment opportunities deriving from the increasing diversification and sophistication of manufacturing industries, and, on the other, by the relatively high, rising, real wages and living standards. Another important aspect of Australia's industrial development has been the considerable degree of import replacement which is partly attributable to the stimulus of the protective tariff. The subject of import replacement is discussed in the next section.

---

48 In J. B. Brigden and others, *The Australian Tariff—An Economic Enquiry*, M.U.P., 1929.

49 For a useful recent discussion of this Brigden Committee conclusion and of the support of it from Australia's experiences since their report, see *Vernon Report*, Vol. I, pp. 356–7.

50 See pp. 88–9 above.

Historically, we can now see the way in which the tariff has helped to provide, through speedier industrial development and diversification, more stability in manufacturing activity than would probably have been experienced without it or with an alternative (for instance, devaluation). This is especially so when we allow for Australia's isolation and the major non-economic influences manifested in two world wars. Australia's industrial development in the inter-war period, and especially in the 1930s (when industrial development was used to assist the national policy of securing a higher level of employment), enabled her to make a more speedy contribution to the war effort through her manufacturing industries. The rapid industrial development since World War II has ensured a greater degree of stability in output and employment by reducing the significance of fluctuations in the prices of primary products.

However, the evolution in economic thought now requiring governments to maintain full employment through appropriate fiscal and monetary policies (see Chapter 9) means that tariff changes are no longer viewed as an appropriate measure to combat short-term fluctuations in economic activity. The Vernon Committee, after considering the burden of the tariff in relation to alternative systems (notably devaluation), concluded:[51] 'The Committee's view is that a tariff system is as good as, and perhaps better than, any alternative[52]. However, we believe that the benefits noted are greater if the tariff is selective.' Most Australian economists and policy-makers would probably support the Committee's general conclusion.

It is the pattern and the size of the tariff about which there continues to be strong economic debate. A leading objective of the Tariff Board has been to assist industries that will be 'economic' and 'efficient'. The Vernon Committee discussed at length[53] the difficulties of interpreting this objective, and suggested that the Tariff Board adopt a 'benchmark', whereby it can give more precision to its judgments of the economics and efficiency of particular industries, and so pursue a selective tariff policy in order to protect industries where the protection is justified. In this way tariff policy may be co-ordinated

---

51 *Ibid*, p. 360.
52 The Committee added (*ibid*, p. 366):
   'Indeed, we believe that the alternative of free trade with devaluation would not have been practicable. However, we have strongly suggested that, despite the difficulty of isolating it, the Tariff has been important in the extension and increased diversity of industry, the development of labour skills, the advance of technology, the ability to absorb a rapid increase in population, involving a high rate of immigration, and the steady increase in capital investment essential to all these achievements.'
53 *Ibid*, pp. 360 and 372–5. See also Tariff Board, *Annual Report for Year 1965–66*, pp. 8–15.

with general economic policy and other protective measures, including exchange devaluation, to foster a more efficient allocation of resources. The need for a more selective tariff policy has grown with the increasing industrial diversification and integration (vertically and horizontally) of the rapidly expanding economy.

When quantitative import restrictions ceased in 1960, the Tariff Board was still pursuing principles established in the 1930s. Competition was then mainly from Britain. The Tariff Board[54], in reporting on the 'changed circumstances' of the 1960s, stated:

'In the 1930s . . . there were substantial tariff preferences in favour of British goods and in certain areas where competition from non-British goods had become important, quantitative restrictions were imposed for "trade diversion" purposes; for example quantitative restrictions were imposed on imports from North America in 1936 under the "Trade Diversion" policy and later against some imports from Japan. Therefore in the 1930s the Tariff Board was primarily concerned with questions of protection arising out of competition from British industry. During the 1960s, competition from countries other than Britain—such as Japan, the United States of America, Federal Republic of Germany and Italy—has been growing steadily with the result that the Board's inquiries are, and will continue to be, increasingly concerned with questions of assistance for local industries against competition from such countries.'

The traditional tariff-making procedures in Australia have involved 'the selection of industries (or parts of industries) on an "ad hoc" basis and largely in response to requests from interested parties seeking greater protection'[55]. Consequently, as the Chairman of the Tariff Board noted, 'the traditional tariff revision procedures have tended to produce a complex and inconsistent structure of protection'[56].

In order to overcome the weaknesses of examining each industry individually and to meet the challenge provided by the increasing diversification and complexity of Australian manufacturing industry, the Tariff Board, in its *Annual Report for Year 1966-67*, stated[57] that it 'proposes a progressive and systematic review of the Tariff consisting of an internal examination . . . of the structure and levels of protection in the Tariff, together with public inquiries into the main areas of production where there has been no recent public inquiry and where the levels of protection are in the medium to high range.'

---

54 *Annual Report for Year 1966–67*, p. 6.
55 *Ibid*, p. 7.
56 G. A. Rattigan, 'The Tariff Board: Some Reflections', *Economic Record*, Vol. 45, March 1969, p. 22.
57 P. 8.

From this study the Board[58] has provided a preliminary classification of products according to whether the level of tariff protection is high, medium, or low. In this way the Board is adopting a benchmark approach, and is establishing a general scale of values to assist in deciding which industries should be encouraged, and which discouraged.

6 THE INFLUENCE OF INDUSTRIALIZATION ON THE STRUCTURE AND SOURCE OF IMPORTS, AND IMPORT REPLACEMENT

The growing industrialization of Australia has been accompanied by significant changes in the composition of imports. Table 38 (see columns 1 to 3) shows that there has been a trend away from finished consumer goods to capital equipment, while the import of producers' material has shown no definite trend. There have been some fluctuations from period to period in the proportion of each class, notably in producers' materials and capital equipment. This has resulted from special factors (e.g. armament expenditure) and from changes in the level of economic activity and the rate and nature of economic growth.

The general trend away from finished consumer goods reflects Australia's greater industrialization and capacity to process raw materials in her own plants. This industrial development has been stimulated by protection. A further significant point is that the proportion of imports essential to maintaining employment and economic development in Australia has risen since the 1930s and approximated 80 per cent by the latter half of the 1960s compared with just over 70 per cent previously.

The changing composition of imports is shown in an alternative way in Table 38 (columns 4 to 6) in terms of the degree of transformation of imports between crude, simply transformed, and elaborately transformed. *Prima facie*, there may seem to be some conflict between the trends in the relative importance of imports as classified in columns 1 to 3 and in columns 4 to 6. But the conflict can be resolved by allowing that the trend, for instance, in column 6 is a combination of the changes shown in columns 2 and 3 in relation to the changes in column 1 on the one hand and columns 4 and 5 on the other. The recovery of 'elaborately transformed' imports in the 1960s follows the sharp increase in the relative importance of capital equipment (see column 2) since the late 1940s. A major component of the decline in finished consumer goods has been the reduction in the proportion of 'road vehicles', as Australian motor vehicle manufacturers have, with the encouragement of official policy, achieved a higher fully

---

58 See its *Annual Report for Year 1967–68*, p. 5 and Apps 3 and 4.

TABLE 38

IMPORTS OF MERCHANDISE ACCORDING TO ECONOMIC CLASSES AND MERCHANDISE IMPORTS AS A PERCENTAGE OF G.N.P., AUSTRALIA, SELECTED YEARS, 1913 TO 1968-9

(Per cent)

Annual averages of financial years	By economic class[a]			By degree of manufacture[a]			Merchandise imports as a percentage of G.N.P.
	Producers' materials	Capital equipment	Finished consumer goods	Crude	Simply transformed	Elaborately transformed	(b)
	1	2	3	4	5	6	7
1913	54	15	31	8	12	80	17·1
1919–20	58	8	34	13	13	74	15·4
1920–21	61	9	30	10	10	80	21·8
1928–30	58	9	33	12	15	73	15·6
1935–40	59	12	29	12	17	71	12·3*
1946–49	63	10	27	12	20	68	14·2
1954–58	54	18	28	17	17	66	14·3
1965–69	55	25	20	14	12	74	13·0

Note: * For period 1935–9.

Sources: (a) R. S. Gilbert, 'Structural Trends in Australian Imports', *Economic Record*, Vol. 35, April 1959, p. 132; and Commonwealth Bureau of Census and Statistics, *Monthly Review of Business Statistics*, October 1969, pp. 16–17.

(b) Computed from data in I. W. McLean, 'The Australian Balance of Payments on Current Account 1901 to 1964–65', *Australian Economic Papers*, Vol. 7, June 1968, pp. 83–6; Commonwealth Bureau of Census and Statistics, *Official Year Book of the Commonwealth of Australia*, No. 54, 1968, p. 1268, *Australian National Accounts*, 1967–8, p. 28, *Balance of Payments* (various issues); and Commonwealth of Australia, *National Income and Expenditure 1968–69*, p.16.

TABLE 39

SHIFTS IN SOURCE OF AUSTRALIAN IMPORTS,[a] 1904 TO 1968-9

Annual Average	Commonwealth countries				Other countries							Total value of merchandise imports (f.o.b.)
	United Kingdom	Canada	New Zealand	Total	France	Germany	Italy	Japan	U.S.A.	Indonesia	Total	
	1	2	3	4	5	6	7	8	9	10	11	12
					Percentage of total							$m
1904–1913	60·1	1·0	4·7	73·2	0·9	5·7	0·5	1·1	11·5		26·8	99
1914/15–1918/19	47·1	2·3	3·0	65·5	0·3	0·4	0·5	5·6	21·8		34·5	137
1920/21–1928/29	45·1	2·9	1·7	57·9	2·6	1·5	0·9	3·0	23·0		42·1	262
1929/30–1938/39	37·9	5·2	1·6	57·5	1·7	3·5	0·9	5·2	16·6		42·5	177
1947/48–1952/53	46·1	3·0	0·7	64·0	1·7	1·6	1·5	1·5	12·5	2·7	36·0	1166
1953/54–1958/59	43·1	2·9	1·3	59·4	1·6	4·4	1·4	2·4	12·6	3·3	40·6	1503
1959/60–1964/65	30·3	3·9	1·7	45·1	1·7	5·7	1·6	6·3	20·7	2·6	54·9	2102
1965/66–1966/67	24·0	3·8	1·6	37·2	3·1	5·4	1·7	9·6	24·8	2·0	62·8	2830
Year												
1967–8	22·1	4·3	1·9	34·7	2·7	5·8	2·2	10·5	25·8	1·7	65·3	3264
1968–9	21·6	4·4	2·2	34·9	1·8	5·8	2·3	12·0	25·4	1·7	65·1	3469

(column 6: West Germany)

Note: [a] Excluding gold.
Sources: Commonwealth Bureau of Census and Statistics *Official Year Book of the Commonwealth of Australia* (various issues), and *Overseas Trade 1968–69*, Bulletin No. 66, pp. 1029–33.

Australian-made content in their vehicles. Thus imports of road vehicles, as a proportion of total imports, fell from about 10 per cent in 1946-9 and 1954-8 to about $2\frac{1}{2}$ per cent in the mid-1960s.

Another interesting structural change has been the shifts in the source of Australian imports. Table 39 shows that the most significant change has been the considerable reduction in the relative importance of imports from the U.K. from about 60 per cent in the decade before World War I to 24 per cent during the mid-1960s, when the U.S. had become Australia's chief source of imports. Imports from Japan and West Germany have also recovered since World War II, and have been relatively larger than in the inter-war period. These changes (as also pointed out in connection with changes in the direction of Australian exports[59]) have resulted largely from 'trade creation' rather than 'trade diversion'. But, 'in addition', as summarized by Dr Snape[60]: 'there have been some trade-diverting factors causing trade to shift from the U.K. On the side of Australian imports, there was a decrease in 1957 in Australia's preference margin for U.K. imports from the range of $12\frac{1}{2}$ to 17 per cent, to $7\frac{1}{2}$ and 10 per cent; an easing of the world's dollar shortage and the removal of discrimination against dollar goods; removal of discrimination against Japanese goods by Trade Agreements of 1957 and 1963; and technological improvements of other countries relative to the United Kingdom. In addition, sentimental and other ties with the U.K. probably declined over the period, and may have caused Australians to be more aware of other suppliers and markets.'

The structural changes in the composition of Australia's imports resulting from the process of industrialization have meant a significant degree of net import replacement. One crude measure of this trend is furnished by the decline in the ratio of merchandise imports to G.N.P., as shown for selected periods from 1913 in Table 38 (column 7). Some allowance should be made for the influence of fluctuations in the level of economic activity. But the broad indication is of a considerable degree of net import replacement, reflecting not only tariff protection but also the expansion of the Australian market with increasing population and the growth of the economy generally[61]. The Vernon Committee estimated that the likely continued net replacement of imports by home-produced goods (which Australian industry would be able to produce efficiently on a competitive basis with

---

59 See p. 92 above.
60 *Op. cit.*, p. 49.
61 'Some of the important industries in which import replacement has been large since immediately before . . . [World War II] are: iron and steel, electrical machinery, motor vehicles, petroleum refining, paper-making and plastics.' *Vernon Report*, Vol. I, p. 365.

imports) during the years to the mid-1970s would involve 'a decline of 0·2 percentage points annually in the ratio of imports to G.N.P.'[62]. Import replacement has certainly assisted Australia to maintain equilibrium in the balance of payments in the face of the unfavourable trends in world markets for her primary exports.

Import replacement is thus a measure of the benefits which have steadily accrued to Australia from the policy of protection and the growth of the Australian market. However, a fundamental question is whether the size of the market is large enough, or growing at a sufficient pace, to enable industrial development to continue to occur rapidly enough. Rapidly enough here means especially in the sense of contributing at an acceptable rate to general economic growth and benefiting from increasing scale. It is in order to meet these potential benefits, and to meet the challenge from the advances in technological developments overseas, that Australian manufacturers should seek to widen their market through exports.

7 THE GROWTH OF MANUFACTURED EXPORTS

With the expansion of Australia's export industries since World War II there has been an increase in the exports of manufactures. In 1953-4 manufactures comprised about 6 per cent of the total value of exports of Australian produce (see Table 20)[63]. Their relative importance has risen significantly since then to just above 9 per cent in the early 1960s and to 16·8 per cent in 1967-8. Iron and steel have grown rapidly, comprising in recent years 20 to 25 per cent of exports of manufactures. Machines and machinery have provided about 15 per cent, while vehicles (and parts) and chemicals just over 10 per cent each.

These industry groups — iron and steel, machinery, vehicles, and chemicals — which are supplying the greater part of Australia's expanding exports of manufactures, have been the leading growth

---

62 *Ibid*, p. 339. See also Appendix K of the Committee's *Report* where it describes the study it made 'of import replacement in the post-war period in terms, first, of replacement in aggregate and in broad classes of goods and, secondly, in terms of replacement by particular industries.' *Ibid*, p. 364.
'The industries which would seem to offer a good deal of scope for import saving are chemicals, machinery and engineering, motor vehicles and parts, cotton, man-made-fibre textiles and pulp and paper-makers.' *Ibid*, p. 339.

63 However, it should be allowed that the classification of product by degree of manufacture is largely arbitrary. There is no universally standard definition of manufactures, semi-manufactures, etc. An illustration of the basic distinctions made by the Commonwealth Statistician is provided by his classification of metals for the purpose of the statistics used for Table 20: ores and concentrates are classed as 'unprocessed' primary produce (col. 7), refined metals (including pig iron) as 'processed' primary produce (col. 8), and metal sheets and other shapes as 'manufactures' (col. 10).

industries since World War II. This partly explains their success as exporters. Their rapid growth with modern, efficient production techniques has been supported principally by growing 'inwardly' through the aid of two traditional avenues of domestic expansion: first, the greater size of the domestic market itself; and secondly, lateral development entailing the replacement of an increasing variety of imports. Both avenues have been largely secured by protection. The achievement of increasing economies of scale through domestic expansion has, in turn, enabled industries to compete more successfully overseas with the large, industrialized countries.

A basic question is whether the traditional pattern of secondary industry development in Australia, depending mainly on the domestic market to secure economies of scale, will be adequate to meet growth expectations without the aid of increasing protection. A senior member of the Tariff Board has explained the question thus:

'The major limiting factor in the growth opportunities of Australia's secondary industries is the size of the domestic market, even though better transport is slowly knitting it into a more homogeneous unit. . . . In terms of many overseas markets the Australian market is minute and, more importantly, in terms of the production technologies being developed to supply these very much larger overseas markets, the Australian manufacturer catering basically for his domestic market is quite often at a growing disadvantage. The most modern and efficient production techniques in an increasing number of instances, just can't be employed economically merely to supply the Australian market. . . . For the Australian manufacturer in this situation it means that his products are becoming uneconomic through the technical obsolescence of hitherto perfectly adequate plant. An important point for national policy purposes is that this is happening increasingly despite the relatively fast growth of domestic demand. It is even more important to note that the fastest possible growth of domestic demand is unlikely to reverse the process in more than a few instances, such are the differences in market sizes, particularly when the product produced overseas can be geared to a growing world-wide market[64].'

Industrialization of the Australian economy during the twentieth century may be epitomized as a race between the size of its economy and the requirement for the minimum economic size of plants. As the Australian economy has grown, technological progress in other

---

64 R. Boyer, *Policies for Growth (Priority as Between Industries)*, a paper delivered at the Autumn Forum of the Victorian Branch of the Economic Society of Australia and New Zealand, May 1969. See also report in the *Australian Financial Review*, 8 May 1969.

advanced industrial economies has continuously increased the optimum scale of plants.

A solution to the handicap of scale is for Australian manufacturing industry to make 'the world its market', and to re-orient itself to exporting a larger proportion of its products, so that industry and the economy can achieve growth expectations[65]. This would prevent manufacturing industries ossifying and stultifying through an inadequate domestic market, and relying on increasing protection. The realism of producing for the world market is already well-established with the leading agricultural and pastoral products, and more recently with a wide range of metals, notably iron ore, alumina, and nickel. Furthermore, a more rapid expansion of exports of manufactures would strengthen Australia's balance of payments and help to meet the increasing demand for imports of goods and services, including the servicing of the considerable overseas investment in Australian manufacturing industries themselves.

Suggestions for further reading

Corden, W. M. 'Protection', *Economic Record*, Vol. 42, March 1966, pp. 129-48; and 'Australian Tariff Policy', *Australian Economic Papers*, Vol. 6, December 1967, pp. 131-54;

Davidson, F. G. *The Industrialization of Australia*, M.U.P., 4th edn, 1969;

Forster, C. *Industrial Development in Australia 1920-1930*, A.N.U. Press, 1964;

Grant, J. McB. and others, *Economic Institutions and Policy*, Chaps 4, 5, and 13;

Hunter, A. (ed.), *The Economics of Australian Industry*, especially Chaps 1, 2, and 6;

Hunter, A. 'Restrictive Practices and Monopolies In Australia', *Economic Record*, Vol. 37, March 1961, pp. 25-52;

Karmel, P. H. and Brunt, M. *The Structure of the Australian Economy*, Chap. 3;

Perkins, J. O. N. *Australia in the World Economy*, Chap. 6;

Samuelson, P. A. and others, *Economics: Australian edition*, Chap. 35;

---

65 This solution has been strongly supported in a paper by the Secretary of the Department of Trade and Industry, Sir Alan Westerman, and reported in the *Australian Financial Review*, 22 May 1969. The *Review* commented: 'Admittedly, the Department of Trade has been calling for an expansion of manufactured exports for some years, but it has never before been so explicit about how the expansion should be achieved, nor so critical of the alternative.'

Stubbs, P. *Innovation and Research: A Study in Australian Industry,*
   Cheshire, 1968;
Vernon Report, Vol. I, pp. 200-16 and Chaps 13 and 14; and Vol.
   II, App. L.;
Wheelwright, E. L. and Miskelly, J. *Anatomy of Australian Manufac-
   turing Industry,* Law Book Co., 1967;
Commonwealth of Australia, *Tariff Board: Annual Report;*
Current Affairs Bulletin, *The Tariff,* Vol. 42, September 1968.

Chapter 7

INSTITUTIONAL DEVELOPMENTS

1 INTRODUCTION

A major reason for the faster rate of economic growth since World
War II has been the action of governments (in Australia and abroad)
in helping to sustain a relatively high, stable level of economic activity
at or near full employment. This has entailed a more extensive range
of economic institutions and policies to meet the changing demands
and strains of society.

It would be beyond the scope of this book to examine the whole
range of economic institutions and policies which have influenced Australia's economic development. This chapter is limited to a review of
the main institutional and organizational developments in the three key
areas of Commonwealth-State financial relations, banking and the
capital market, and wage determination. This will set the stage for a
discussion of living standards in the next chapter and of Australia's
major economic policy objectives and problems in Chapter 9.

2 COMMONWEALTH-STATE FINANCIAL RELATIONS

(a) The Dominant Role of the Commonwealth

In the seventy years since the establishment of Australia's Federal
structure of a Commonwealth and six States, the power structure has
changed significantly. Much of the change concerns the increasingly
dominant role of the Commonwealth Government in economic, social,
and political affairs. This has followed partly from favourable judicial
interpretation of the Commonwealth Constitution, and has meant a
considerable increase in the general authority and specific powers of
the Commonwealth, sometimes in ways not anticipated by the
Founders. But since World War II extension of the Commonwealth's
powers in the fields of banking and civil aviation has been effectively
limited by Section 92 of the Constitution. This provides that 'trade,
commerce, and intercourse among the States, whether by means of
internal carriage or ocean navigation, shall be absolutely free'.

Some of the increase in the Commonwealth's economic and social
powers may be seen as resulting spontaneously from the rapid, closer
economic development of the Australian economy. The Commonwealth is naturally the central, leading partner in many fundamental

aspects of the Federation. Thus some of its increase in power has resulted from co-operation with the States in order to meet changing economic and social circumstances. This has been partly so in respect to the financial arrangements between the Commonwealth and the States, as discussed further shortly. The changes have not always taken place without serious argument, with the leaders of each of Australia's constituent, competitive parts eager to preserve or further their individual interests (political, economic, and social). The growing dominance of the Commonwealth has led to the misunderstanding among some observers that Australia has evolved from a Federation into a unitary state in which the States' main function is to act as administrative agencies of the central government[1].

Specific areas in which the Commonwealth influences economic development (within certain limits in some respects) include the tariff, public finance, immigration, the arbitration system, banking, the encouragement of rural development, and social services. The Commonwealth acquired from the colonial governments a tradition of active government participation in economic affairs. The 'free trade' spirit of the Commonwealth Constitution, involving the abolition of (the differing) tariffs between the States, necessarily gave the Commonwealth monopoly control of customs duties at the national borders. A corollary was the conferring on the Commonwealth of a monopoly of excise taxes, including, with legal support, sales tax[2]. During the early years of its life the Commonwealth relied for its revenue mainly on the large amounts of customs and excise duties which it gathered. The victory of the 'protectionists' in 1908 meant that the Commonwealth's monopoly power over customs and excise was thenceforth more actively used to protect domestic industries as well as to raise revenue[3].

(b) The Commonwealth's Control of Income Taxation

An important change in taxation occurred in 1915-6 when the Commonwealth Government moved into the field of income tax in

---

1 For a more detailed discussion of this misunderstanding, see W. Prest, 'Federalism in Australia: The Role of the Commonwealth Grants Commission', *Journal of Commonwealth Political Studies*, Vol. V, March 1967, pp. 3–7.

2 'In Australia sales taxes have long been held by the Courts to be excise duties and therefore the prerogative of the Commonwealth Government, whereas in other federations they are levied by both State and Federal Governments and in the U.S.A. and Canada they are the most important single source of State or provincial revenue.' W. Prest, 'Federal–State Financial Relations', *Economic Papers*, The Economic Society of Australia and New Zealand, New South Wales and Victorian Branches, No. 20, October 1965, p. 20.

3 See p. 143 above.

order to raise funds for war. With the expansion of Commonwealth social services and then the demands of World War II (in particular, the increasing war expenditure and the need to reduce personal consumption and prevent inflation), the Federal Labour Government of Mr John Curtin exercised its legal right to make first claim on income, and introduced in 1942 a scheme of income tax, including company tax, which meant that that field became exclusively Commonwealth. It has remained so despite the opposition of some of the States and two High Court cases challenging its constitutional validity[4].

Previously income tax was a complex matter with different income tax systems in each State and the general severity of taxation varying considerably from one State to another. At the same time the incidence of taxation upon incomes at different levels varied widely between the States. By contrast, the Constitution (in Section 51, ii) provides that taxation levied by the Commonwealth shall be uniform throughout Australia without discrimination 'between States or parts of States'[5].

The introduction of uniform income taxation meant much more than the simplification of taxation. It marked a major further shift in economic power from the States to the Commonwealth. This was not an unexpected or sudden change. Since Federation the influence of the Commonwealth in financial matters had increased greatly.

(c) Commonwealth-State Financial Agreement of 1927 and the Loan Council

The Australian governments have traditionally been heavy borrowers for economic development. In the 1920s, following substantial borrowing overseas independently and competitively by the States and the Commonwealth, it was recognized that there would be definite

---

4 The stamp duty tax on receipts for income (at the *ad valorem* rate of one cent in $10) which was first levied in Western Australia from February 1967 and in Victoria from February 1968 has elements of an income tax to the extent that it applies to wages and salaries. The Commonwealth has objected to this tax apparently on the grounds that it could weaken and limit Commonwealth control and its degree of freedom in raising taxes. In June 1970, the Victorian Government announced that this tax would cease from 1 July 1970.

5 Nevertheless, in 1945, the Commonwealth introduced a system of zone allowance deductions on income as an encouragement to development. 'Zone allowance deductions are prescribed for residents of isolated areas subject to uncongenial climatic conditions and high costs of living. Two zones A and B have been prescribed and the allowances are: Zone A [which includes the northern sparsely settled area of Australia], $540 plus an amount equal to half the total deductions allowable for the maintenance of dependents; and Zone B [covering isolated areas of the southern States, including Broken Hill and the South-west of Tasmania], $90 plus an amount equal to one-twelfth of the total deduction allowable for the maintenance of dependents.' *Official Year Book of the Commonwealth of Australia*, No. 55, 1969, p. 765. Victoria is the only State with no area in either zone.

advantages in the co-ordination of Australia's public borrowing. This led to the Financial Agreement of 1927, which set up the Australian Loan Council, representing both Commonwealth and States[6]. This body has effectively limited the power of the States to borrow on their own behalf. Under the agreement a major function of the Loan Council is to determine the size and allocation of loans for State public works and housing, and the Commonwealth became the sole borrowing authority for most Australian public purposes. The amendment of the Constitution by referendum, necessary to hand over these powers to the Commonwealth, is one major change of the Constitution that has been ratified by the Australian people[7].

Through the Loan Council the whole process of governmental borrowing is closely co-ordinated on the basis of annual programmes, with the Commonwealth exercising a dominant position. It can do so since it has the voting strength. Each State has one vote, the Commonwealth has two deliberative votes and a casting vote. Thus the Commonwealth needs the support of only two other States to obtain agreement to its policy. In practice, the Commonwealth has usually been able to ensure adherence to its policy. On occasions it has been outvoted at the Loan Council. But the Commonwealth's control of federal finance (and of the Reserve Bank, as explained below), means that it has been able to influence greatly the overall funds available to the States.

(d) Imbalance Between Commonwealth and States in Allocation of Incomes and Functions

The financial and constitutional position which has developed in Australia is one of imbalance between the Commonwealth and the States, in the allocation of revenue and functions[8]. The revenue collected by the States during the 1960s totalled just under one-fifth of that collected by the Commonwealth, whereas expenditure (current and capital) by the States amounted to about four-fifths the size of

---

6 For a critical account of the history and functions of the Loan Council, see J. A. Maxwell, *Commonwealth–State Financial Relations in Australia*, M.U.P., 1967, Chap. 4.

7 The only other major change of the Constitution was in 1946 when the Commonwealth was empowered to legislate for the provision of social services in addition to invalid and old-age pensions. The additional services specified are: 'maternity allowances, widows' pensions, child endowment, unemployment, pharmaceutical, sickness and hospital benefits, medical and dental services (but not so as to authorize any form of civil conscription), benefits to students and family allowances.' *Official Year Book of the Commonwealth of Australia*, No. 55, 1969, p. 12.

8 For a recent, more detailed account of this imbalance see Prest, 'Federal–State Financial Relations'.

TABLE 40
RECEIPTS AND OUTLAY OF COMMONWEALTH AND STATE
GOVERNMENTS, 1968-9

	Commonwealth		States	
	$ million	% of total	$ million	% of total
Outlay	*		*	
Current expenditure[a]	1,735	41·3	1,462	45·3
Capital expenditure[b]	593	14·1	871	27·0
Transfer payments				
Cash benefits	1,406	33·5	36	1·1
Interest	16[d]	0·4	480	14·9
Other	417	9·9	151	4·7
Net advances[c]	33[e]	0·8	225	7·0
Total	4,200	100·0	3,225	100·0
Receipts				
Taxation	5,484	93·0	836	70·7
Non-tax	415	7·0	347	29·3
Total	5,899	100·0	1,183	100·0
Excess or deficiency	+1,699		−2,042	
Grants from the Commonwealth	−1,419		+1,419	
Net increase (+) or decrease (−)				
in indebtedness	−280		+623	

Notes: [a] Includes expenditure on education, public health, welfare, defence,
and other services
[b] Consisting of fixed capital expenditure on new assets plus increase
in stocks.
[c] To State authorities (e.g. housing) and local authorities.
[d] Represents the interest paid by the Commonwealth to the private
sector after excluding interest paid on behalf of the States.
[e] Excluding loans raised on behalf of the States.
Source: *Commonwealth of Australia, Supplement to the Treasury Information
Bulletin: National Accounting Estimates of Public Authority Receipts
and Expenditure, December 1969, Tables 1, 3, and 5.

the Commonwealth's expenditure[9]. Details of the financial position of
the Commonwealth and the States for 1968-9 are shown in Table 40.

While the Commonwealth has become financially dominant there
has been no corresponding transfer of functional activities. The States
retain their constitutional responsibility for important services such as
education, hospitals, and roads, and they control leading public
utilities such as railways and electricity.

---

9 Commonwealth of Australia, *Supplement to the Treasury Information
Bulletin: National Accounting Estimates of Public Authority Receipts and
Expenditure,* December 1969, Tables 1, 3, and 5.

TABLE 41

COMMONWEALTH PAYMENTS TO THE STATES PER HEAD OF POPULATION AND TOTAL FOR AUSTRALIA, 1968-9

	N.S.W.	Victoria	Queens-land	South Australia	Western Australia	Tasmania	Total	Total Australia
	$	$	$	$	$	$	$	$m
	Per head of population							
General revenue grants								
Financial assistance	75·23	74·65	89·04	99·29	133·20	108·14	84·92	1018
Special grants	—	—	—	—	0·63	43·58	1·45	17
Special revenue assistance	0·90	0·89	1·07	2·95	1·39	1·29	1·17	14
Total	76·13	75·54	90·11	102·24	135·22	153·02	87·54	1050
Specific purpose payments								
Under Financial Agreement								
Interest	1·32	1·27	1·25	1·24	1·02	1·38	1·27	15
Sinking fund	1·63	1·55	1·59	2·50	2·27	3·85	1·80	22
Universities	3·92	3·61	3·17	3·83	3·05	3·41	3·63	44
Tuberculosis hospitals	0·97	0·98	1·34	0·50	0·65	0·91	0·96	11
Other	1·82	3·30	2·12	2·46	2·11	1·95	2·36	28
Total	9·66	10·71	9·47	10·53	9·10	11·50	10·02	120
Specific purpose capital grants								
Universities	1·71	2·11	1·00	0·95	0·79	2·34	1·59	19
Roads	10·68	9·87	17·75	17·11	32·86	22·04	14·18	170
Other	4·23	3·46	8·91	10·16	16·03	6·18	6·24	75
Total	16·62	15·44	27·66	28·22	49·68	30·56	22·01	264
Specific purpose loans	1·57	1·04	1·63	12·45	8·04	12·66	3·32	40
Total Payments	103·98	102·73	128·87	153·44	202·03	207·74	122·89	1473

Source: Commonwealth of Australia, *Commonwealth Payments To or For the States 1969–70*, pp. 62 and 64.

(e) Commonwealth Payments to the States and the Commonwealth Grants Commission

The imbalance between revenues and functions in Australia is met by massive transfers of funds from the Commonwealth to the States. The forms and size of these transfers for 1968-9 are shown in Table 41.

The Commonwealth Constitution provided in Section 96:

> 'During a period of ten years after the establishment of the Commonwealth and thereafter until the Parliament otherwise provides, the Parliament may grant financial assistance to any State on such terms and conditions as the Parliament thinks fit.'

Special grants in aid of general revenue were paid annually to Western Australia from 1910-1, Tasmania from 1912-3 and South Australia from 1929-30. From 1934-5 onwards these special grants were paid on the recommendation of the Commonwealth Grants Commission. This Commission (of three members) was established in 1933 in the midst of deep depression, considerable difficulties in State finances, and a campaign for secession in Western Australia. The Commission's main duty was to enquire into and report upon claims of any State for a grant of financial assistance.

The Commission at first determined special grants for the three so-called 'claimant' States of South Australia, Western Australia, and Tasmania on the argument of financial weakness resulting from Federation. As was seen in the previous chapter, manufacturing development in New South Wales and Victoria benefited from the establishment of the customs union at Federation. Soon after its establishment, however, the Commission adopted a more general criterion for special grants. In its *Third Report* (1936) the Commission's basic principle was explained thus:

> 'Special grants are justified when a State through financial stress from any cause is unable efficiently to discharge its functions as a member of the federation and should be determined by the amount of help found necessary to make it possible for that State by reasonable effort to function at a standard not appreciably below that of other states.'

This principle of 'financial need' has, in the words of Professor Prest, a former member of the Commission, meant that 'the claimant States receive special grants sufficient to balance their budgets (or at least to reduce their deficits to the same *per capita* level as the standard States), subject to their showing reasonable effort in raising revenue and economy in spending it. This principle remains unimpaired, but over the years alterations in the methods of applying it have naturally occurred as the inevitable result of changing circumstances[10].'

The special grants to claimant States have helped to reduce more quickly regional dualism in Australia by closing the gaps in productivity and income among the States. The relatively more developed, industrialized, and wealthy States with higher taxable capacities — notably New South Wales and Victoria — have assisted the less developed to secure more quickly essential social capital, which should, in the long run, stimulate a more rapid, balanced development of the Australian economy.

From 1969 only Tasmania has sought a special grant through the Commonwealth Grants Commission. South Australia ceased doing so in 1959[11], and Western Australia in 1968. The special grants formerly paid to both the latter States have been embodied in the financial assistance grants which are paid by the Commonwealth to the States, and which in 1959 took the place of what were formerly regular tax reimbursement grants to each State instituted under uniform taxation. The system of financial assistance grants was agreed upon at the 1959 Premiers' Conference. This agreement provided for the grants to be determined each year by adjusting the amounts paid in the previous year according to a formula which takes account of wage changes, population changes, and a betterment factor (equal to 1·1 times the percentage increase in average wages for Australia as a whole between the two previous years).

The financial assistance payments, which constitute the largest type of grant received by the States (see Table 41), may be spent in any way the State determines. The disbursements bear no relation to the tax collections in the States, a source of continuing unrest in some States, especially Victoria. In fact, total Commonwealth payments *per capita* to Western Australia and Tasmania in recent years have been twice as high as those to New South Wales and Victoria, largely reflecting the Commonwealth's assessment of the variations in the budgetary resources of the States[12]. As shown in Table 41, the Commonwealth also makes payments and capital grants to the States for specific purposes such as education, roads, and water conservation.

The principle which is applied by the Commonwealth in determining general revenue grants is basically the same as that followed by

---

10 W. Prest, 'Maxwell on Federal–State Finance', *Economic Record*, Vol. 44, June 1968, p. 237. 'After 1959 the only standard States were New South Wales and Victoria.' *Ibid*, p. 238.

11 However, the South Australian Government has accepted the Commonwealth Government's offer at the Premiers' Conference in June 1970 to apply again to the Commonwealth Grants Commission for extra assistance.

12 See Prest, 'Federal–State Financial Relations', p. 27.

the Commonwealth Grants Commission. The Prime Minister (Mr. J. G. Gorton), in opening the Premiers' Conference in Canberra in June 1970, stated:

'The general principle underlying the distribution of the general revenue grants is that each State should be enabled to provide Government services of a standard broadly comparable with those of each other State without imposing higher taxation or other charges[13].'

The Prime Minister pointed out that

'the principle is rather easier to state in general terms than it is to apply in practice and there are many problems both of a practical and conceptual nature which arise in attempting to determine the correct distribution of the grants[14].'

Since the general revenue grants form so large a proportion of each State's revenue, it is felt by the Commonwealth 'that it would be desirable to have independent investigation and advice on this question for the next review of the arrangements' and that if the States agree 'to accept this the best approach might be for the Commonwealth Grants Commission to be given this task'[15].

New Commonwealth-State financial arrangements in 1965 and 1970 have contained broadly the same basic formula adopted in 1959 with several modifications in each arrangement. In 1965 the modifications were: first, the arrangement was to run for five years instead of six like the previous. Secondly, the base amounts have as before been the grants paid to each State in the previous year, but provision was made for special increases in Victoria's base of $1·2 million in the first year (1965 6) only and in Queensland's of $2 million annually. The additional grant to Victoria reduced the difference between the *per capita* grants to Victoria and New South Wales to approximately the same level as in 1959-60. The increase in Queensland's share was mainly to compensate for that State's large area and sparsity of population. Thirdly, the betterment factor was increased from what, in effect, meant an average overall amount of 0·4 per cent a year to a fixed additional 1·2 per cent on the base amounts after adjustment for population and wage increases[16]. Finally, some minor changes were made in the population factor by the inclusion of Aborigines and a reduced time-lag by measuring population increases in the year ended December of each financial year, instead of the previous July 1.

The amendments in the new financial arrangement of June 1970 were: first, the betterment factor was raised from 1·2 per cent to 1·8

13 As reported in *The Australian*, 26 June 1970.
14 *Ibid.*
15 *Ibid.*
16 See Prest, 'Federal–State Financial Relations' pp. 23–5.

per cent, applying from 1971-2. Secondly, the Commonwealth increased the general revenue grants to the States by $40 million in 1970-1, to be distributed between the States in the same proportion as their new 1970-1 formula grants. This amount is to be included in the base for determining the formula grants from 1971-2. Thirdly, the special increase in Queensland's base of $2 million annually would continue, as in the previous quinquennium. Fourthly, the *per capita* grant of New South Wales and Victoria was increased by $2 a head, providing New South Wales with about $9 million extra in 1970-1 and Victoria $6·8 million. This additional grant was made because of the tendency for the *per capita* differentials between the grants to New South Wales and Victoria and those to other States to widen. These *per capita* grants to New South Wales and Victoria will not form part of the base for purposes of determining the grants payable to both States under the grants formula, but will be added each year on the basis of population. Fifthly, the Commonwealth gave Western Australia an undertaking to continue the provision of $15·5 million which it had been receiving formerly as a special grant through the Commonwealth Grants Commission and which from 1968 had been embodied in Western Australia's financial assistance grants, as noted above; but this figure will be reduced progressively as a grant over the next five years and be offset with an increase in loan allocation.

Finally, substantial assistance was granted by the Commonwealth specifically directed at reducing the burden of interest and sinking fund charges on State public debt. This assistance is in two forms:

(i) The Commonwealth agreed to provide an interest-free capital grant of $200 million in 1970-1 to be used for non-income earning works, e.g. schools and administrative offices. This sum is to increase in future years at the same rate as the total works and housing programmes.

(ii) The Commonwealth has undertaken to assume the interest and sinking fund burden of an additional $200 million of State debt in each of the next five years. Thus by 1974-5 the Commonwealth will have assumed the responsibility for existing State debt totalling $1,000 million.

These two proposals will mean a saving to the States of $11·5 million in 1970-1, rising to $118·3 million in 1974-5, and an overall saving of $320·5 million over the next five years.

Both these proposals are of considerable importance to State finances. The importance of the interest-free capital grant stems from the fact that previously these sums have been provided by the Commonwealth entirely in the form of loans. They have taken the form of subscriptions from Commonwealth revenue to the loan programme of the Loan Council to meet the shortfall of loans raised in the domestic market or borrowed overseas for the States' works and housing programmes. The size of this assistance has varied from year to year according to the state of the loan market, but was considerably greater in the 1950s when Commonwealth assistance totalled about 39·0 per cent of the States' programmes compared with 17·0 per cent in the 1960s[17]. This assistance has been officially referred to as 'Commonwealth subscriptions to Special Loans'. A source of grievance with the States has been that the Commonwealth has charged interest on these loans. The provision in the 1970 arrangement for the interest-free capital grant will probably make these special subscriptions unnecessary. The starting point of this capital grant of $200 million in 1970-1 is just over double the average annual size of Commonwealth subscriptions to loans during the 1960s.

The assistance to the States' loan and debt situation and the improvement in both the amount and the rate of growth of the financial assistance grants themselves provided in the 1970 arrangement seem to have improved appreciably the States' financial outlook for the next quinquennium. The unrest in the States over their financial arrangement with the Commonwealth has also stemmed partly from the States' lack of a significant, flexible growth tax built into their main revenue sources, such as the Commonwealth possesses in progressive income taxation. This lack, as explained in Chapter 9, has attained significance because of creeping inflation. However, the 1970 financial arrangement provides that the States should share in Commonwealth revenue in the form of general revenue grants at a rate of growth roughly in line with the rate at which income tax receipts have been increasing[18] It is the base figure on which these increases are computed that the States would still like to see raised significantly in order to ease their expenditure responsibilities.

An important factor behind the assistance of the Commonwealth in reducing the debt burden of the States has been the marked divergence in the net public debt positions of the Commonwealth and the States. During the 1950s and 1960s State debt grew tremendously while the Commonwealth's declined. This, as the States pointed out at the Premiers' Conference in February 1970, resulted from the

---

17 Commonwealth of Australia, *Commonwealth Payments To or For the States* (various issues).

18 The rate of increase in general revenue grants during the period 1970–1 to 1974–5 is estimated by the Commonwealth to be on average nearly 13 per cent annually. This approximates the average annual rate of increase in income tax receipts during the period 1964–5 to 1968–9. Source: Commonwealth of Australia, *Supplement to the Treasury Information Bulletin: National Accounting Estimates of Public Authority Receipts and Expenditure*, August 1969, p. 7; and *The Australian*, 26 June 1970.

TABLE 42
PUBLIC DEBT OF THE COMMONWEALTH AND THE STATES
($ million)

COMMONWEALTH

Date (at 30 June)	Recorded securities on issue	*Less* internal treasury bills	Public securities on issue	*Less* public securities held for Commonwealth purposes	*Less* direct loans to States	Net public debt
1950	3731	—	3731	22	123	3586
1965	3134	632	2502	868	1264	370
1969	3682	859	2823	1148	1879	−204

STATES

Date (at 30 June)	Recorded securities on issue	*Add* direct loans by the Commonwealth			*Less* sinking fund balances	Net public debt
		Housing	Other	Total		
1950	2367	123	—	123	6	2484
1965	7091	1159	105	1264	5	8350
1969	8831	1624	255	1879	34	10,676

Source: The Financial Relationships of the Commonwealth and the States, p. 12; see p. 171, n. 19 of text.

ability of the Commonwealth from the early 1950s 'to provide the whole of its capital and development works out of current funds and actually to reduce its net public debt so greatly that it is now effectively a net creditor government'[19]. Table 42 shows that when adjustment is made to the recorded securities on issue on account of the Commonwealth for (i) internal treasury bills, (ii) securities held by the Commonwealth on its own account, and (iii) direct loans to the States, the public debt of the Commonwealth has declined from $3,586 million at 30 June 1950 to a negative amount of $204 million at 30 June 1969 By contrast, the net public debt of the States over the same period has increased by more than four times from $2,484 million to $10,676 million.

The Commonwealth has been able to achieve its net creditor position almost entirely as 'the result of the natural growth [of its revenue through income tax] rather than from increased tax rates and charges'[20]. The Commonwealth left the States to obtain whatever funds could be raised on the bond market, and it assisted them, as noted above, by meeting any shortfall in their loan programme by special loans.

The use of taxation revenue to finance the Commonwealth's public works and to assist the loan programme of the States has resulted in nearly three-fifths of Australia's public fixed capital expenditure since World War II being financed from taxation revenue. This is an important change in Australian public finance. In the nineteenth century the colonial governments borrowed heavily overseas. They did so again, though on a smaller scale, in the 1920s when borrowing from the Australian public by the sale of government (Commonwealth, local, and semi-government) securities was undertaken. However, since World War II, the public sector has relied relatively little on overseas borrowing for capital expenditure.

The shift from borrowing to compulsory saving, that is taxation, to finance the bulk of public works has resulted partly from the insufficiency of private savings to meet the demands of the public and private sectors. Anyway the Commonwealth has been unwilling to borrow overseas on a large scale on public account. Rather the Commonwealth has preferred to leave this to the private sector, having indeed encouraged and assisted the private sector in doing so[21]. The use of central bank credit through the issue of treasury bills as an additional source

---

19 *The Financial Relationships of the Commonwealth and the States*, p. 3, being a paper prepared by the States for the Premiers' Conference in February 1970 and printed in Victoria, *Parliamentary Debates*, 10 March 1970.
20 *Ibid.*
21 See pp. 113–7 above.

of funds has not been favoured (except as a temporary measure), since this would have strengthened the inflationary forces through excess demand.

The heavy financial dependence of the States on the Commonwealth under the Financial Agreement and uniform taxation has greatly reduced the influence of State Budgets on Australian fiscal policy. Nevertheless, the States possess considerable control over what they do with the funds at their disposal. The Commonwealth's main power and hence its overall control of fiscal policy derive from the control it exercises in determining the total amount of the funds available to the States as revenue or loans. In effect, this means that the Loan Council no longer fulfils its function. It also means that the States have responsibility for spending revenue but not for raising it. This has been held to be a weakness of Australian public finance. But it is difficult to prove — either quantitatively or qualitatively — claims that economic efficiency in the allocation of limited resources among competing ends has suffered any more under the present system than it may have under alternative schemes.

(f) Growth of 'co-operative federalism'

Despite the growth of Commonwealth power, which has been emphasized above, there has been considerable friendly co-operation between governments, or at least consultation on matters affecting more than one State. Before Federation the State Governments had met and co-operated. They continued to do so after Federation at Premiers' Conferences, which have been held at least annually at the time of Loan Council meetings. There has also been a growth in recent years of Ministerial conferences between the States and the Commonwealth, covering a wide range of interests including agriculture, transport, regulation of various business activities, education, and social problems. These conferences have led to complementary legislation passed by the Commonwealth and States in a number of fields. These have included the marketing of wheat, the provision of uniform social laws relating to the adoption of children and to divorce, the passing of uniform company legislation, and the establishment of a joint Commonwealth and State system controlling the exploration of off-shore oil resources.

Australia's experiences with the Loan Council, Premiers' and Ministerial Conferences, and Commonwealth Grants Commission may be described as 'co-operative federalism'[22]. The considerable changes

---

22 See Prest, 'Federalism in Australia: The Role of the Commonwealth Grants Commission', pp. 4–7.

that have accompanied the rapid growth of the Australian economy have not meant a change of the Federation into a strictly unitary state. As mentioned earlier, the States remain responsible for a wide range of functions. With the rapid growth of the Australian economy and the increasing interdependence between the States, especially through the greatly improved means of communications and a breaking down of 'the tyranny of distance', it is in the interests of the States to co-operate with each other and with the Commonwealth in the pursuit of their common economic policies. Nevertheless, important economic and social differences between the States persist, and have continued to be a subject of detailed discussion in the annual report of the Commonwealth Grants Commission.

Only in respect to the increasing financial dominance of the central government is there an implication of subordination of the States. However, even in the field of finance, it is necessary for the Commonwealth — for political as well as economic reasons — to recognize the needs of the States and to co-operate with them. With the increasing influence of government in economic affairs, a greater concentration of power in the hands of the central government for control of the economy through positive economic policies has been inevitable. The increasing role of government and the main objectives of economic policy will be examined further in Chapter 9.

3 BANKS AND THE CAPITAL MARKET

The objective in this section is to review the major institutional and structural changes which have been made in Australian banking and the capital market in general for the purpose of making monetary policy an effective branch of economic policy. This will prepare the way for a discussion of the role of monetary policy in the overall objectives of Australia's economic policy in Chapter 9.

(a) Development of the Central Bank[23]

An essential institution in any country under modern conditions is a central bank which acts as government banker, controls the note issue, and manages the country's monetary policy by controlling the trading and savings banks and foreign exchange transactions. The Commonwealth Bank of Australia was established in 1911 as a government-owned trading and savings bank, but it was not empowered with central bank functions until 1924, when it became the Australian note

---

23 For more detailed accounts of this subject, see: H. W. Arndt and C. P. Harris, *The Australian Trading Banks*, Cheshire, 3rd edn, 1965, pp. 172–9; and L. F. Giblin, *The Growth of a Central Bank*, M.U.P., 1951.

printing and issue authority. Its central bank functions were originally modelled on those of the Bank of England. However, its development as a central bank as now conceived for Australian conditions was at first very slow. Emergency wartime legislation and legislation by the Chifley Labour Government in 1939 and 1945, respectively, provided the Commonwealth Bank with powers of a 'modern' central bank.

One of the most important powers devised in 1941 for wartime use but continued in 1945 involved the establishment of the special account system whereby the Commonwealth Bank was able to freeze (and itself hold) part of the trading banks' funds and so control the volume of credit which the banks could grant. The Bank, with the approval of the Commonwealth Treasurer, was also empowered to issue directives on bank advance policy and to control bank interest rates.

The private trading banks strongly opposed the 1945 legislation, which not only continued into peace-time the wartime banking powers bestowed on the Commonwealth Bank, but also instructed the Bank to engage in active competition for trading bank business. As noted in the previous section, the extension of the Commonwealth Government's powers over banking has been checked by Section 92 of the Constitution. In particular, the judicial interpretation of this Section blocked the Chifley Government's attempted nationalization of the trading banks in 1947. Nevertheless, during the 1950s the Commonwealth Bank expanded its trading bank business in active competition with the private trading banks. Legislation[24] in 1953 further developed the Commonwealth Bank as a central bank, and established the Commonwealth Trading Bank to take over most of the general trading bank functions of the Commonwealth Bank. But this did not go far enough for the private banks in their demands for amendments to the 1945 legislation. Their continued resentment of the competition from the Commonwealth Trading Bank and of the fact that it was not subject to special account provisions led to further legislation in 1959. The Commonwealth Treasurer (Sir Arthur Fadden), when first introducing the 1959 legislation, stated:

'Since there will no doubt be a great deal said about the attitude of the private banks, I think I should state explicitly the point of view they have put to the Government. It is this—

(a) they recognize the need for a strong central bank and they say that, if it functions as a true central bank, they are prepared to accept its leadership;

---

24 By the Liberal and Country Party Government of Mr (later Sir) Robert G. Menzies. This party began what is still an unbroken period of rule in 1949 at an election in which banking was a major political issue.

(b) they do not object to the competition of the Commonwealth Trading Bank as long as it is fair competition;

(c) they do, however, consider the Trading Bank to gain unfair advantages from its connexion with the central bank and they fear the use that might be made of a trading bank, so linked with the central bank, if a government hostile to their interests came to power[25].'

The 1959 legislation drastically reorganized the Commonwealth Bank, which ceased to exist under that name. It was replaced by two separate institutions: one is the Reserve Bank of Australia, which preserves the central bank in a climate of closer co-operation with the trading banks in respect to monetary policy[26]; the other institution is the Commonwealth Banking Corporation, which comprises three large government banks: the Commonwealth Trading Bank, the Commonwealth Savings Bank, and the Commonwealth Development Bank. The last took over the former Mortgage Bank and Industrial Finance Department of the Commonwealth Bank, and continues their functions, in particular the provision of credit to primary producers and industrial undertakings (especially small ones), which would otherwise find it difficult to secure credit on reasonable terms.

Under the new legislation the special accounts were replaced by a system of statutory reserve deposits. This system is examined in more detail shortly. The Commonwealth Trading Bank is now also required to keep a statutory reserve deposit with the Reserve Bank of the same ratio as in force for all the major trading banks. In order to bring the Commonwealth Trading Bank further into line with the private trading banks, it has now been made liable to Commonwealth income tax. In short, the Commonwealth Trading Bank operates now on

---

25 Commonwealth of Australia, *Parliamentary Debates*, Vol. H. of R. 17, 1957, p. 1766. This legislation was first introduced in 1957, but the Menzies Government had to wait until 1959 before it held a majority in the Senate and could thus have the legislation passed.

26 The legislation continues the central bank's powers to issue directives on bank lending and to control interest rates. 'The Reserve Bank is able to influence interest rates generally through its open market operations. More specifically, the Bank, with the approval of the Treasurer, has authority under the Banking Act to make regulations relating to the control of rates of interest paid or received by banks or others in the course of any banking business transacted by them. By influencing the terms on which banks borrow and lend, the Bank is able initially to affect the flow of funds to and from banks and, to the extent that other borrowers and lenders respond to changes in the terms of bank financing, ultimately to influence the general level of interest rates.

Bank interest rates have not been formally determined under the Banking Act but maximum rates have been fixed after discussion between the Reserve Bank and the banks, and with the approval of the Treasurer.' *Reserve Bank of Australia: Functions and Operations*, Sydney, 1969, pp. 15–16.

precisely the same basis as the private banks so far as the provisions of the Banking Act 1959 are concerned.

Since the mid-1950s Australia's central bank has permitted or instituted a number of changes. These have meant the development of a more diverse, sophisticated capital market, which is more suited to the requirements of the rapidly growing Australian economy. These changes have included a relaxation of the rigid, somewhat negative monetary restrictions which were imposed by the central bank during the first decade after World War II in its attempt to restrain the inflationary forces. The dynamic changes have included: (i) the development in co-operation with the major private trading banks of a liquidity convention which has permitted a more effective control of monetary policy by the central bank; (ii) a widening of the facilities which trading banks are able to offer their customers; and (iii) the establishment of the short-term money market under the supervision of the Reserve Bank. We will look at important features of each of these changes.

(b) The Operation of the S.R.D. System and the Evolution of the Liquidity Convention.

A trading bank's capacity and willingness to lend depend on many factors, but a dominant one is its liquidity. This is determined by its holdings of cash and assets which can be exchanged quickly for cash with little risk of capital loss. The effectiveness of monetary policy depends partly on the ability of the central bank to influence the state of liquidity of the trading banks. This may be attempted indirectly through variation in interest rates, or it may be attempted directly through regulating the liquidity of trading banks. In Australia considerable reliance has been placed on direct regulation.

The Reserve Bank's powers to regulate directly trading bank liquidity derive from two complementary systems: the S.R.D. (statutory reserve deposit) system (special accounts) and the L.G.S. (liquid assets and government securities)[27] convention.

The S.R.D. system is the main method by which the Reserve Bank controls the trading banks' liquidity and hence the volume of credit which they can make available. Under the S.R.D. system the Reserve Bank determines the minimum amount which each bank must deposit in its S.R.D. account at the Reserve Bank. This amount is determined as a proportion of each bank's current level of Australian deposits, the Reserve Bank withholding (or releasing) a proportion of the banks'

---

27 'L.G.S. assets are defined as notes and coin, cash with the Reserve Bank, Commonwealth Treasury bills and notes and other Commonwealth Government securities.' *Ibid*, p. 9.

funds in the light of the economic conditions prevailing from time to time. The 1959 banking legislation specifies that this proportion, or S.R.D. ratio as it is known, is uniform for each trading bank. The ratio can be increased with one day's notice, provided it does not exceed 25 per cent of total deposits; and subject to certain conditions and with 45 days' notice the ratio can be increased beyond 25 per cent of deposits.

The apparent success of the S.R.D. system as an instrument of monetary control owes much to the evolution of the L.G.S. convention in the mid-1950s. The central bank had earlier recognized that effective administration of special account policy, particularly to achieve restraint under inflationary conditions, required the willing co-operation of the trading banks. What was lacking was a conventional liquidity standard which could complement special account policy so that the central bank could affect the capacity and willingness to lend by altering the distribution of assets that determine liquidity between special accounts and L.G.S. assets. Furthermore, what each trading bank regarded as a safe minimum varied.

The central bank at first asked the trading banks to conduct their advance policy so as to maintain an average L.G.S. ratio over the year of 25 per cent. But this proved unsuccessful, the major reason being the refusal of most of the trading banks to follow the central bank's policy. Nevertheless, the latter persisted with its search for a convention. It realized, as its Governor explained, that:

'in the absence of a convention, it could only revert to the practice of keeping the least liquid banks with little more than till money and thus continuously dependent on the Central Bank for loans. This was an arrangement which banks could scarcely find palatable[28].'

Hence, in 1956, the central bank made a second attempt, this time successful, to establish a liquidity convention according to which the trading banks agreed not to allow their L.G.S. ratio to fall below the uniform minimum of 14 per cent[29]. This 'Convention . . . has no statutory basis but is a formal expression of certain firm understandings which had been reached between the central bank and the major trading banks'[30] Although the central bank viewed a minimum of 14 per cent as too low for a longer-term objective, the establishment of

---

28 H. C. Coombs, *The Conditions of Monetary Policy in Australia*, R. C. Mills Memorial Lecture, University of Sydney, 1958, p. 32.

29 For accounts of the establishment of this convention and of the earlier unsuccessful attempt, see: Coombs, *op. cit.*, pp. 28–34, and Arndt and Harris, *op. cit.*, pp. 196–9.

30 *Reserve Bank of Australia*, Sydney, 1966, p. 19.

the convention was a considerable help to it. Previously it could never be sure that some banks, in providing advances, would not allow their liquidity to fall below 14 per cent. The minimum ratio has since 'been increased, by agreement with the banks, on two occasions — to 16 per cent in 1959 and to 18 per cent in April 1962'[31].

Adherence to the L.G.S. convention has allowed the central bank to direct the S.R.D. system in the light of the trading banks' 'margin of free liquidity'. As the Reserve Bank has explained:

'The margin of "free" liquidity in the banks' hands at any time (as measured by the difference between the actual level of the L.G.S. ratio and the conventional minimum level) serves, after allowing for seasonal fluctuations, as a support for credit policy. If, for example, the Reserve Bank thought a more restrictive policy were needed, it would, in addition to informing the trading banks of this view, consider the desirability of administering Statutory Reserve Deposits so as to bring the actual L.G.S. ratios of the banks closer to the conventional minimum. If a more expansive credit policy were appropriate, the Reserve Bank, as well as so informing the banks, would tend to administer the Statutory Reserve Deposits so as to increase the banks' L.G.S. ratios and their margin of free liquidity, thereby providing them with the means for expanding their lending[32].'

This convention of behaviour is similar to those operating in other countries. It has now become an accepted part of the Australian banking system. The convention acts as a guide to both the central bank and the trading banks in their working relationship.

(c) The Increasing Range of Activities of the Trading Banks and the Growth of Non-bank Finance Companies

While the relationship between the trading banks and the central bank has been put on a firm basis in Australia, there has been a considerable decline in the relative importance of bank credit[33]. This in part reflects the rapid growth and diversification of hire-purchase and other finance companies since World War II. Substantial growth and diversification of non-bank finance companies have also occurred in Britain, the United States, and other countries. In Australia, in the quinquennium 1934-5 to 1938-9 bank credit approximated 56 per

---

31 *Ibid.*
32 *Ibid*, p. 20.
33 For a more detailed discussion of this decline and statistical estimates of bank and non-bank credit in Australia for the period since 1934–5, see Arndt and Harris, *op. cit.*, pp. 81–6.

cent[34] of total credit granted by major financial institutions, while hire-purchase companies provided about 2 per cent. In the quinquennium 1958-9 to 1962-3 the share of bank credit had fallen to only 8 per cent, while hire purchase totalled 7 per cent, and other instalment credit provided 5 per cent. During this twenty-four year period the share of stock exchange new issues rose from 18 per cent to 56 per cent, housing finance provided by savings banks and building societies grew from 3 per cent to 16 per cent, and the share of new loans of life assurance companies fell from 20 per cent to 7 per cent.

Hire-purchase and instalment credit facilities have contributed greatly to the development of Australia's manufacturing industries by helping consumers to purchase durable goods including motor vehicles and household equipment. However, the activities of these financial institutions, including the considerable volume of credit which they grant, lie outside the direct control of the central bank. Under the Commonwealth Constitution the Commonwealth Government has power, through the central bank, to control the activities of all banks, both trading and savings, except State banks trading in their own State. It is believed that hire-purchase and other finance companies do not come within the Commonwealth's constitutional power, but this question has not been tested. Thus to the extent that monetary policy relies on direct action through the banking system it has been operating in a relatively contracting field. But, indirectly, the central bank — through open market operations and an active interest rate policy, and its control of foreign exchange transactions and the money supply — may influence the general state of liquidity and a wide range of credit facilities. Furthermore, 'while the Banking Act gives the Reserve Bank no formal control over the lending policy of financial institutions other than trading banks and savings banks, the Bank now maintains regular contact with some of these institutions (notably the hire-purchase finance companies and the life offices) and endeavours, with some success, to persuade them to adopt a lending policy consistent with that laid down for the banks'[35].

It is now recognized that a weakness of monetary policy in the 1950s was the artificially low interest rate policy with funds relatively easy to get. This assisted the rapid expansion of finance companies, particularly hire-purchase companies, that generally prospered outside the direct control of the central bank. The finance companies met

---

34 This estimate and those that follow in this paragraph are from Arndt and Harris, *op. cit.*, p. 82.
35 J. McB. Grant and others, *Economic Institutions and Policy: An Australian Introduction*, p. 320.

demands that the banks were, by policy directions, prevented from meeting owing to the restraint of credit aimed at controlling the inflationary forces in Australia. The background to the problem has been described thus by Dr Coombs in a post-mortem on his own term of Governorship of the central bank during the period of restrictive monetary policy:

'The official reluctance to see the prices of government securities, pressure-sold to many small holders during the war years, fall drastically caused the authorities to support these prices by bank purchases in the market — a procedure which clearly undermined the effectiveness of their own policies of restraint.

There is no doubt finance companies would in any case have emerged as a significant element in the Australian financial scene. They emerged the more quickly and the more explosively because banks were precluded from doing this business and because interest rate policy enabled them easily to outbid the traditional yields offered by banks and governments. . . . The "mortal sin" was the refusal to allow the price of government securities to fall and interest rates to rise[36].'

The trading banks have countered the competition from non-bank finance companies by themselves participating in the expansion of new forms of financial institutions. In the mid-1950s all the seven major private trading banks entered the field of hire-purchase finance, either by establishing wholly owned subsidiary companies, or by investing on a large scale in the share capital of existing companies. The close association with the banks has greatly strengthened the hire-purchase companies' credit standing and access to customers through branch offices of the banks. The banks in turn have shared in the profitable business of hire-purchase finance, but have also accepted perhaps a considerable responsibility for the continued solvency of these companies.

At the same time the central bank has permitted the trading banks themselves more scope in competing for business. An important widening of trading bank activity which took place between 1956 and 1962 was the establishment by the seven major private banks of savings bank subsidiaries. This step was taken largely to meet the competition for trading bank business of the Commonwealth Trading Bank, which it was believed was at a distinct advantage through its close association with the Commonwealth Savings Bank. The move has proved highly

---

36 H. C. Coombs, 'A Look Back and Forward', *Economic Record*, Vol. 45, December 1969, p. 488.

successful for the private savings banks. By 1969 they had attracted just over one-third of total savings bank deposits in Australia.

Other new facilities which the trading banks have been permitted to provide in order to widen the range of services they can offer customers include: (i) 'term lending' (introduced in April 1962) to rural, industrial, and (to a lesser extent) commercial fields for capital expenditure for fixed terms from about three to eight years; (ii) a new fixed deposit (introduced in April 1964) with a period of 30 days to 3 months (for amounts of $100,000 and over) which meant a reduction from 3 months of the minimum term for which trading banks could accept large fixed deposits, thus enabling banks to compete more fully with the short-term money market and inter-company loan market for short-term funds; (iii) 'personal loans' (as distinct from traditional overdraft lending) instituted in March 1967; (iv) in May 1968 'lease financing' was introduced on a moderate scale. This 'was a relatively new development in Australia but had become increasingly important over recent years, particularly in dealings in the industrial equipment field'[37]. (v) In March 1969 'marketable certificates of deposit' were introduced for the first time in Australian trading bank practice. As the Reserve Bank explained:

'the introduction of these certificates, which combine the characteristics of interest bearing deposits with those of marketable assets, was designed to help maintain the competitiveness of banks in markets for short-term funds. Certificates of deposit have been issued in amounts of $50,000 or over for terms ranging from three months to two years at yields of up to 4·75 per cent. Banks are not permitted to buy back certificates issued by themselves[38].'

Another important innovation of the major trading banks, with the support of the Reserve Bank, has been the establishment of a new corporation named the Australian Resources Development Bank[39]. This bank began business in March 1968 for the purpose of making loans available, both directly and mostly through refinance loans to trading banks[40], for the large-scale development of Australia's natural

---

37 Reserve Bank of Australia, *For the Press: Lease Financing*, 21 May 1968.
38 Reserve Bank of Australia, *Report and Financial Statements 1968–69*, p. 21.
39 See Australian Resources Development Bank Limited, *Annual Reports*.
40 'The speed of development of the Bank has been possible because most of its advances are in the form of refinance loans made to the shareholding trading banks. Those banks first negotiate the terms with the ultimate borrower, then make the loan to him, accepting the credit risk themselves, either individually, or in consortium with other banks. The funds they outlay in this way are recouped by the arranged refinance loan. In this way, the tasks of assessing complex projects and settling loan agreements, as well as the credit risks

resources. The bank's direct lending has been partly supported by fixed interest funds raised overseas. Special emphasis has been given to the development of mineral ores, oil, and natural gas, and to the retention as far as possible of Australian equity in their ownership. Some loans have also been provided for the establishment of new projects involving the processing and manufacturing of natural resources. The Resources Bank's policies (including interest rates) are determined in consultation with the Reserve Bank.

There has been a recent move towards greater rationalization of Australia's banking system. Previous mention has been made of seven major private trading banks. In 1970 the number was reduced to six with the merger of the Australia and New Zealand Bank and the English, Scottish and Australian Bank into the Australia and New Zealand Banking Group Ltd. This was the first merger between major trading banks in Australia since 1951. Mergers have steadily reduced the number of major Australian trading banks from twenty in 1900 to twelve in 1939 to seven at present (including the Commonwealth Trading Bank). There have been merger discussions between at least four of the remaining major private banks. It is almost certain that these will not materialize, although some feel that 'Australia is over-banked'[41]. Rationalization has occurred and could probably be taken further by the closing down of duplicated branch offices in more sparsely settled areas (so concentrating business into larger offices) and by the fuller utilization of costly electronic equipment at head offices.

(d) Short-term Money Market[42]

An important recent development under the supervision and encouragement of the central bank has been the establishment of the official short-term money market. During the 1950s an unofficial money

---

themselves, are spread through the trading bank system, while most of the assets of the Resources Bank consist of undoubted loans made to the major trading banks.' Australian Resources Development Bank Limited, *Second Annual Report—Year ended 30 September 1969*, p. 2.

During the bank's first 18 months of operation loans and advances amounted to about $91 million, and firm commitments had been made for further loans of $234 million. (*Ibid.*)

41 *The Economist*, supplement on 'Boundless Banking—An international survey', 15 November 1969, p. 46.

42 For a more detailed account of the functioning of this market, see P. J. Rose, *Australian Securities Markets*, Cheshire, 1969, especially Chap. 7. See also: Arndt and Harris, *op. cit.*, pp. 99–103; R. R. Hirst and R. H. Wallace (eds), *Studies in the Australian Capital Market*, Cheshire, 1964, Chap. 8; and Reserve Bank of Australia, *The Short-Term Money Market in Australia*, mimeographed, 22 September 1969.

market (mainly provided by leading stockbrokers) had developed in Australia to meet deficiencies through the limited opportunities for the secure placement of short-term funds (available for periods of less than three months) at a remunerative rate of interest. The chief alternative had been to hold these funds with a trading bank as a demand deposit on which no interest was paid (the trading bank deposit terms on which interest was paid at that time being periods of 3, 6, 12, and 24 months).

In February 1959 the central bank came to arrangements with authorized dealer companies whereby the dealers accept loans over-night, at call, or for fixed periods from minimum amounts of $50,000 up to limits approved by the central bank, and they invest these funds in 'money market securities', defined as Commonwealth Government securities with currencies not exceeding three years. The arrangements also provided for the dealers to buy and sell these securities in parcels of $100,000 and over[43]. The central bank undertook to grant 'lender of last resort' facilities to the authorized dealers. This facility means that dealers may borrow from the central bank against the lodgement of securities, thus freeing them of the risk of substantial capital losses. 'Until February 1959, the business had been hampered by the fact that in Australia's narrow and irregular bond market, a considerable risk attached to holding bonds which might have to be liquidated suddenly to meet call money withdrawals[44].'

The accredited dealers originally numbered four, but by October 1960 had grown to the present number of nine. Shareholders in the companies comprise stockbroking firms which had been active in the earlier unofficial market, insurance companies, and other financial institutions. Trading banks are not permitted to hold a direct equity interest in any dealer company, for it was considered at the time of the establishment of the official market that this might lead to pre-ferential discrimination between individual banks and dealers, which would not be conducive of an efficient, unprejudiced market. But trading banks have benefited through the additional asset of call money facilities provided by the short-term money market. The trading banks have generally been the largest lenders to dealers[45]. This asset is not recognized by the Reserve Bank as 'liquid' for purposes of the L.G.S. convention, but it can generally be turned into L.G.S. assets on demand[46].

---

43 Reserve Bank of Australia, *Report and Financial Statements, 1900*, p. 24.
44 Arndt and Harris, *op .cit.*, p. 100.
45 See Rose, *op. cit.*, pp. 114–6.
46 For a critical discussion of the central bank's case for excluding loans to dealers from L.G.S. assets, see Rose, *op. cit.*, pp. 116–7, and Arndt and Harris, *op. cit.*, pp. 101–2.

The dealers have been permitted steadily to widen their activities: in March 1965 they were allowed to include in their transactions the discounting of bank-endorsed or accepted commercial bills maturing within 120 days; in March 1969 they were allowed to deal in bank certificates of deposits maturing within two years; and in April 1969 more significant changes were permitted by the central bank when the dealers were afforded more flexibility through greater scope to deal in and hold a wider range of assets. These assets could comprise government securities maturing within five years instead of three years as previously, 'bank bills without formal limit as to maturity, bank certificates of deposit maturing within five years and non-bank bills maturing within 180 days; in addition a small part of dealers' funds could be held in such other assets as they might choose'[47].

A number of important advantages have followed the establishment of the short-term money market, and have justified the support and encouragement given by the Reserve Bank. The market has meant more effective competition for short-term funds and their more efficient use. From the point of view of the Commonwealth Treasury the market has increased the marketability of government securities by directly widening the short- and medium-term bond market and indirectly widening the market for long-term issues. As Dr Rose[48] concluded:

'Investors now have better opportunities for selecting those securities which suit their requirements. The attractiveness of government bonds as an investment has thereby been enhanced. Dealers' demand for bonds also gives the government opportunities to issue short-dated securities, thus benefiting by the lower rates which generally apply to these securities.'

For the Reserve Bank the official money market has established facilities for more effective open market operations whereby (through purchase or sale of bonds as the need arises) it can influence the general state of liquidity of the trading banks and the public, and indicate its monetary policy more effectively through changes in interest rates. Finally, the money market has assisted the establishment, also under the supervision of the Reserve Bank, of an orderly commercial bills market. The latter market, to the extent that it replaces the unofficial private bills market that has developed in recent years mainly in the form of an inter-company loan market, should further improve the effectiveness of monetary policy by widening the central bank's direct coverage of the capital market.

---

47 Reserve Bank of Australia, *For the Press, Short-Term Money Market*, 24 April 1969.
48 *Op. cit.*, p. 137.

4 WAGE DETERMINATION

(a) Origins and Development of the System of Compulsory Arbitration

An outstanding feature of the determination of wage rates and the conditions of employment in Australia has been the widespread acceptance of the system of compulsory arbitration. In most other countries the usual system is collective bargaining, involving the settlement of industrial disputes by conciliation and voluntary arbitration. Much conciliation and voluntary arbitration also take place in Australia, but it is within the formal setting of compulsory arbitration.

Australia's compulsory arbitration system has its roots in the strikes of the early 1890s. Previously collective bargaining had been introduced to Australia from Great Britain. The trade unions in Australia in the important mining, shipping, and pastoral industries had become very strong at a time when the right of workers to organize themselves through unions was questioned by employers. During the prolonged nation-wide 'maritime strike' in 1890 (which involved all of the above industries), and during later strikes, there was a general reluctance of employers and employees to meet and negotiate settlements. But it was felt that there was no need for a new country such as Australia to experience the conflicts of industrial Britain. This led to the growing support for a system of compulsory arbitration in place of the system of collective bargaining. Compulsory arbitration was seen as a way to avoid the economic disruption of industry, the losses of income, and the hardship suffered by workers and their families during strikes and lock-outs. Furthermore, many concerned with industrial relations were impressed by the apparently successful system of compulsory arbitration introduced in New Zealand in 1895.

Another important factor which strengthened the grounds for the establishment of a legal system of wage determination was the presence of 'sweated' labour in industries where union organization was absent or weak. One major industry where this was so was the clothing trades. In Victoria the position was met by the introduction of Wages Boards in 1896 in a number of industries to determine minimum wage rates and working conditions. In N.S.W. legislation providing for compulsory arbitration was introduced in 1901[49]. These measures reflected

---

49 The strikes in 1890 and the defeat of the unions also led to the formation of the New South Wales Labour Party. This set the pattern in other States, and later in the Commonwealth sphere. The unions thereby moved away from relying entirely on industrial action and turned to the judicial procedure as well to achieve economic justice. This contributed to the establishment of the independent industrial tribunals by the States and the Commonwealth, as noted further below.

the strongly held belief that through the intervention of an impartial arbitrator just, peaceful solutions could be found to the problems of industrial relations, 'sweating', and poverty.

A decisive step towards the establishment of Australia's system of compulsory arbitration was taken in the Commonwealth Constitution, which, under Section 51 (xxxv) empowers the Commonwealth Government to legislate with respect to 'conciliation and arbitration for the prevention and settlement of industrial disputes extending beyond the limits of any one State'.

The Commonwealth's powers are thus strictly limited to making laws about the two methods of 'conciliation and arbitration'; and any action must be limited to interstate industrial disputes. The States, on the other hand, have full powers to legislate on industrial matters confined within their own boundaries.

The original Commonwealth *Conciliation and Arbitration Act* was passed in 1904. The Court which it established began to function the following year. By 1912 the States had also exercised their rights in establishing independent industrial tribunals for the control of wages, hours, and industrial disputes, compulsory arbitration being adopted in New South Wales, Queensland, and Western Australia, a wages board system in Victoria and Tasmania, and a combination of the two systems in South Australia.

The importance of conciliation in the individual systems, as differentiated from compulsion, varies. But in the Commonwealth and most of the State systems the stage is reached where, the parties having failed to agree, a compulsory award may be made. The details of the individual systems need not concern us. Attention will be concentrated on the Commonwealth system since, as explained in more detail shortly, it is this system that has become the leading exponent of wage determination in Australia.

(b) The Functions of the Commonwealth Conciliation and Arbitration Commission

Since World War II there have been two major changes in the Commonwealth system. One is the separation of the judicial from the conciliatory and arbitral functions. This was provided for in extensive amendments to the *Conciliation and Arbitration Act* in 1956. The Commonwealth Industrial Court was formed to deal with the judicial matters under the Act; and the Commonwealth Conciliation and Arbitration Commission (commonly referred to as the Commission, and the body with which we are mainly concerned) was formed to handle the functions of conciliation and arbitration. This separation has helped to overcome the traditional view that wage fixing is essentially a judicial process; in particular, it has contributed to a greater acceptance of the relevance of the economic and social implications of the deliberations and decisions of the Commission[50].

The second major change concerns the division of the work of the Commission between Presidential members who have the qualifications and status of judges and Conciliation Commissioners who have experience in industrial relations in private industry or the public service. There is a clear division between the work of the Presidential members and the Commissioners. This dual system was provided for by amendments to the Commonwealth *Conciliation and Arbitration Act* in 1947, and then further developed by the legislation in 1956.

The Presidential members, constituted in a bench of at least three members, are empowered to make awards or to certify agreements on matters of national importance concerning the 'total wage', the standard hours of work, long-service leave, and a minimum rate of pay for women. The powers of the Presidential members are thus restricted to broad general questions, while jurisdiction in all other matters is given in the first instance to an individual arbitrator, who may be a Presidential member or Commissioner assigned to particular industries or the Commonwealth Public Service Arbitrator. The Commission in June 1970 was comprised of a President, five Deputy Presidents, a Senior Commissioner, and fifteen Commissioners.

When a matter raises issues affecting the public interest, the *Conciliation and Arbitration Act* provides that it may be heard by prior reference or on appeal by a bench constituted of at least three members of the Commission, including at least one Presidential member. Each Commissioner has been assigned to a particular industry or group of industries, his prime objective being to encourage employers and employees to prevent or settle disputes by conciliation, with arbitration being resorted to only when conciliation has failed. The terms of an agreement reached by conciliation may be registered by the Commission or incorporated in an award. However, the forces at work within Australia's compulsory system have tended to lean quite heavily towards arbitration, thus weakening the aim to encourage conciliation. This has been so in individual industries (especially in some key sectors such as the coal industry and on the water front) as well as in the fixing of award rates on a national scale.

(c) The Development of a Uniform National Wage Policy
The Commonwealth Conciliation and Arbitration Commission determines awards for unions whose members work in more than one State.

---

50 See J. E. Isaac, *Wages and Productivity*, Cheshire, 1967, p. 137.

A union or an employers' association may obtain an award by registering with the Commission, hence also bringing itself under the general authority of the Commission. Some members of a union may be covered by the award of a State tribunal and others by an award of the Commission. In 1963, 42·3 per cent of male employees and 31·0 per cent of female were directly affected by Commonwealth awards[51]. The Commission's ability to extend the coverage of its awards is limited by Section 51 (xxxv) of the Commonwealth Constitution (previously quoted). But, as the Vernon Committee noted:

'the interpretation of this provision by the High Court has been generally favourable to the extension of the Commission's authority, and the principal reasons for many employees being outside the scope of Commonwealth awards are industrial rather than constitutional in character, especially the preference of the trade unions[52].

Though the Commission's awards do not cover a majority of the labour force, its influence goes much further than those on Commonwealth awards. It also has a considerable indirect influence on wages and terms of employment not covered by its awards. The Commission 'obviously gains in influence from being the most important single authority from the prestige accorded to a national tribunal whose awards prevail over State awards where there is a conflict between the two, and from the status that has been acquired by the Federal basic wage'[53]. Largely for these reasons the State tribunals have frequently followed the Commission in major cases. In short, the Commission has set the main pattern of wages and conditions of employment throughout Australia in all industries and for nearly all levels of occupation. This has occurred despite the limited legal basis of the Commonwealth tribunal. An important advantage which many see in the Australian highly centralized system of wage fixation is that — especially in comparison with other developed free-enterprise countries — it provides a suitable instrument for the administration of a uniform national wage policy. This aspect will be examined further below.

(d) The Main Pattern of Wages

Until June 1967, the concept of basic wage was common to wage

---

51 For statistics of the proportion of employees affected by State awards, see Commonwealth Bureau of Census and Statistics, *Labour Report*, No. 53, 1967, p. 53.

52 *Vernon Report*, Vol. I, p. 133. See also J. H. Portus, 'Aspects of the Commonwealth and State Division of the Industrial Power', *Journal of Industrial Relations*, Vol. 5, April 1963.

53 *Vernon Report*, Vol. I, p. 133.

rates determined by Commonwealth and State industrial authorities. The 'basic' wage, or the 'living' wage as it was first known in Australia, was initially interpreted as the 'minimum' wage necessary to maintain 'a family of about five' in a reasonable state of comfort[54]. The most famous of the Australian pronouncements of the concept of a living wage was the 1907 Judgment of Mr Justice Higgins. This judgment established the so-called 'Harvester standard'. Justice Higgins concluded that a 'fair and reasonable' wage for an unskilled labourer in Melbourne must be an amount adequate to cover 'the normal needs of an average employee regarded as a human being living in a civilised community'[55]. This wage, in 1907, Higgins felt was 7/- a day, or £2-2-0 per week.

Though the Commonwealth basic wage initially applied directly only to workers on Commonwealth awards, it soon became the benchmark for the pay of most workers, since a basic wage was fixed by State tribunals as well.

In addition to the basic wage, 'secondary' wage payments have been determineed by the Commonwealth and State industrial tribunals. These secondary payments include margins for training, skill, or experience, and loadings and other special considerations peculiar to an occupation or industry. The basic and secondary wage together comprise the total wage for a particular occupation.

In 1967 the Commission accepted the employers' claim for the adoption of the 'total wage' concept, comprising the former basic wage and any secondary wage. Thus, for Commonwealth awards, the concepts of basic wage and secondary wage (or margins) have been discontinued. This total wage varies from one job classification to another. The pattern of wages which exists is basically the result of the market forces of demand and supply. These forces influence the wages awarded by industrial tribunals for various occupations and also reveal themselves in over-award payments, contributing to a diverse occupational wage structure within an industry and from one industry to another[56].

(e) The Consolidation of the System of Compulsory Arbitration

The system of wage determination in Australia, which has been largely centred on the Commonwealth tribunal, has played a key role in the consolidation of Australia's compulsory arbitration system. As this

---

54 *Official Year Book of the Commonwealth of Australia*, No. 33, 1940, p. 700.
55 *Ibid.*
56 For detailed discussions of (i) the demand and supply forces and of the wage structure in the Australian setting, and (ii) over-award payments, see Isaac, *op. cit.*, Chap. 2 and pp. 108–15, respectively.

system evolved during the twentieth century, it seemed to satisfy largely two important and closely related objectives for a majority of Australians: first, it provided a considerable measure of social justice and industrial peace, hence allowing a more rapid development of the Australian economy; and secondly, most Australians seem to favour the characteristic of egalitarianism inherent in Australia's arbitration system through its ensuring legally at least a basic pay, and increases or decreases in that pay, for the main body of workers.

A consequence of the development of Australia's compulsory arbitration system is that Australia has become one of the most highly unionized industrial countries in the western world. In 1966 about 54 per cent of total wage and salary earners in Australia were members of a trade union[57]. This compares with about 42 per cent in Great Britain[58] and 30 per cent in the United States[59].

After more than sixty years of compulsory arbitration this system is well-established in Australia. Despite its imperfections in securing and preserving industrial peace, it seems highly doubtful whether any move to abandon arbitration would command any substantial support from employers or unions. This is not only because of the usual reluctance to depart from the status quo, but more particularly because there appears to be no suitable alternative system which would be more successful in maintaining industrial peace with steady growth while ensuring that workers in general receive their fair share of rising productivity. The close attachment to the arbitration system makes of considerable importance the principles underlying the Commission's fixation of wages in Australia.

(f) The General Principles of Wage Determination

The total wage may change as the result of two types of enquiry which may be brought before the Commission: first, through a 'national' wage case, when the total wage of all workers on Commonwealth awards may be varied; and secondly, through 'work-value' enquiries, when the difficult task of assessing the relative work-value of particular jobs is undertaken. Not the least of the difficulties with Australia's highly centralized arbitration system is the characteristic of

---

57 Commonwealth Bureau of Census and Statistics, *Labour Report*, No. 52, 1965 and 1966, p. 247. The proportion has been declining from a peak of 62 per cent in 1954 to 59 per cent in 1961 and 50 per cent in 1969. *Sources:* Commonwealth Bureau of Census and Statistics, *Labour Report* (various issues), and *Trade Union Statistics*, December 1969.

58 Computed from data in H.M.S.O. Central Statistical Office, *Annual Abstract of Statistics*, No. 105, 1968, pp. 113 and 133.

59 Computed from data in *Statistical Abstract of the United States*, 1966, pp. 230 and 246.

egalitarianism which is expressed in Australian industrial relations as the principle of 'comparative wage justice'. As Professor Isaac[60] said: 'under this principle, relative wage rates should be fixed in terms of the requirements of jobs — skill, responsibility, effort, etc. Work involving the same requirements should be paid the same wage. The pay or "work value", to use a common expression of the Australian labour market, of different jobs should be proportioned to their relative job requirements.'

The characteristic of egalitarianism in wage determination first revealed itself with the basic wage which applied to the unskilled labourer. Changes in the basic wage, and now in the total wage by the Commonwealth tribunal have usually been adopted almost immediately by the State tribunals. The egalitarian characteristic has, as indicated in the above quotation, also manifested itself in the secondary wage, or work-value adjustments to total wage. This has been so under the conditions of mostly full employment since World War II.

The wage rate that has become the yardstick for adjusting wages in other industries is that of the fitter in the metal trades. The key role of the fitter was already evident in the 1920s. But the considerable unemployment throughout the inter-war period prevented the development of the close relationship between wages that has applied in recent years, when variation in the fitters' wage — as in the case of variations in the basic or total wage — has been the signal (on considerations of industrial peace and wage justice) for a general, proportionate change in wages in all industries[61]. The responsibility for this change has fallen largely on the Commission because of its dominant role in wage determination in the metal trades.

Thus, in keeping with comparative wage justice, the relative pay position between different groups of workers has tended to be largely maintained. However, this may engender an undesirable degree of rigidity in the pay structure which may hinder economic progress. There must be sufficient flexibility in marginal changes in wages to ensure sufficient mobility of labour so that labour can move or become available in accordance with changes in the supply of and demand for various skills.

As noted earlier, the basic wage was initially conceived in terms of the 'needs' of an average family. Later the capacity of the economy to pay became a leading principle[62]. This was clearly revealed in 1931

---

60 *Op. cit.*, p. 17.

61 See Isaac, *op. cit.*, pp. 11 and 103.

62 For detailed reviews of the principles that have historically played an important part in the Commonwealth tribunal's determination of wages, see: K. Hancock, 'The Wages of the Workers', *Journal of Industrial Relations*, Vol. II, March 1969; Isaac, *op. cit.*, Chap. 5, especially pp. 100–8; and *Vernon Report*, Vol. I, pp. 140–7.

CHART 9
INDEXES OF CONSUMER PRICES, AVERAGE MINIMUM WEEKLY WAGE
RATES, AND AVERAGE WEEKLY EARNINGS, AUSTRALIA, SEPTEMBER
QUARTER 1947 TO MARCH QUARTER 1970
(Ratio Chart)

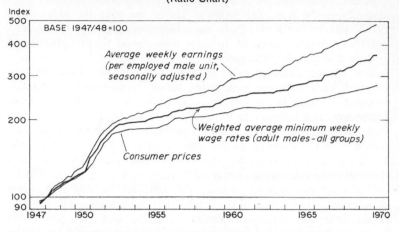

Sources: Commonwealth Bureau of Census and Statistics, *Wage Rates and Earnings* (various issues), and *Monthly Review of Business Statistics* (various issues).

when the Commonwealth tribunal reduced the basic wage by 10 per cent (and State tribunals soon made similar cuts) in view of the substantial fall in export income and the severe economic depression. Since 1931 the capacity to pay principle has gained in importance. By 'capacity to pay' economists generally mean the highest real wage that a country can sustain without inflationary consequences which might create balance of payments difficulties (by reducing the country's ability to export and compete with the imports of the main competitor countries) and which might lead to unemployment and a slower rate of growth.

Since World War II the Commonwealth tribunal's task of assessing capacity to pay has been greatly complicated by the considerable inflation of costs and prices. The inflation has been caused partly by 'demand-pull' elements and partly by 'cost-push'. 'Demand inflation' is generated by the aggregate demand for goods and services exceeding the potential supply of goods and services. This theory fits especially a situation of full employment when the shortages of goods, production bottlenecks, and competition for workers generate price increases, including wage increases.

'Cost inflation' occurs through rising unit costs brought about by spontaneous increases in wages (including award wages) and profits which are at least partly independent of the state of demand and which cannot be absorbed by rising productivity. The aim of the increase in wages or profits is to increase the share of the factor in the total product. An essential characteristic of cost inflation is the use of some monopoly power (exercised by unions or employers) leading to price increases which would not have occurred in a perfectly competitive market. In practice, both demand and cost inflation have been operating, and it becomes impossible to distinguish properly between them.

Chart 9 provides a broad picture of Australia's inflationary experience, and shows that the greater part of the increases in wages and earnings have been absorbed in higher prices. Between the third quarter of 1947 and the same quarter of 1969 consumer prices rose by about 179 per cent and average weekly wage rates by 264 per cent, providing an increase in the real value of award rates of 31 per cent. Most wage-earners have done better than this, since average weekly earnings over the same period rose by 396 per cent and real earnings by 78 per cent[63].

The divergence between earnings and award rates is referred to by economists as 'wage' or 'earnings drift'. Since a ratio scale is used in Chart 9, changes in the distance between average earnings and award rates are a measure of the earnings drift. The rate of change in average earnings (apart from changes in award rates themselves) is determined by a number of factors including overtime pay, increases in pay achieved by direct negotiation leading to over-award pay, the effects of payments by results, changes in the occupational and industrial composition of the labour force, and changes in the proportion of female and junior workers.

Earnings drift has been an important aspect of wage history in most other countries too since World War II[64]. It appears to be a special feature of a full-employment economy. In Australia the conditions of full employment have favoured workers' obtaining over-award payments and overtime. Earnings drift raises special problems in the fixing of award wages if the Commission is to take account of the limits imposed on wage increases beyond which inflation will result.

One of the complex problems which the Commonwealth tribunal has faced since World War II is the question of what adjustments, if

---

63 For more detailed studies of the inflation of wages and prices in Australia, see: Hancock, *op. cit.*, especially pp. 25–30; and *Vernon Report*, Vol. II, App. F.

64 For fuller discussions of the problem and the measurement of earnings drift in Australia, see: *Vernon Report*, Vol. I, pp. 128–32 and Vol. II, pp. 606–9; Isaac, *op. cit.*, pp. 108–15; and K. Hancock, 'Earnings Drift in Australia', *Journal of Industrial Relations*, Vol. 8, July 1966.

any, should be made on account of rises in the cost of living in order to safeguard a given real wage against rising prices. In the Commonwealth arbitration system the adjustment of wages by an amount reflecting changes in prices originated with Higgins' decision in 1913 to adjust the basic wage prescribed by the Harvester standard[65]. The system of automatic quarterly cost-of-living adjustments of the basic wage was adopted in 1921[66]. This system received the general support of unions and employers, and continued without challenge, until 1953 when on application from employers, the Court abolished automatic adjustments.

The background to this decision in terms of the sharp rise in award rates and prices may be seen in Chart 9. Between August 1946 and August 1953, the 'six capitals' basic wage for adult males had increased from £4.18.0 to £11.16.0, an increase of £6.18.0, or 141 per cent, in seven years. Four-fifths of this increase had resulted from quarterly adjustments.

One reason for the abandonment of the quarterly adjustments was their accelerating inflationary effects, notably in 1951 and 1952. Another reason given by the Court was that there was 'no ground for assuming that the capacity to pay will be maintained at the same level or that it will rise or fall co-incidentally with the purchasing-power of money'[67]. The rate of inflation decreased considerably after 1953, partly because of the abandonment of quarterly adjustments by the Commonwealth tribunal[68], partly because of the recession following the Korean war boom, and also because of improvements in the economic management of the economy through fiscal and monetary policies in controlling demand inflation. The Commonwealth tribunal has continued to take movements in prices into account in making new awards[69]. Indeed, it has been continually pressed to do so by the unions in national wage cases[70].

The real question is whether price changes do increase an economy's ability to pay higher wages. There are six possible causes of price

---

65 In the previous year the Commonwealth Statistician had commenced the publication of retail price index numbers.
66 For a discussion of the significance of this system, see Hancock, 'The Wages of the Workers', p. 20.
67 Judgment in the 'Basic Wage and Standard Hours Inquiry 1952–1953', p. 21.
68 Only the State tribunal in South Australia permanently discontinued quarterly adjustments to the State basic wage in 1953. The position regarding quarterly or periodic adjustments to other State basic wages has varied between and within the other States from time to time. See *Official Year Book of the Commonwealth of Australia* (various issues).
69 For a survey of the recent history of the cost-of-living principle in the Commission's decisions, see *Vernon Report*, Vol. I, pp. 140–2.
70 This has been an important part of the union's case for the adoption of the principle of 'prices plus productivity' from 1959 onwards. *Ibid*, pp. 144–6.

change, four of which clearly do not provide ground for a wage increase while two might. Price increases which result from increases in *import prices* and unfavourable *seasonal conditions* do not provide an increase in capacity to pay; nor do price increases resulting from higher *indirect taxes,* which the government has imposed presumably to reduce spending power; and nor do price increases which result from *corresponding proportionate increases in wages and profits* which in turn have increased unit costs. But if higher prices are caused by higher *export prices* and higher *profit margins* in a monopolistic situation, this would provide prima facie evidence of increased capacity to pay, and may justify the Commission's raising wages[71].

However, when account is taken of (i) the changes in the detailed items of the consumer price index, as published by the Commonwealth Statistician in recent years, (ii) the relative constancy over the long run of the share of G.N.P. accruing to wages and profits[72], and (iii) the generally unfavourable trend in export prices (see Chart 7), there appears to be no firm grounds on account of price changes to justify on economic grounds any major, permanent increase in wages. Moreover, export prices tend to fluctuate widely, and would not provide a suitable criterion on which to base wage changes, especially since wages tend to be 'sticky' in a downward direction. Furthermore, selective government policies such as legislation against restrictive trade practices and the taxation of monopoly profits would probably provide more effective measures to promote a competitive market than general wage increases.

The Vernon Committee asserted that the application of the cost-of-living principle 'is one cause of the inflationary bias in the Commission's decisions. Whenever the price level is disturbed for whatever reason, the cost-of-living criterion involves magnifying the disturbance . . . We reject any suggestion that price increases add to the economy's ability to pay higher wages[73].' While this rejection may need to be qualified at times on grounds of the last two causes of price changes listed above, as a generalization of the economic history of Australia since World War II, the assertion fits the evidence fairly well.

By contrast, the principle of capacity to pay appears to offer a more appropriate criterion for determining wages. A major problem

---

71 See: R. I. Downing, 'Prices, Productivity, Wages and Inflation', *Economic Record,* Vol. 36, March 1960, especially pp. 120–2; and R. I. Downing and J. E. Isaac, 'The 1961 Basic Wage Judgment and Wage Policy', *Economic Record,* Vol. 37, December 1961, especially pp. 487–90.

72 See Isaac, *Wages and Productivity,* Chap. 3; and *Vernon Report,* Vol. I, pp. 126–8 and 137–8. The Vernon Committee concluded: 'The conception of wage increases as an assault on profits must be regarded as a delusion.' (*Ibid,* p. 138.)

73 *Vernon Report,* Vol. I, pp. 141–2.

has been the measurement of the capacity to pay and changes in it. Acceptance of the usefulness of the concept of national productivity for wage-fixing purposes has grown.

This concept formed an increasingly important part of the submissions of the parties before the Arbitration Commission in national wage cases during the 1960s[74].

The ability of the parties to make estimates of the historical increase in productivity (though only approximate), has naturally led to a clearer appreciation than previously of the usefulness of the concept in the Commission's traditional task of assessing capacity to pay. In the deliberations of the Commonwealth tribunal until about 1965 the concept of capacity to pay held some close reference to the recent and existing state of economic activity[75]. But a productivity-geared wage policy, as envisaged for an incomes policy aimed at preventing (or restraining) cost-push inflation, is concerned with the future increase in capacity, although the historical trend of productivity is likely to be a major basis of prediction.

Similarly, the capacity to pay principle should be fundamentally concerned with the ability to pay in the future, in particular, the ability to increase wages during the next year or so, without adding to costs per unit of output. The important point is that if average earnings rise faster than productivity, and if the relative shares of the total product beween wages and profits remain fairly constant (as noted earlier has tended to be so), then unit costs and prices will rise by approximately the percentage by which the increase in earnings exceeds that in productivity.

Probably the nearest that we have approached defining the limit of the increase in economic (or real) capacity is the measure of productivity. The statistical evidence on trends in earnings, prices, and productivity supports the central conclusion of the Vernon Committee that the Commission should base movements in money wages primarily on the *prospective* increase in national productivity. This does not mean that the prescriptions which the Commission may follow are clear-cut. Another complicated aspect to be taken into account is the outlook of the balance of payments. For this purpose, the concept of 'effective productivity' which (along with that of national productivity) has received attention in proceedings before the Commission,

---

74 It was not until 1963 that the Commonwealth Bureau of Census and Statistics began publishing estimates of G.N.P. at constant prices to permit more reliable estimates of the trend in productivity.

75 The Vernon Committee remarked that 'capacity to pay has never been defined in concrete terms . . . . In our view, the only proper interpretation of capacity to pay is capacity to pay increased wages without inflationary consequences.' *Vernon Report*, Vol. I, pp. 143 and 144.

especially in the union's submissions[76], takes into account not only changes in the productivity of Australian industry, but also changes in the purchasing power of export incomes in terms of imports[77]. The considerable importance of changes in real income in Australia arising through the balance of payments gives support to the concept of effective productivity as a useful, relevant one for the Commission which would be worth taking into account along with national productivity[78].

It is also important for the Commission to follow criteria which will ensure the fixing of wages that are 'fair and reasonable' on grounds of equity, so fostering industrial peace. There is — in the interests of workers, employers, and the community in general — the further problem of the effective integration of wage policy with general economic policy. It is clearly important for the Commission to have a flexible approach to its task. This would rule out any *rigid* adherence to the productivity criterion.

However, what the productivity criterion does mean is that, by paying close attention to prospective increases in national (or effective) productivity and taking into account the likelihood of earnings drift, the Commission — in the words of the Vernon Committee — 'can assess the consequences on price levels of increases in award wages'[79]. The importance of knowing the effects on prices stems from the policy objective of achieving price stability as far as possible. This is a matter which is examined further in Chapter 9, where the problems of inflation and of keeping wage increases within prescribed limits will be examined in more detail in the context of the long-run objectives of economic policy.

5 CONCLUSION

The institutions which have been reviewed in this chapter perform key functions in Australia's economic development: in the field of public finance to ensure that fiscal policy is properly formulated; in banking to provide effective monetary policy; and in wage policy to curb wage inflation and to contribute towards the desired income distribution. It is debatable whether the development of the institutions

---

76 See *Vernon Report*, Vol. I, p. 144.
77 The complications of 'the open economy' for wage determination in Australia are discussed in detail by Isaac, *op. cit.*, pp. 63–6 and 71–3.
78 The Vernon Committee, while favouring prime attention being paid to national productivity, felt that 'the Commission might proceed with somewhat more liberality when the balance-of-payments outlook is favourable and with more restraint when it is unfavourable'. *Vernon Report*, Vol. I, p. 148.
79 *Ibid*, p. 145.

and their policies have been as successful as could be. But probably few would deny the need for these institutional developments to ensure that growth prospects are not impaired.

A basic requirement (for the achievement of the policy goal of steady growth at full employment, which is discussed in the concluding chapter) is that the institutions and their economic policies should be flexible and adaptable to meet the changing economic conditions and the desired ends. It is also highly desirable that there be close co-ordination between the Governments (Commonwealth and States), the central bank, and the wage-fixing authorities to ensure that the policies each is pursuing are consistent and complementary. The analysis in this chapter has particularly indicated the considerable progress which has been made since World War II in respect to the much greater degree of overall control which is now exercised by the Commonwealth Government over fiscal policy and by the central bank over monetary policy. The significance of this greater overall control will be seen more clearly in the concluding chapter where attention is given to (i) the growing importance of the government sector in total economic activity, and (ii) the much greater co-ordination between the Commonwealth Government and the central bank. The part played by wage policy is also considered further in the next chapter in connection with living standards, while in the final chapter consideration is paid to the case for an incomes policy to assist fiscal and monetary policies in checking inflation.

Suggestions for further reading

Commonwealth-State Financial Relations
  Boxer, A. H. (ed.), *Aspects of the Australian Economy*, Chap. 2;
  Grant, J. McB. and others, *Economic Institutions and Policy*,
     Chap. 9;
  Samuelson, P. A. and others, *Economics: Australian edition*,
     Chaps 8, 9 and 19;
  Commonwealth of Australia, *Commonwealth Payments To or For
  the States 1969-70*;
  Commonwealth of Australia, *Commonwealth Grants
     Commission: Report* (Annual);
  Prest, W. *The Economics of Federal-State Finance*, Joseph
     Fisher Lecture, University of Adelaide, 1954;
     'Federal-State Financial Relations', *Economic Papers*, The
     Economic Society of Australia and New Zealand, New
     South Wales and Victorian Branches, No. 20, October 1965,
     pp. 19-32; and 'Federalism in Australia: The Role of the

Commonwealth Grants Commission', *Journal of Commonwealth Political Studies,* Vol. 5, March 1967, pp. 3-17.

Banks and the Capital Market
Arndt, H. W. and Harris, C. P. *The Australian Trading Banks,* Cheshire, 3rd edn, 1965;
Grant, *op. cit.,* Chaps 7 and 8;
Hirst, R. R. and Wallace, R. H. (eds.), *Studies in the Australian Capital Market,* Cheshire, 1964, especially Chaps 4, 7, and 8;
Samuelson, *op. cit.,* Chaps 15-18;
Reserve Bank of Australia, *Report and Financial Statements* (Annual);
Reserve Bank of Australia: Functions and Operations, Sydney, 1969;
Vernon Report, Vol. I, Chap 10; and Vol. II, App. I;
Current Affairs Bulletin, *Australia's Changing Financial Structure,* Vol. 26, October 1960, reprinted in Arndt, H. W. *A Small Rich Industrial Country,* Chap. 5.

Wage Determination
Isaac, J. E. *Wages and Productivity,* Cheshire, 1967;
Isaac, J. E. and Ford, G. W. (eds.), *Australian Labour Economics: Readings,* Sun Books, 1967; and *Australian Labour Relations: Readings,* Sun Books, 1966;
Samuelson, *op. cit.,* Chap. 7;
Vernon Report, Vol. I, Chap. 7; and Vol. II, App. F.

Chapter 8

LIVING STANDARDS

Like everything else economic growth has its costs. If economic growth could be achieved without any disadvantages, everybody would be wholly in its favour. But since growth has real disadvantages, people differ in their attitude to growth according to the different assessment which they give to its advantages and disadvantages. . . . The case for economic growth is that it gives man greater control over his environment, and thereby increases his freedom. (*Lewis*, The Theory of Economic Growth, *pp. 420–1.*)

Once we descry the sort of world towards which technological growth is bearing us, it is well worth discussing whether humanity will find it more congenial or not. (*Mishan*, The Costs of Economic Growth, *p. 176.*)

There is no country and no people, I think, who can look forward to the age of leisure and of abundance without a dread. For we have been trained too long to strive and not to enjoy. It is a fearful problem for the ordinary person, with no special talents, to occupy himself, especially if he no longer has roots in the soil or in custom or in the beloved conventions of a traditional society. (*J. M. Keynes, 'Economic Possibilities for our Grand-children (1930)', in* Essays in Persuasion, Macmillan, 1931, *p. 368.*)

1 INTRODUCTION

At the beginning of this book reference was made to the considerable attention that has been paid since World War II to economic development in practically all countries as a major objective of government policy. It will be fitting in this chapter to review the end result of this development in terms of the trends in Australia's living standards.

The study of living standards concerns material and non-material living conditions. This involves an examination of the degree to which the people's needs and wants are satisfied, and this largely depends on the level of real income. In economics a study is made of the level and trend in real income in reference to living standards, since the level and trend of real income largely determine the level and trend of the material welfare which flows from the consumption of the goods and services which may be obtained with that income. An increase in material welfare on balance usually means an increase in general welfare which will provide greater satisfaction of human wants.

In view of the multiplicity and diversity of people's needs and wants, there are many aspects of the standard of living, some of which are vague and involve value judgments. What is important in life varies among different groups and classes in the community and from time to time as desires and consumer patterns change. Each person's living standard is a complicated combination of many factors. Some factors are material and measurable, others are of a non-material nature, subjective and incapable of exact measurement.

The changes in the material and non-material elements may conflict. This does not prevent us from noting the level and trend of statistical measures or from making observations on the wider social aspects of the general trends in living standards. For analytical purposes, the factors determining living standards are usually divided into four broad groups, which are closely interrelated: general measures, specific measures, non-material elements, and the distribution of income[1].

2 GENERAL MEASURES

Three important general measures of the trends in living standards are real personal income per head, real personal disposable income per head, and real personal consumption expenditure per head (Table 43). The strong uptrend in these three measures in Australia since World War II is generally believed to indicate a rise in the community's living standards, for it indicates in respect to income an increase in the power to buy more of the goods and services which people may wish to buy, and in respect to consumption expenditure the process of doing so.

There are no comparable estimates of real personal income before 1938-9 in order to show the goods and services *available* per head. The position can be broadly seen by comparing the trend rates of real G.N.P. (that is, goods and services *produced*) per head shown in Table 3 (column 6), Table 4 (column 3), and Table 44 (see also Chart 1). This comparison indicates in particular that while there has been a generally sustained, rapid increase in real G.N.P. per head since 1938-9 of just over 2 per cent per annum, during the first four decades of the twentieth century there had been only a comparatively slow advance of about ½ per cent per annum. We noted in Chapter 2 that the advance has at no time been a completely steady one. But, whereas the fluctuations in economic activity since World War II

---

1 See *Vernon Report*, Vol. I, Chap. 6; and Vol. II, App. E.

TABLE 43

SELECTED INDICATORS OF LIVING STANDARDS, AUSTRALIA, 1938-9 TO 1968-9

(At 1959-60 prices)

Year	Total personal income per head $	Personal disposable income per head $	Personal consumption expenditure per head $	Index Nos (Base 1948-9=100)		
				Total personal income per head	Personal disposable income per head	Personal consumption expenditure per head
	1	2	3	4	5	6
1938-39	617	588	553	66	70	73
1948-49	938	838	758	100	100	100
50	992	896	778	106	107	103
51	1164	1012	808	124	121	107
52	965	842	780	103	100	103
53	953	842	744	102	100	98
1953-54	952	856	781	101	102	103
55	994	902	815	106	108	108
56	1012	918	819	108	110	108
57	998	902	810	106	108	107
58	962	875	819	103	104	108
59	997	908	827	106	108	109
1959-60	1045	949	864	111	113	114
61	1054	951	862	112	113	114
62	1058	959	861	113	114	114
63	1106	999	900	118	119	119
64	1189	1068	935	127	127	123
65	1220	1088	961	130	130	127
1965-66	1213	1076	962	129	128	127
67	1273	1124	986	136	134	130
68	1267	1113	1017	135	133	134
69	1356	1183	1031	145	141	136

Computed from data in various issues of the following: Commonwealth of Australia, *National Income and Expenditure*; Commonwealth Bureau of Census and Statistics, *Australian National Accounts*, *Monthly Review of Business Statistics* (for consumer price index to deflate the original figures for cols 1 and 2) and *Quarterly Summary of Australian Statistics*.

TABLE 44
AVERAGE ANNUAL RATES OF INCREASE* IN SELECTED MEASURES OF
LIVING STANDARDS AND IN G.N.P. (AT 1959–60 PRICES), AUSTRALIA,
EXPRESSED PER HEAD AND PER PERSON EMPLOYED, 1953 4 TO 1968–9
(Per cent)

	Total	Per head	Per person employed
	1	2	3
Real G.N.P.	4·6	2·5	2·5
Real G.N.P. adjusted for terms of trade	4·4	2·3	2·3
Selected measures of living standards			
Real personal income	4·4	2·3	2·3
Real personal disposable income	4·2	2·1	2·1
Real personal consumption expenditure	4·0	1·9	1·9

Note: * From trends fitted by least squares.
Source: As for Table 43.

have generally been minor with the recessions short lived and the underlying trend continuing strongly upwards, the first four decades were marked by periods of significant stagnation or decline in real income and hence in living standards, notably during World War I and the depression in the early 1930s.

There are several comments that should be made in reference to the quality and interpretation of the statistics under consideration here. As previously noted, the statistical estimates, particularly before 1938-9, are only approximate. For purposes here this may be especially so because of the weaknesses of the data used to deflate for price changes and because no allowance was made in the deflation process for changes in the quality of commodities and services. Allowance should also be made for changes in the pattern of consumption and distribution of income; both these aspects are discussed shortly.

Another qualification is that the estimate of G.N.P. is not an absolute measure of all goods and services produced in the community. For example, it does not include the services of housewives or of consumer durables apart from dwellings Provided the relative size of these services does not change greatly from one period to another, their omission does not limit the usefulness of the estimates of real income and consumption expenditure. Their omission means, however, that the estimates of real income and consumption are more appropriately viewed as indexes rather than as absolute measures of material welfare.

Total real income should also be viewed in relation to the number of workers as well as total population, since the number of dependents of each worker influences the nature and size of his personal consumption expenditure. Table 44 shows that there was no apparent difference in the trend rates between G.N.P. per head and G.N.P. per person employed over the period 1953-4 to 1968-9 as a whole. This was because the growth in total population and in persons employed increased at approximately the same rate over this period. However, over shorter periods since World War II this was not so since there were marked changes in the age structure of the population[2]. In the earlier post-war years population rose faster than employment; but during the 1960s the position was reversed (see Table 3, columns 4 and 5), involving a reduction in the proportion of dependents. But the income per worker may not always be a true indication of a family's standard of living. For instance, when a dependent takes a job at a lower wage than the national average, it does not necessarily mean a lower standard of living per worker if the total income per family unit is greater, as may occur when a married woman enters the labour force.

The explanation of the slightly slower average annual rates of increase of the measures of living standards shown in Table 44 than in real G.N.P. per head lies partly in the decline in Australia's terms of trade during the period. This accounts for about 0·2 percentage points. The difference for this reason was greater in the earlier post-war years[3]. When the terms of trade move unfavourably, Australia receives less in imports for each dollar's worth of exports.

To summarize, the trend in the general statistical measures indicates that there has been a much accelerated, sustained advance in living standards over the last three decades at roughly four times the average annual rate of advance during the first four decades of this century. Furthermore, the rapid advance is continuing.

3 SPECIFIC MEASURES

In addition to general measures, observations on living standards are provided by specific quantitative indicators relating to such matters as health, nutrition, housing, and education. Unlike the general measures, the study of these specific indicators entails some value judgments as to their importance in living standards. However, there tends to be general agreement on a number of social aspects. Thus 'a rising trend in public expenditure on education or health is judged

---

2 *Vernon Report*, Vol. I, pp. 105–6.

3 During the period 1953–4 to 1962–3 there was a difference of 0·4 percentage points between G.N.P. per head at constant prices and G.N.P. per head at constant prices adjusted for the terms of trade. See *Vernon Report*, Vol. I, pp. 104–5.

to denote an improvement in living standards because education and health are considered good things in their own right'[4].

Strong evidence of a sustained improvement in the standard of health in Australia appears to be indicated by the continued decline in death rates throughout this century. The infant mortality rate has fallen from just above 100 per 1,000 births at the beginning of the century to a little below 20 in recent years; that is, the infant mortality rate is now less than one-fifth what it was 70 years ago[5]. Over the same period the general death rate has declined from about 12 per 1,000 to between 8 and 9 per 1,000, a fall of over 25 per cent.

Another aspect of the declining death rate is the increase in the expectation of life. A male born between 1901-10 could have expected at birth to reach an age of about 55 years — but a male born in the 1960s could expect to live to almost 70. For a female the increased expectation of life at birth is from 59 years to about 74. The decline in death rates and the longer expectation of life are largely the effect, but also partly the cause of rising living standards. Elements increasing the expectation of life are better nutrition, the considerable advances in medicine and progress in treating the sick, including the control, cure, and prevention of diseases which previously claimed many lives — for instance, pneumonia and tuberculosis. The rapid growth of real income per head has allowed the full realization of these gains to Australia.

A notable aspect of housing is the spread of home ownership. This is highly valued by Australians, as is indicated by the high proportion of owner-occupied houses (including purchaser by instalment). This proportion has grown from 53 per cent at the Censuses in 1933 and 1947 to 63 per cent and 71 per cent at the 1954 and 1966 Censuses, respectively[6].

Having one's own house on one's own block of land sets a high standard, but at the same time it has created the suburban sprawl, which in turn has brought its own problems, especially with the rapid growth of Australia's population. In the newly developed fringe areas of the capital cities, increases in the standard of living have often been retarded by the inability to provide immediately (owing partly to the problem of allocating scarce resources among competing ends) adequate roads, transport, sewerage, shopping, and specialized personal services. Also with the growing suburban sprawl, much time is spent travelling to work, thus tending to limit the time available for more

---

4 *Ibid*, pp. 108-9.
5 The statistics in this and the next paragraph are from Commonwealth Bureau of Census and Statistics, *Demography*, Bulletin No. 84, 1966.
6 *Official Year Book of the Commonwealth of Australia*, No. 54, 1968, p. 227.

fruitful or recreational activities. While these sociological aspects are generally considered to be bad for living standards, their significance varies between individuals.

There have also been marked improvements in the quantity and quality of housing, particularly since World War II. The quality of housing has improved in both design and construction, providing what are generally considered improvements in living standards through more healthy living conditions and greater comforts. These improvements have followed the equipping of homes with consumer durable goods in the fields of lighting, heating, cooking, radio, television, and so on. But there is still room for improvement, especially in the clearance of sub-standard houses. These are not entirely confined to the cities. In the rural areas there are still a number of houses which lack amenities more generally available in the city, such as running water in the kitchen with a kitchen sink. But the rapid spread of electricity through rural areas since World War II has meant a marked improvement in housing standards. The proportion of occupied private dwellings connected with electricity in rural areas increased from 48 per cent at the 1947 Census to 81 per cent at the 1961 and 93 per cent at the 1966[7]. 'Among the least satisfactory features of Australian housing standards is the relatively high proportion of houses not yet connected to a sewerage system. In 1947 the proportion with flush toilets, even in urban areas, was only 70 per cent, the deficiencies being mainly in Sydney and Brisbane. No later information is available[8].'

The relatively high level of national production in Australia provides the potential to achieve a high standard of diet, health, housing, and education. It is this position which, together with subjective observation, partly justifies the view that, in terms of average living standards, Australia ranks among the half-dozen top countries in the world[9]. Specific evidence that Australia is a relatively affluent community is also held to be manifested in the wide range of consumers' choice, including, for example, items of household durable consumer goods and the motor car.

The number of motor cars registered has risen from just over half a million in 1946 to about $3\frac{3}{4}$ million in 1970, and the number of motor vehicles (i.e. motor cars, commercial vehicles, and motor cycles) from nearly one million to nearly 5 million[10]. Thus there is now on average one motor car for just over every three persons, compared to one car for about every fourteen persons in 1946. Ownership

---

7 *Ibid*, p. 228, and *Vernon Report*, Vol. I, pp. 111–2.   8 *Ibid*, p. 112.
9 See p. 34 above; and *Vernon Report*, Vol. I, p. 108.
10 *Official Year Book of the Commonwealth of Australia* (various issues).

of a car has meant independence in transport — for travelling to work, on holidays, and for the weekend excursion. But against these private gains should be set any social disadvantages and their external dis economies — the greater noise and pollution of the air, the increasing traffic problems and congestion, and the associated mounting road toll. These diseconomies justify taxing the use of motor vehicles to finance remedial measures.

However, motor vehicles are not the only source of external dis-economies. The external impact of a number of activities in a modern industrial society is contributing to the growing problems of pollution of water, air, and soil. In short, economic growth creates wants as well as satisfies them. Increasing attention is being given to the introduction of effective controls of environmental pollution associated with affluence; but there is much more that remains to be done.

4 NON-MATERIAL ELEMENTS

There are a number of important non-material elements influencing the standard of living, particularly in the areas of freedom, justice, and security. Two elements in which considerable advances have occurred in Australia are social security and working conditions.

The outstanding feature of the improvement in social security since the early 1940s has been the virtual elimination of the fear of un-employment because of the absence of periods of prolonged, large-scale unemployment. This aspect is discussed further shortly in con-nection with the distribution of income.

Substantial improvements in working conditions have been marked by a reduction in the number of hours worked and increased periods of annual leave. At the beginning of the century there was a 48-hour standard working week. A permanent reduction to a 44-hour week was made in 1925. Certain workers had achieved reductions at an earlier date, but in some of these cases it was only temporary. In 1947 the standard working week was further reduced to 40 hours. Apart from Australia, only the United States and New Zealand have an effective 40-hour standard week, though the actual number of hours worked approximates this in other countries for particular industries, such as manufacturing[11].

Paid annual leave of one week was first introduced in awards of the Commonwealth Court of Conciliation and Arbitration in 1936. In 1945 the Commonwealth tribunal extended the annual leave period to two weeks, and in 1963 to three weeks. Other improvements obtained by an increasing number of workers in Australia, especially

---

11 *Vernon Report*, Vol. I, p. 113.

since World War II, have included superannuation, sickness benefits, and long-service leave. One important positive effect of the improvements in working conditions has been the considerable reduction in time lost through industrial disputes[12]. This in turn has helped to raise national productivity and so helped to meet the additional costs of the improved working conditions.

5 DISTRIBUTION OF INCOME

The subject of income distribution raises some difficult questions. What would be considered the best distribution of income involves political theory as much as economics. In a capital-hungry country such as Australia there appears to be a choice between on the one hand a pattern of income distribution that would support an adequate flow of savings to finance a rapid rate of economic growth which may lead to more rapid increases in living standards in the longer run, and on the other a more equal distribution of income with a lower level of savings and a slower rate of growth. A difficulty is that little is known about the economic effects of different income distributional patterns, such as the incentive to take risks and to invest. A major reason for this lack of knowledge is the lack of statistical information on income distribution in Australia.

A discussion of living standards that relies on averages like the per head measures of real personal income and consumption expenditure can be misleading unless something is known about the variation about the average. If a country's real income is mostly concentrated in a few hands, while the majority live in conditions of poverty, a measure of its real income per head considered alone will be meaningless as far as standard of living is concerned.

The conclusion which was drawn in the earlier analysis of the general measures, that rising trends in real income per head and consumption expenditure per head indicate generally rising living standards for the community, rests on a close relationship existing between real income and consumption per head and the typical (or modal) standard of living of the community. Though there are major gaps in Australian statistics on income distribution, there nevertheless appear to have been favourable influences which support strongly the conclusions which have been drawn above in respect to the relationship between real income and consumption expenditure and living standards.

One of the major sources of improvement in living standards of the community and of a more equal distribution of income since the early

---

12 See Commonwealth Bureau of Census and Statistics, *Labour Report*, No. 53, 1967, pp. 284–90; and *Vernon Report*, Vol. I, pp. 113–4, and Vol. II, p. 583.

1940s has been the absence of periods of prolonged or widespread unemployment. Since World War II the annual percentage unemployed has been mostly less than 1½ per cent of the total labour force (see Chart 3). Unemployment has risen a little in each recession period, but to nowhere near the levels reached in the downswings in economic activity, or even generally applying, before World War II. Consequently real incomes and hence living standards have been held at higher levels than when unemployment was greater.

The high level of employment strengthens the use which was made above of the per head measures of real income and consumption for the period since the early 1940s. When there is a considerable loss of income through unemployment, use of the national averages of income and consumption as a guide to the trends in the living standards of the community is weakened.

On the subject of the actual distribution of income, the evidence suggests that incomes in Australia have been more evenly distributed than in most other countries. There are no standard statistics for an international comparison of income distribution. A study of the distribution of employment income (that is, income from wages and salaries) by Professor Lydall for the Vernon Committee showed that (for the period 1952 to 1961)

'employment incomes, before tax, and probably after tax as well, in Australia are more equally distributed than in the United States, the United Kingdom, Canada, Germany, and Poland. They are distributed very similarly to employment incomes in Sweden, before tax, but less evenly than those of New Zealand, both before and after tax[13].'

Lydall also found that during the period 1952 to 1961 both pre-tax and post-tax incomes had become less equally distributed. On this the Vernon Committee commented:

'This is not necessarily a bad thing for the standard of living. It is arguable that the gains in equity from evenness in wage and salary incomes may be offset at some point by the losses in incentives, and it follows that pursuit of an even distribution of living standards may react against the improvement of those standards. We should not conclude, however, that the actual dispersion that Professor Lydall refers to had any desirable incentive effect with respect to any particular occupation or industry. To determine this, further research would be necessary[14].'

---

13 *Vernon Report*, Vol. II, p. 588.
14 *Vernon Report*, Vol. I, p. 114.

The characteristic of egalitarianism inherent in Australia's system of wage determination, and also the principle of fixing wages according to the capacity of industry to pay, as discussed in the previous chapter, have contributed to the more equal distribution of employment income in Australia, and have themselves also contributed to the fairly close relationship concluded above to exist between real income and consumption per head and the typical standard of living. The Vernon Committee noted approvingly:

'There has been widespread acceptance in Australia of the view that a given aggregate of incomes distributed evenly is better than the same aggregate distributed unevenly. Australia probably justifies its reputation of being an egalitarian society in terms of income as well as status, but the statistics to demonstrate this are not easy to produce[15].'

Two important aspects of government policy have contributed to a more equal distribution of income in Australia since World War II: first, the greater incidence of direct taxation which is progressive in character[16] and has increased relatively to indirect taxation[17]; and secondly, the large increase in and the widening range of 'cash benefits to persons' (or cash social service benefits as they used to be called) permitted by the substantial increase in taxation[18]. As a proportion of G.N.P., total taxation (direct and indirect) rose from 15 per cent in 1938-9 to between 22 and 25 per cent since World War II[19].

The widening range of social service benefits and in most respects the real increases in the amounts paid have ensured that the general rise in real income per head in Australia has been shared fairly equally[20]. The main classes of social service benefits provided by the

---

15 *Ibid.*

16 That is, the proportion of income taken by the government rises as income increases.

17 The proportion of total tax revenue derived from direct taxes has increased from 34·5 per cent in 1938–9 to an annual average of 51·9 per cent during the period 1948–9 to 1967–8. Source: A. H. Boxer, 'Public Finance' in Boxer (ed.), *Aspects of the Australian Economy*, p. 34.

18 Cash benefits to persons, as a proportion of G.N.P., rose from 3·3 per cent in 1938–9 to 5·0 per cent in 1948–9 and 5·3 per cent in 1968–9. Source: Table 45 below.

19 Computed from data in Commonwealth of Australia, *National Income and Expenditure* (various issues).

20 The maximum age pension payable during 1948–9 averaged $4·20 per week. The current maximum is $15·00. Source: Commonwealth Bureau of Census and Statistics, *Quarterly Summary of Australian Statistics* (various issues). In real terms, that is adjusted for the rise in the consumer price index, the maximum pension has risen about 45 per cent. This approximates the rise in real personal income per head over the period and is slightly better than the rise in real personal disposable income per head (see Table 43). The estimates of the real increase in the pension exclude the favourable effects of changes in eligibility and increased fringe benefits available to pensioners.

Commonwealth are: age and invalid pensions (which were introduced quite early in this century, in 1909 and 1910, respectively), child endowment (introduced by the Commonwealth in 1941), widows' pensions (1942), unemployment and sickness benefits (1945), hospital benefits (1946), pharmaceutical benefits (1950), and medical benefits (1953)[21].

6 SOCIAL GROUPS EXPERIENCING POVERTY[22]

Though the evidence is extensive that, for the majority of Australians, standards of living are high, and in most respects are continuing to rise, there are specific groups in the community still experiencing hardship. These are people who find the 'protective circle' provided by Australia's system of wage determination and social services inadequate to meet their basic needs. In consequence they are experiencing relatively low standards of living with only dim prospects of improvement. A survey of living conditions in Melbourne concluded that 'approximately one person in every eighteen appears to be living in poverty'[23].

People in these groups include the aged, families with a large number of dependent children, and unskilled recent migrants. Yet another, somewhat special group experiencing economic hardship are part-Aborigines, particularly those living on the fringes of country towns.

Some progress has been made in recent years in meeting the special requirements of these groups. In particular, low rental housing and increased social service payments and special provisions have relieved the poverty and economic hardships being experienced. But there are still some who, it can be strongly claimed, have not been provided for adequately or quickly enough when the need arises and is urgent.

Suggestions for further reading

Australian Institute of Political Science, *Poverty in Australia*, Angus & Robertson, 1969;

Hancock, K. (ed.), *The National Income and Social Welfare*, Cheshire, 1965;

---

21 For a more detailed review of Commonwealth 'cash benefits to persons', see Boxer (ed.), *op. cit.*, pp. 25–6.

22 See Australian Institute of Political Science, *Poverty in Australia*, Angus & Robertson, 1969, especially Chap. 3 by R. F. Henderson, 'The Dimensions of Poverty in Australia', and Chap. 4 by J. Paterson, 'The Causes and Relief of Poverty'; and R. J. A. Harper, 'Survey of Living Conditions in Melbourne—1966', *Economic Record*, Vol. 43, June 1967.

23 *Ibid*, p. 288.

Harper, R. J. A. 'Survey of Living Conditions in Melbourne—
1966',—*Economic Record,* Vol. 43, June 1967, pp. 262-88;
Mishan, E. J. *The Costs of Economic Growth;*
Samuelson, P. A. and others, *Economics: Australian
edition,* Chap. 6;
Vernon Report, Vol. I, Chap. 6; and Vol. II, App. E.

Chapter 9

ECONOMIC STRATEGY

It may well be that we will never wholly solve the problem of combining economic stability with full employment and development but it is a task worthy of our best intelligence and our utmost devotion. (H. C. Coombs, The development of monetary policy in Australia, E.S.&A. Bank Research Lecture, 1954, University of Queensland Press, p. 23.)

Where inflation is concerned nearly everyone finds it convenient to confine himself to conversation. All branches of the conventional wisdom are equally agreed on the undesirability of any remedies that are effective. (J. K. Galbraith, The Affluent Society, Hamish Hamilton, 1958, pp. 164 5.)

1 INTRODUCTION

This concluding chapter reviews the strategy underlying Australian economic policy since World War II. It also examines further the problem of wage and price inflation, and discusses its significance for current policy. Inflation is perhaps the major unsolved economic problem of the period, being largely a product of the post-war strategy itself.

By the term strategy is meant the formulation of the longer-run goals of the economy and the art of directing economic activity for their achievement. Strategy differs materially from tactics; the latter concerns the short-term management of the economy aimed at meeting the former. Hence tactics play a vital role in determining the degree of success or failure of a strategy[1].

2 GOAL OF STEADY GROWTH AT FULL EMPLOYMENT

One could easily construct a long list of economic objectives. About many of them there would be considerable debate. In a democracy there needs to be widespread acceptance of an objective before it may become a successful government policy[2].

---

1 See A. Smithies, 'Australian Economic Strategy', *Economic Record*, Vol. 39, March 1963, pp. 24–5.
2 See P. H. Karmel, *Economic Policy in Australia—Ends and Means*, The G. L. Wood Memorial Lecture, 1954, M.U.P.

Australia's economic strategy since World War II has been largely dominated by the mandate to achieve maximum steady economic development at a full employment level of real income. There are other aggregative goals associated with full employment. In 1945 the Commonwealth Government in a 'White Paper' entitled 'Full Employment in Australia' set out the overall objective of national economic policy as entailing the maintenance of (i) full employment, (ii) stability of prices, (iii) equilibrium in the balance of payments, and (iv) a rapid rate of economic development.

These economic and social objectives, with the emphasis initially on full employment[3], were generally adopted by governments in other countries as well. The objectives have been appropriately viewed as centring round the problems of maintaining internal and external balance[4]. The maintenance of internal balance requires that economic policy is directed towards achieving a balance between the aggregate supply of and aggregate demand for goods and services corresponding with some acceptable definition of full employment consistent with a reasonable degree of price stability; and externally economic policy aims to maintain a sound balance between the supply of exports and demand for imports, after allowing for financial transfers.

The origin of the emphasis on attaining the maximum steady economic growth and progress at full employment, through direct government action, if necessary, dates back to the 1930s. The wastes and distress during the severe economic depression in the early 1930s and the subsequent economic stagnation strengthened the case for positive government intervention. Then the Keynesian revolution[5] in economic thought gave new hope that something positive could be done through fiscal and monetary policy to prevent the marked fluctuations in economic activity that meant periods of heavy unemployment. Out of this came the policy declarations on full employment. Largely as a by-product of this objective, the emphasis soon turned to the maintenance of steady economic growth.

---

3 An early United Nations report stated: 'Commitments to a policy of full employment are . . . contained in various Government declarations, in formal statements of policy published in the form of official documents, and in legislative enactments. In the United Kingdom, Canada and Australia, the employment policies of the Governments are stated in White Papers presented by command to Parliaments. In New Zealand and the United States, employment policies are embodied in Employment Acts'. Source: United Nations, *Maintenance of Full Employment*, New York, 1949, p. 9.

4 For recent discussions of policies for meeting internal and external balance, see Snape, *International Trade and the Australian Economy*, Chaps 4 and 5; and Perkins, *International Policy for the World Economy*, Chaps 2 and 7.

5 This followed the publication of J. M. Keynes' *General Theory of Employment, Interest and Money*, Macmillan, 1936.

3 ECONOMIC REASONS FOR THE EMPHASIS ON GROWTH

Economic growth was one of the first main interests of economists. But, as noted in Chapter 1[6], the conscious concern about growth as the central objective of economic policy is really a phenomenon of the period following World War II. Growth received emphasis because it was seen as the necessary means to avoiding a return to depression and large-scale unemployment. Growth is also seen as the means of raising productivity, so checking cost and price inflation.

The essential characteristic of growth is that it involves real investment which absorbs the potential savings of a fully employed economy. Furthermore, the investment may incorporate technical progress thereby helping to increase national productivity. The increase in productivity in turn permits the increase in living standards which people in contemporary society firmly desire. Thus the emphasis of economic policy today is not only on social security with full employment, but also social security with national progress through increasing productivity thereby providing the rise in living standards for everyone, either directly through the increase in real personal disposable income or indirectly through the growth of social services.

4 OTHER POLICY OBJECTIVES

There are many other economic and social goals which form part of Australia's overall economic strategy. Important goals have been indicated at various points in this book. They include, in particular, a high rate of immigration supported by heavy capital inflow on private account and the growth of industrialization. The latter has been aided by protection, and includes the associated objectives of import replacement and promotion of manufactured exports. Exports of rural products and minerals have also been fostered. Other important projects have included the considerable housing programme and the development of public assets, including major specific works such as the Snowy River Scheme (providing hydro-electric power and additional water for irrigation) and the Ord River Project in Western Australia.

Commonwealth and State Governments have provided slightly more adequate education and training for the increasing population. Government expenditure on education as a proportion of G.N.P. has risen on both current and capital accounts (see Table 45). More could be done in this field, especially for the poor, so that doors which at present are closed because of the lack of education, may be opened

---

6 See also A. H. Boxer and R. D. Freeman, 'Aspects of Post-War Economic Growth', in Boxer (ed.), *Aspects of the Australian Economy*, p. 113.

TABLE 45

GOVERNMENT* EXPENDITURE ON GOODS AND SERVICES AND TRANSFER PAYMENTS AS A PROPORTION
OF G.N.P., AUSTRALIA, SELECTED YEARS, 1938-9 TO 1968-9

Type of outlay	1938-9 $m	1938-9 % of G.N.P.	1948-9 $m	1948-9 % of G.N.P.	1958-9 $m	1958-9 % of G.N.P.	1968-9 $m	1968-9 % of G.N.P.
A Net expenditure on goods and services								
(a) Current:								
War and defence	26	1·4	89	2·0	363	2·9	1012	3·7
Education	} 92	} 5·0	53	1·2	236	1·9	739	2·7
Public health and welfare			48	1·1	165	1·3	428	1·6
Other†			166	3·7	451	3·6	1151	4·2
TOTAL CURRENT	118	6·5	356	8·0	1215	9·7	3330	12·3
(b) Capital:								
Education			6	0·1	69	0·6	204	0·8
Public health			6	0·1	38	0·3	77	0·3
Development of resources and assistance to industry			45	1·0	170	1·4	338	1·2
Transport and communication			125	2·8	483	3·9	1209	4·5
Power, fuel, and light			44	1·0	242	1·9	432	1·6
Other††			64	1·4	115	0·9	293	1·1
TOTAL CAPITAL	112	6·1	290	6·5	1117	8·9	2553	9·4
(c) Total Current and Capital	230	12·6	646	14·4	2332	18·6	5883	21·7

B Transfer payments:								
Cash benefits to persons	50	3·3	223	5·0	698	5·6	1442	5·3
Interest	106	5·8	182	4·1	320	2·6	666	2·5
Subsidies**	6	0·3	60	1·3	49	0·4	226	0·8
Other***	—		34	0·8	47	0·4	205	0·8
TOTAL TRANSFERS	172	9·4	499	11·2	1114	8·9	2539	9·4
C Gross national product	1824		4471		12,524		27,114	

Notes:
    * Includes all public authorities.
    † Includes law, order, and public safety, repatriation, development of resources and assistance to industry, immigration, civil aviation, and all other.
    †† Includes welfare, housing, and other.
    ** Subsidies are designed to aid particular industries such as dairying, wheat, ship-building, and oil exploration.
    *** Includes overseas grants and contributions, and grants towards private capital expenditure.
    Gaps indicate that data are not available.

Sources: Commonwealth of Australia, *National Income and Expenditure, 1954–55* and *1968–69*; and Commonwealth Bureau of Census and Statistics, *Australian National Accounts, 1948–9* to *1962–3*, and *1967–8*.

to them. Resources are also absorbed in meeting the needs of defence. In general, the policies are directed at the promotion of political and social stability, freedom, and security within an environment of steady economic growth providing rising living standards.

Even where there has been substantial agreement and acceptance of particular objectives there has still, of course, been considerable room for divergent views between different political parties about the best or fastest tactics for their achievement. Differences arise through variations in the order of priorities of the objectives or through interpretations to be given to alternative policies. In a situation of mostly full employment, as has been experienced in Australia since World War II, differences have ensued between the Commonwealth and the State Governments about the best allocation of Australia's scarce resources of labour and capital among the many competing ends. The economic strategy to follow would be to allocate the labour and capital where they would be most productive[7]. Differences have also arisen over the interpretation of the interrelationship between key economic variables and over the appropriate economic policy to achieve internal and external balance.

5 THE GROWING IMPORTANCE OF GOVERNMENT

The active participation of governments in promoting a strategy of rapid economic development of the Australian economy with rising living standards has entailed a substantial increase in the proportion of G.N.P. generated by government expenditure on goods and services. This change since the 1930s justifies the characterization of Australia as having become 'a semi-planned economy'. Table 45 shows that total government expenditure in 1938-9 equalled about 12·6 per cent of G.N.P. In 1948-9 the proportion was only a little higher at 14·4 per cent. Since then there has been a considerable increase, reaching about 22 per cent in the years 1967-9[8].

As Chart 10 indicates, the increase of government expenditure has not been at a steady rate. After rising steeply to 21 per cent in 1951-2, it declined to a level of between 18 and 19 per cent during the period 1953-4 to 1963-4. Then a sharp recovery occurred, mainly through

---

7 This allocation may be assisted by using appropriate techniques of investment appraisal which are described as benefit-cost analysis. For an explanation of the main features of this approach, see Commonwealth of Australia, *Supplement to the Treasury Information Bulletin: Investment Analysis*, July 1966.

8 Nevertheless, 'the government sector's share in overall activity is lower in Australia than in most of the leading western countries including the United States, Canada, the United Kingdom, France, and Sweden'. Boxer, 'Public Finance', in Boxer (ed.), *op. cit.*, p. 23.

CHART 10
GOVERNMENT EXPENDITURE ON GOODS AND SERVICES AND TRANSFER PAYMENTS AS A PROPORTION OF G.N.P., AUSTRALIA, 1938–9 AND 1948–9 TO 1968–9

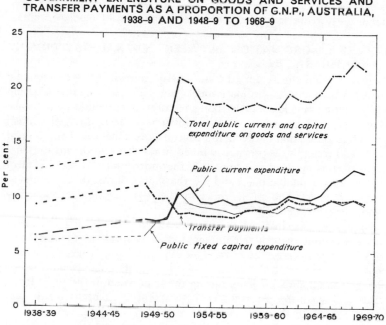

Sources: As for Table 45

current expenditure (notably in defence and education), and to a smaller extent through capital expenditure.

By contrast, transfer payments[9] as a proportion of G.N.P. (see Table 45 and Chart 10) have overall been fairly steady in recent years at about the proportion of 1938-9 but there have been significant changes in the relative importance of sub-items. In particular, the share of cash benefits to persons has been significantly higher throughout the post-war period than in 1938-9. This has been compensated for by the substantial fall in the burden of the public debt (that is, interest as a proportion of G.N.P.). Table 45 shows that while the total interest bill has risen by just over five times between 1938-9 and 1968-9, the burden has fallen by a little over half. The reduced interest burden reflects partly the fact noted in Chapter 7 that a major part of public capital expenditure since World War II has been

---

9 Transfer payments are conventionally treated in the national income statistics as not contributing to G.N.P.

financed from taxation (and hence the total debt has not increased as fast as might have been so). The interest burden has also been significantly reduced by the considerable inflation of money income.

6 CLOSE CO-ORDINATION BETWEEN CENTRAL GOVERNMENT AND CENTRAL BANK

A major requirement for the successful pursuit of the economic goals has been close co-ordination between the various bodies initiating and directing policies. Two striking features of economic policy since World War II compared to the 1930s have been, first, the much greater co-ordination between the central government and the central bank; and secondly, as previously noted in reference to the institutional developments outlined in Chapter 7, the much greater overall control now exercised on the one hand by the Commonwealth Government over fiscal policy, and on the other by the central bank over monetary policy.

Because of the close co-ordination between the central government and the central bank it is common today to speak of them as one, namely, the monetary authority. The days have gone when the central bank could dictate to the Loan Council what its policy should be, as did the Commonwealth Bank during the depression in the early 1930s when it forced the Australian Governments (Commonwealth and State) to reduce their deficits by increasing tax rates and reducing expenditure[10]. Moreover, bank legislation ensures that this relationship will not arise again. The major post-war objectives of Australia's economic policy, as outlined above, were written into or implied in the 1945 legislation which set out the functions of Australian central bank activities. These objectives have been repeated in the *Banking Act 1959-66* thus:

'It is the duty of the Board, within the limits of its powers, to ensure that the monetary and banking policy of the Bank is directed to the greatest advantage of the people of Australia and that the powers of the Bank . . . are exercised in such a manner as, in the opinion of the Board, will best contribute to —
   (a) the stability of the currency in Australia;
   (b) the maintenance of full employment in Australia; and
   (c) the economic prosperity and welfare of the people of Australia[11].'

---

10 See Giblin, *The Growth of a Central Bank*, Chap. 6.
11 As quoted in *Reserve Bank of Australia: Functions and Operations*, 1969, p. 4.

The Act also

> 'lays down the procedure which would be followed in the event of a difference of opinion arising between the Government and the Bank Board as to whether the monetary and banking policy of the Bank is directed to the greatest advantage of the people of Australia (as required under the Bank's charter), but these provisions have never been called into use.
>
> The Act provides that if a difference of opinion cannot be resolved by discussion between the Treasurer and the Board, the Treasurer may make a recommendation to the Government which may, by order, determine the policy to be adopted by the Bank[12].'

7 THE PROBLEM OF INFLATION

While most developed countries have maintained high levels of employment or mostly full employment with fairly rapid growth since World War II (as seen in Chapter 2), and Australia's performance has been one of the most successful especially in respect to employment, it has not been without other serious economic problems. For Australia (as for most countries) there have at times been serious strains on the balance of payments, requiring restrictive policies to reduce imports and safeguard the level of international reserves in order to preserve external viability. The periods of restriction, in particular the more severe ones, have contributed to recessions in economic activity[13].

Explanation of the balance of payments difficulties lies largely in the interrelationship between the forces of aggregate supply and aggregate demand associated with the degree of full employment and the relation between internal and external prices. In general, a high and rising level of economic activity has been associated with increasing prices and balance of payments pressures. Australia's marginal propensity to import has tended to rise as full or over-full employment is reached. This tendency appeared to be particularly strong in the 1950s and early 1960s, and contributed to Australia's balance of payments crises during that time[14].

The objective of price stability, as well as that of the maintenance of full employment, has been given considerable emphasis in practically all countries. Nevertheless, most countries have experienced periods of more or less severe inflation of costs and prices, though

---

12 *Ibid*, p. 3.
13 See Boehm, 'Economic Fluctuations', and Snape, 'International Trade', being Chaps 3 and 4, respectively, in Boxer (ed.), *op. cit.*
14 *Ibid*, especially pp. 51–5.

CHART 11
RELATION BETWEEN INFLATION AND UNEMPLOYMENT, AUSTRALIA, 1956–69

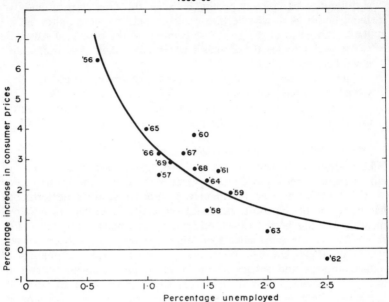

Sources: Increase in consumer prices computed from data in Commonwealth Bureau of Census and Statistics, *Monthly Review of Business Statistics* (various issues); and percentage unemployed as for Chart 3.

there have been some significant differences between individual countries in the rate of inflation at particular times. This may be seen in Table 46, which shows, for certain countries, index numbers of consumer prices for selected years during the 1950s and 1960s. The Table indicates that the increase in consumer prices in Australia, in particular in the 1960s, has not been greatly different from that in other developed countries, but distinctly better than in certain developing countries[15].

8 THE 'PHILLIPS CURVE'
The problem of cost and demand inflation has been illuminated for several countries by showing the relationship between the percentage unemployed and the percentage change in prices in terms of a diagram

---

15 For a detailed analysis of the trends in prices and cost in Australia during the period 1939–64 in comparison with the countries with which she trades, see *Vernon Report*, Vol. II, pp. 590–9.

called the Phillips curve (after Professor A. W. Phillips)[16]. A Phillips curve for Australia is presented in Chart 11. In order to make the values of the two variables contemporaneous, the percentage change in the consumer price index between calendar years (shown on the vertical scale) is related to the percentage unemployed in the year ended six months earlier (shown on the horizontal axis)[17].

The chart is presented principally in support of the notion that there is an inverse correlation between the change in prices and the level of unemployment. The inverse relation is illustrated by the fitted curve[18]. A curvilinear relation between the change in prices and the unemployment rate would seem to describe the demand and cost forces: prices rise increasingly faster as the economy moves to full employment and over-full employment, and prices change only slowly as the unemployment rate increases from a situation near full employment. The scatter of the points clearly demonstrates that the relationship is a loose one. Indeed, though it is possible, it would be surprising to find an exact relation with the points falling neatly on a smooth curve. The economic system is far more complex and variable than that.

Two interrelated factors contributing to the scatter of the points are, first, the varying time-lags associated with the demand and cost forces pushing up prices, and secondly, structural and institutional changes. The regression analysis suggested that the major part of the influence of lags has been allowed for in the contemporaneous figures on an annual basis. But some part of the demand and cost forces (possibly a variable proportion from year to year) would almost certainly affect prices in a later period.

The lag may vary not only from time to time but also from enterprise to enterprise. Some structural changes contributing to the scatter of the points would tend to be stronger in the short run, and would include especially the influence of the weather on the state of the harvest, overseas disturbances, and the state of the trade cycle. In

---

16 For a brief theoretical exposition of this curve and a critical discussion of 'an Australian Phillips curve', see P. A. Samuelson, K. Hancock, and R. Wallace, *Economics· Australian edition*, pp. 386–7 and 844–6.

17 Regressions of the change in prices on the unemployed percentage were computed for the periods 1954–69, 1956–69, and 1959–69 with the variables taken contemporaneously and with the changes in prices lagged three months and six months. The most significant results were obtained for the data shown in the chart.

18 The fitted curve to the points in the chart was computed from the regression

$$y = -1 \cdot 01 + 4 \cdot 65 \cdot \frac{1}{x}$$
$$(0 \cdot 69)$$

where y is the percentage change in prices and x is the percentage unemployed. The proportion of the variance of y explained by the regression equation (R^2) is 79·4 per cent.

TABLE 46

INDEX NUMBERS OF CONSUMER PRICES IN SELECTED COUNTRIES, 1951–1969
(Base of each index: Year 1963=100)

Year	Argentina (Buenos Aires)	Australia	Canada	France	Germany (West)	India	Indonesia (Djakarta)
1951	6	66	85	62	81	77	
1954	10	82	87	69	81	75	
1957	15	91	92	73	87	82	
1960	55	97	96	92	92	92	13
1961	63	100	97	95	94	94	17
2	81	100	98	95	97	97	46
3	100	100	100	100	100	100	100
4	122	102	102	103	102	113	205
1965	157	106	104	106	106	124	830
6	207	110	108	109	110	137	9,502
7	268	113	112	112	111	156	25,612
8	311	116	117	117	113	160	57,712
Quarter							
Sept. 1969		120	123	125	116		
Dec. 1969		121	124	126	117		

Year	Italy	Japan	Netherlands	New Zealand	Sweden	United Kingdom	United States of America
1951	71	65	78	67	68	67	85
1954	78	77	81	80	74	77	87
1957	83	79	89	86	83	87	92
1960	87	83	94	94	91	91	97
1961	89	87	94	96	93	94	98
2	93	93	96	98	97	98	99
3	100	100	100	100	100	100	100
4	106	104	106	104	103	103	101
1965	111	111	110	107	109	108	103
6	113	116	116	110	116	113	106
7	118	121	120	117	121	115	109
8	119	128	125	122	123	121	114
Quarter							
Sept. 1969		136		129		127	121
Dec. 1969		137		129		129	122

Note: Gaps indicate that data are not available.
Sources: Commonwealth Bureau of Census and Statistics, *Monthly Review of Business Statistics*, June 1970, p. 28; and *Official Year Book of the Commonwealth of Australia* (various issues; 1951, 1954, and 1957 recomputed to base 1963 = 100).

respect to the latter, a price increase resulting from a wage increase which cannot be absorbed by an increase in productivity tends to take place more slowly in recession phases, when trade is more competitive. Some price increases may also be delayed for political reasons.

The scatter of the points does mean, however, that the usefulness of the Phillips curve is limited as a means of predicting precisely what the result will be at a particular time. Nevertheless, it is a helpful theoretical device for illustrating the dilemma which has faced policy-makers since World War II regarding the underlying relationship between wages, prices, and unemployment. It also helps to clarify the objective of economic policy: namely, to push the Phillips curve downwards and to the left in the direction of getting a smaller rise in prices for the situation of full employment (which corresponds with about 1 per cent of unemployment).

The downward slope from left to right of the Phillips curve suggests that an increase in unemployment would moderate or elimi-nate the price inflation. Empirical research indicates that the level of unemployment at which price stability would be attained varies for different countries because of structural and institutional differences between them. The level may vary for the same country over time also for structural and institutional changes. Tentative results initially obtained by Phillips for Australia from an analysis of the relationship between unemployment and wage increases indicated that about 3 per cent unemployment could be expected to lead to price stability[19]. In fact, since World War II price stability in Australia has been achieved with a lower rate of unemployment of between 2 and 2·5 per cent. But this was only for a brief period[20]. Only twice has the annual unemployment rate reached or been higher than 2 per cent. In 1961-2 the percentage unemployed was 2·5 per cent and in 1962-3 it was about 2 per cent. These were also years of price stability in Australia (see Table 46).

---

19 A. W. Phillips, *Wage Changes and Unemployment in Australia, 1947–1958*, Economic Monograph No. 219 of the Economic Society of Australia and New Zealand, N.S.W. Branch, and Monograph No. 14 of the Victorian Branch.

20 It is the years of higher unemployment that are not well represented by the fitted curve in Chart 11. This is probably partly because of the limited experience of price stability.

An extrapolation of the regression result in Chart 11 suggests that for the period 1956–69 an unemployment rate of 4·6 per cent would have been required to restrain the demand and cost forces sufficiently to provide price stability. But this is very hypothetical. The regression result which was obtained for the period 1959–69, namely

$$y = -2·10 + 6·47 . \frac{1}{x} \qquad (R^2 = 76·3 \text{ per cent}),$$
$$(1·20)$$

indicates that an unemployment rate of 3·1 per cent would have led to price stability.

For the United Kingdom[21] an unemployment rate of $2\frac{1}{2}$ per cent and for the United States[22] of 5 to 6 per cent may be required to maintain pay increases compatible with productivity increase and price stability[23]. Society it seems faces a choice of either low unemployment with creeping inflation, or high unemployment with price stability.

The social and political choice of Australians has been for the maintenance of as high a level of employment as possible[24]. Full or near-full employment has provided not only greater social security and a basic self confidence in workers about the future, but it has almost certainly also ensured more rapid rates of economic growth and productivity increase than would have been achieved with higher levels of unemployment. Higher unemployment would have led to slower population growth, particularly through a lower rate of immigration. What Australians have been doing instead, in not abandoning the strategy of a high rate of growth, is learning to live with a tolerable rate of inflation[25].

9 SOCIAL AND ECONOMIC EFFECTS OF INFLATION

It is important to recognize that the above choice of 'low unemployment with creeping inflation' is only a 'second best' strategy, and that

---

21 A. W. Phillips, 'The Relation between Unemployment and the Rate of Change of Money Wage Rates in the United Kingdom, 1861–1957', *Economica*, Vol. 25, November 1958.

22 P. A. Samuelson and R. M. Solow, 'Analytical Aspects of Anti-Inflation Policy', *American Economic Review*, Vol. 50, May 1960.

23 For a critical examination of the relation between unemployment, wages, and prices, and of the implications for Australia, see Isaac, *Wages and Productivity*, pp. 84–8.

24 The Vernon Committee echoed the choice of Australians thus:

'We wish to stress that, while there may be some level of unemployment, probably greater than that experienced in Australia in the past 15 years, which would eliminate internal pressure on prices, we utterly reject the notion that contriving of such a level would be a proper means for securing price stability. . . . Such a proposition [would] offend against generally accepted social values.' *Vernon Report*, Vol. I, p. 43.

25 Evidence of the official attitude towards, and apparent tolerance of, the creeping inflation experienced during recent years is implied in the following passage through the concern expressed, in mid-1969, that the rate of price inflation may have been accelerating: 'There is some evidence . . . that upward pressures on prices have intensified. It is true that in the year to the June quarter of 1969 the consumer price index increased by only 2·9 per cent. Between the June quarters of 1967 and 1968 the index also rose by 2·9 per cent. . . . The *danger*, once costs and prices begin to climb *faster*, is that business and other calculations will be based on inflationary expectations.' Source: Commonwealth of Australia, *The Australian Economy 1969*, Canberra, July 1969, p. 14, italics added.

The *Australian Financial Review* (in its 'leader' of 20 April 1970) described the public's attitude to inflation thus: 'Current convention seems to make 3 per cent an acceptable annual average, though good economic management should make it less, subject to the vagaries of drought.'

there are some serious problems and complex tactical policy implications flowing from the creeping inflation. This raises a number of questions which are well beyond the scope of this book. But there are several aspects which can be referred to briefly here.

A major problem is that the effects of inflation are conflicting and uncertain. In some circumstances inflation stimulates economic activity and growth by a favourable influence on profit expectations. There is an incentive to produce at the current lower prices. It is easier to correct errors in a market that is increasing in real and money terms. In a competitive society the inflationary tendencies through both demand and wage pressures encourage the introduction of labour-saving techniques, thereby increasing labour productivity and so supporting the higher wages.

Another favourable effect of inflation is that it reduces the burden of debt. People purchasing homes and consumer durable goods have found the burden of interest payments and the repayment of loans progressively lightened as their wages have risen during the inflation. Similarly, the inflation has, as already noted, contributed appreciably to the reduction of the interest burden of the public debt.

Statistical studies in other countries of the relationship between inflation and productivity have been quite inconclusive, some showing a favourable relation, others unfavourable[26]. The considerable inflation in recent years in Argentina and particularly Indonesia has not been accompanied by rapid growth in either country (see Tables 5 and 46); in fact, in Indonesia, as noted in Chapter 2, there appears to have been retrogression during the period 1958-66.

There are five unfavourable effects of inflation which justify the continuing attempt to prevent or restrain it. First, a danger of inflation for an 'open' economy such as Australia in which international trade plays a major role is that the internal inflation will be faster than in competing countries. This was particularly so for Australia from the early 1950s to the early 1960s and contributed to her balance of payments crises in 1955-6 and 1960-1, and hence to the introduction on those occasions of more restrictive monetary and fiscal policies. These policies in turn contributed to recession periods during which the rate of economic growth slowed down. But, in the 1960s, the rate of inflation in Australia was mostly slightly less than that in other countries, so the influence of the inflation on the balance of payments has not appeared important.

Secondly, inflation leads to distortions in the structure of the economy. The distortions may not reveal themselves immediately, but may have a cumulative destabilizing influence on the future level of

---

26 For a review of these studies, see Isaac, *op. cit.*, p. 83.

economic activity. Structural maladjustments may occur in the public
sector as well as in the private. The inflation in Australia has been a
particularly important disruptive influence on Commonwealth-State
financial relations. This disruption highlights the imbalance between
the Commonwealth and the States in the allocation of incomes and
expenditure. It especially emphasizes the fact that the States' finances
— unlike the Commonwealth's — have suffered under inflation because of their lack of an adequate growth tax which, as noted in
Chapter 7, the Commonwealth possesses in the inbuilt flexibility of
progressive income tax. The States have felt the full brunt of inflation on the cost side, for their expenditure has risen proportionately
with the inflation of costs and prices, thereby effectively reducing or
restricting the real resources available to them. This effect of inflation
has been a major reason for the dissatisfaction of the States over their
financial relations with the Commonwealth.

A third serious weakness of inflation is that it stimulates speculation.
This, in fact, may contribute to the structural distortions. Rash
speculation may lead to inflationary pressures and bottlenecks in the
supply-demand nexus by diverting scarce resources from sounder projects which will be more productive and efficient in the long run.
Speculative activities contributed to the exuberant spending boom in
1960 in Australia, when there was a strong optimism supported by
the belief that inflation would continue. This contributed to a growing
willingness to substitute less liquid assets (e.g. land and industrial
shares, whose prices tend to rise with the general price level) for bank
deposits in anticipation of higher incomes from dividends or earnings
and/or capital gain. The position was quickly reversed during the
1961 recession and the scramble for liquid assets. The real side of the
boom involved an exaggeration of anticipated demand which in turn
led to an oversupply of certain goods and services, notably houses,
land sub-divisions, and consumer-durable goods. While the excess
capacity was worked off, recovery was delayed.

Fourthly, major social and economic problems arise from the redistribution of income and wealth caused by inflation. This problem of
redistribution has also been part of the difficulties underlying Commonwealth-State finances. In general, the redistribution is most serious
for those on fixed incomes, for retired persons and widows[27]. These

---

27 The unfavourable effects of inflation have materially contributed to the
substantial increase since World War II in the proportion of people of pension-
able age actually drawing the pension. In 1948–9, 39·2 per cent of persons
eligible by age drew the pension, but by 1967–8 the proportion had reached 54·6
per cent.* Relaxation in the means test on income and property to which the
payment of the pension is subject would also have contributed to this increase.
*Source: *Official Year Book of the Commonwealth of Australia*, (various issues).

people may suffer much from the erosion in value of their savings, superannuation benefits, and fixed property income. Others whose real income may be squeezed by internal inflation are farmers and exporters whose prices are fixed on the world market.

Finally, there is the real danger that the rate of inflation may accelerate, particularly as the result of speculation and attempts to safeguard income and wealth against the effects of continually rising prices. It is the experience of persistently rising prices that has led a number of countries[28] to attempt to apply an incomes policy, though no country has found such a policy easy to establish or maintain.

10 THE CASE FOR AN INCOMES POLICY

An essential objective of an incomes policy is to restrain the rate of increase in money wages and other incomes (including profits) to a rate compatible with productivity increases and stable prices. This would greatly improve upon the 'second best' policy situation described above, in particular it would better safeguard the balance of payments and protect those not able to hedge against or to benefit from inflation.

It is an economic fact, not a political one, that the emphasis in an incomes policy must be on wage restraint. This is because of the importance of wages in prime costs and because a large number of consumer prices are fixed on the basis of a constant percentage mark-up on prime costs. Thus it is a natural development that serious attention should be given to containing increases in money wages within productivity increases. If mark-ups remain constant, it follows that profits will rise proportionally with money wages. This helps to explain the relative constancy of the share of G.N.P. accruing to wages and profits, as noted in Chapter 7.

An incomes policy has appeared necessary because of the lack of any alternative means of constraining the inflationary effects of pay and price decisions. In the conditions of full or near-full employment and creeping inflation, as has been experienced since World War II, employers (for both demand-pull and cost-push reasons) have finally allowed — or not been greatly disturbed when — wages and costs have risen faster than productivity. This is because they know that they can raise prices fairly easily to cover that part of the increase in unit costs which cannot be absorbed by an increase in productivity.

The facts for Australia are that while national productivity has risen during the period 1953-4 to 1968-9 at an average rate of about $2\frac{1}{2}$ per cent per annum, average weekly earnings have increased at the

---

28 These countries have included France, the Netherlands, Sweden, United States of America, and United Kingdom.

rate of about 5 per cent per annum. The difference between these two rates of 2½ per cent is also approximately the rate at which the consumer price index has risen. It must be allowed that the consumer price index is not a general index of all prices. Nevertheless, the price inflation which Australia has experienced simply reflects the fact that earnings (including award wages[29]) and profits have both increased at a rate substantially faster than would be the objective of an incomes policy in which the ideal would be for incomes to increase in step with national productivity.

Most wage earners have shared, though not all in equal proportion, in wage increases which have been faster than the increase in productivity. They have shared through award payments rising faster than productivity and also through over-award payments which have contributed to earnings drift.

In view of the creeping inflation, the Arbitration Commission's introduction of a 'minimum wage' (for adult male employees only) in 1966 was especially appropriate[30]. The minimum wage ensures that lowly paid workers, who have benefited little or not at all from the substantial wage increases granted through margins and over-award payments, could share more fully in the increase in material welfare[31]. They can share more fully because the increases in the minimum wage in 1966 and 1969, which were greater than the general wage increases granted by the Commission in those years, compensated for

---

29 Between June 1954 and June 1969, the average minimum weekly wage rate index (adult males, all groups) rose from 99·5 to 175·6, respectively (base: 1954 = 100·0). This gives a compound rate between the terminal years of 3·8 per cent a year. Source of wage index: Commonwealth Bureau of Census and Statistics, *Wage Rates and Earnings* (various issues).

30 In the 1966 National Wage Judgment (in which the basic wage was increased by $2), the Commission unanimously provided for a minimum wage which it set at the basic wage plus $3·75. Three State tribunals (South Australia in 1966 and Western Australia and Tasmania in 1967) have followed the Commission in prescribing rates of minimum wage for adult males, mostly the same as in the Commonwealth awards.

The minimum wage has been increased as a result of the decision of the Commission in subsequent national wage cases; in 1967 by $1·00 a week, in 1968 by $1·35, these being the same increases as granted in total award wages. But in the 1969 National Wage Judgment, while the total weekly wage was increased by 3 per cent the minimum wage was increased by $3·50, or about 9 per cent. Source: Commonwealth Bureau of Census and Statistics, *Wage Rates and Earnings* (various issues).

31 It was the adoption of the total wage concept that has enabled the Commission to apply more effectively a minimum wage which is more appropriate to a 'needs' standard. For a fuller discussion of this aspect, see J. E. Isaac and G. W. Ford (eds), *Australian Labour Economics: Readings*, Sun Books, 1967, pp. 17–20. As Isaac and Ford explain: 'To have increased the basic wage element to a level regarded by the Commission as being more appropriate to a "needs" standard would have involved a rise in the wages of all other workers with the possibility of a severe rise in prices.' *Ibid*, p. 19.

some erosion of wage increases by price inflation, since wage increases in the aggregate (award and non-award) have exceeded the increase in productivity. If collective bargaining was to grow in importance in Australia in the determination of wages, the minimum wage would also become more important in its protection of workers whose bargaining power is relatively weak.

Australia has no incomes policy in the narrow sense defined in the opening paragraph of this section. Nevertheless, the principles of wage determination which the Arbitration Commission has taken into account in recent years go some considerable way towards meeting the essential requirements of an incomes policy. In recent years the Commission appears to have recognized more fully its responsibility in avoiding wage inflation. Its decision to combine the basic wage and secondary wage into a total wage should lessen the risk of wage increases which are beyond capacity to pay. At the same time, the Commonwealth Government, in intervening in national wage cases in the public interest, has become more helpful and positive in the advice it offers to the Commission concerning the Government's views on the state of the economy and the capacity to absorb increased wages.

Indeed, whether the Commission likes it or not, it has, in the words of the Vernon Committee, 'become an incomes tribunal de facto even though its statutory duty is to settle industrial disputes'[32]. Furthermore, as noted in Chapter 7, the Commission's influence is considerable. It has become a national wage-fixing body and should recognize its concern with economic policy as a whole so that its decisions complement as far as possible fiscal and monetary policies. But this assumes that demand inflation is effectively controlled.

11 ECONOMIC FORECASTING AND PLANNING

The degree of success of Australian economic strategy — in particular the goal of maximum steady economic growth with full employment and a satisfactory degree of price stability — depends greatly upon the choice and successful integration of appropriate economic policies. The choice of policies and their direction highlight the need for accurate diagnoses and forecasts of the state and future course of economic activity. This need has increased markedly with the growth of the semi-planned economy involving the dual and closely related aspects of the greater size of government income-generating expenditure and the mandate to guide the economy towards its goals by effective policies. It is for these reasons that 'indicative planning'

---

32 *Vernon Report*, Vol. I, p. 145.

involving long-term economic forecasting and planning have come increasingly into the focus of interest of policy makers in recent years. The Vernon Committee observed that:

> Most developed economies appear to have recognized the need for the orderly consideration of long-term trends and long-range problems as a supplement to the ordinary processes of short-term economic management. We believe that Australia could, with great advantage, move in the same direction[33].'

In France the setting of targets in terms of five-year plans has become an integrated part of economic policy since early after World War II. In the United Kingdom, Sweden, and Canada medium and long-term prognoses have at least been used as sources of information by public authorities and private enterprise in the planning of future policy[34].

The Vernon Committee recommended the establishment of an 'Advisory Council on Economic Growth' on the lines of the Economic Council of Canada which was established in 1963. The Committee felt that the Canadian 'seems to be more relevant to the Australian situation'; and it added:

> 'the Economic Council of Canada . . . has the broad function of advising "how Canada can achieve the highest possible levels of employment and efficient production, in order that the country may enjoy a high and consistent rate of economic growth and that all Canadians may share in rising standards of living"[35].'

The Committee rejected the suggestion that Australia should adopt 'anything in the nature of a national economic plan involving individual industry targets . . ., as this would require elaborate machinery and, in all probability, a considerably higher degree of government intervention in the economy than would be acceptable in this country'[36]. But the Committee favoured 'periodical statements by the

---

33 *Vernon Report*, Vol. I, p. 451. See also J. B. Condliffe, *The Development of Australia*, Ure Smith, 1964. It is significant that in this privately sponsored report by the Stanford Research Institute for the Australian Research Development Foundation, it was stated (p. 15): 'The most important recommendation of this report in respect of the public sector of the economy, is that the Commonwealth Government should create a National Development Council to serve as a fact-finding body at the service of both the States and the Commonwealth.'

34 Active steps towards longer-term economic planning are also being taken in New Zealand. See A. R. Low, *Indicative Planning—The New Zealand Experience*, paper presented at the Conference of Australian and New Zealand Economists, University of Melbourne, May 1970.

35 *Vernon Report*, Vol. I, p. 452.

36 *Ibid*, p. 450.

Government that long-term policies will be directed to the achievement of a certain rate of economic growth'[37] which for the next decade the Committee set at 5 per cent per annum.

The Prime Minister (Sir Robert Menzies), in a statement revealing some misunderstanding of the Committee's recommendation regarding an Advisory Council, declared:

'We unhesitatingly reject this idea. . . . In the Australian democratic system of government based upon the consent of a free community, no government can hand over to bodies outside the government the choice of objectives and the means of attaining them in important fields of policy, particularly when such bodies would, through the power of publication, come to exercise what I have described, I hope not extravagantly, as a coercive influence upon governments[38].'

A constitutional precedent for the proposed Council already exists in the Tariff Board, which acts in an advisory capacity only, with no decision-making authority. But the Advisory Council on Growth was envisaged as operating without any specific reference from the government, which would be free to reject or accept the Council's advice as the government saw fit.

Rejection of this important Vernon Committee proposal does not mean that there is no medium-range or long-range forecasting or planning by government departments for their independent, internal use. But only three government instrumentalities publish regular projections: (i) the Commonwealth Bureau of Census and Statistics twice a year publishes a short-term forecast of private capital expenditure based on a sample survey of businesses; (ii) the Bureau of Agricultural Economics has made quarterly medium-term forecasts of rural production and exports since 1957; and (iii) the Department of National Development has furnished annually a medium-range and long-range projection of mineral exports since 1967[39]. Economic programming is clearly evident in many specific areas and for important aspects of the whole economy, outstanding examples being the Commonwealth and State budgets (containing forecasts for a twelve-month period[40]) and the migration programme. A long-term projection has been made of the population of Australia (see Table 9).

---

37 *Ibid.*
38 Commonwealth of Australia, *Parliamentary Debates*, Vol. H. of R. 47, 1965, p. 1085.
39 See pp. 73–4 above.
40 However, the Commonwealth Treasurer, Mr L. Bury, has forecast a major change in the Government's economic planning through the annual budget. Mr Bury (in Commonwealth Treasury, *Press Release*, No. 53, 8 June 1970) stated that it was his 'ambition as Treasurer to produce the first published set of forward estimates of Commonwealth expenditure' which 'go beyond the

Planning is also evident with the balance of payments, as seen in the efforts to promote exports rather than restrict the demand for imports. Special encouragement has been given to the development for export of Australia's natural resources, notably minerals and manufactured exports[41]. Benefits have followed the establishment in 1958 of both the Export Development Council and the Manufacturing Industries Advisory Council. The former, which comprises about forty members with industrial, commercial, and professional interests and government representatives, was formed to 'advise the Government on all aspects of the development of Australia's exports'[42]; while the latter, which comprises about twenty-two business leaders from various sectors of industry, was established to 'obtain objective and forward-thinking advice on the ways the business man saw the economy, and his views on possible ways of meeting the problems inherent in rapid growth'[43]. There are a number of other public and private bodies or societies which contribute to Australia's economic development in their individual fields by undertaking research work and assisting the better organization of economic activity, and also by providing a forum for debate and the dissemination of knowledge.

However, Australia lacks official, comprehensive, integrated economic forecasts and plans. It is in order to fill this gap that a need has been seen for a body such as a National Economic Advisory Council. This body could represent all major interests of private management and trade unions, and be at the service of the Commonwealth and State Governments and private businesses, its aims being to assist in a national plan to achieve the desired rate of sustained growth. Its task could include a continuing review of the economy, taking account of medium term and long-term trends and setting realistic target growth rates for major sectors, regions, and the economy as a whole, as is being attempted in other western countries. It could also undertake research and issue reports to help inform the public on the nature of economic problems and the appropriate policies

---

traditional twelve-month period'. No indication was given of the period the estimates will cover.

The Treasurer added: 'The main value in making forward estimates is that such estimates could provide us with a much wider body of knowledge and a better framework in which to make new policy decisions. In short, forward estimates could help to promote informed decisions' and become 'an integral element in planning programming budgeting'. The Treasury has already done a considerable amount of work on this task and hopes to introduce the new system in time for the 1971 budget.

41 See pp. 71–4 and 94 above.
42 *Vernon Report*, Vol. II, p. 1032.
43 Manufacturing Industry Advisory Council, *Australian Manufacturing Industry in the Next Decade*, April 1959.

to meet them. This could contribute towards a readier acceptance of desirable economic policies, hence making their success more likely.

Indicative planning requires a considerable degree of understanding and sophistication of the community. Confidence should not flag if the actual rate of growth is less than the target rate, or lead to complacency if the actual rate exceeds the target. Divergences from target would certainly call for a review of economic policy and private business decisions, and for an examination of whether the targets were realistic in the circumstances. Fluctuations could occur for independent reasons. The actual rate could vary in any year from the projected average according to such closely related influences as the overseas economic situation, the trade cycle, and the weather.

The introduction of target growth rates does not imply the imposition of a totalitarian plan. Rather it would provide a pool of common information, which should mean a more efficient management of the economy with consequent improvement in growth performance and increase in material welfare. The stock of common information would permit the assessment of the adequacy of exports, imports, capital formation, the expenditure on education and training, and other variables which play a vital part in the efficient management and desired growth of the economy.

The need for a continuing review of the economy taking account of longer-term trends has been recognized by several private institutions. The Institute of Applied Economic and Social Research at the University of Melbourne was the first body in Australia to make publicly available[44] from 1968 a quarterly review of current economic trends and fluctuations of selected indicators, together with a general view of future economic prospects in both the short and medium terms. Certain private economic and market research organizations[45] provide regular forecasts for their clients, and from the late 1960s have supplemented their detailed accounts of the current economic trends with medium-range and long-range forecasts of key sectors and of the overall growth prospects of the Australian economy into the 1980s. These private reviews and forecasts, which have the advantage of independence of political interests[46], are filling a major gap in our economic knowledge, and should facilitate more rational long-term planning for investment and consumption expenditures. They should also assist the adoption of appropriate tactics to meet the problems of short-term management in both the private and public sectors.

---

44 In *Australian Economic Review*.
45 Notably, Philip Shrapnel & Co. and W. D. Scott & Co.
46 See H. F. Lydall, 'The Economy as a Whole: Policies for Growth', *Economic Record*, Vol. 42, March 1966, p. 148.

The generally favourable economic climate and balance of payments with a fairly rapid rate of economic growth in Australia since the Vernon Committee reported in 1965 have perhaps contributed to the apparent complacency and lack of official attention to this important subject. The Vernon Committee was established with widespread support early in 1963 after considerable criticisms of the inadequacies of the short-term and long-term economic management and performance of the Australian economy. The criticisms concerned the 'stop-go' record of the 1950s and the worst post-war recession in the early 1960s involving balance of payments crises and slower rates of economic growth. But since the Committee reported there has been an absence of any serious setbacks, save for a minor recession in 1965-6, and this could be partly attributed to the severe drought conditions over much of central and eastern Australia.

However, we can never expect the economic system to perform ideally. Furthermore, our understanding of it is imperfect. Nevertheless, our knowledge of it is continually improving and enabling us to evolve institutions and policies which will meet gaps and weaknesses and make for a more successful attainment of our economic goals. By better economic management, as indicative planning should promote in both public and private enterprises, we would assist the most efficient and acceptable allocation of our scarce resources among the many competing ends. In these ways, too, we would foster the appropriate circumstances for the achievement of both maximum steady growth with social security and the desired improvements in the quality of life for everyone.

Suggestions for further reading

Arndt, H. W. *A Small Rich Industrial Country*, Part 1;
Arndt, H. W. and Corden, W. M. (eds.), *The Australian Economy*, Cheshire, 1963;
Corden, W. M. 'Australian Economic Policy Discussion in the Post-War Period: A Survey', in *American Economic Review*, Vol. 58, No. 3, Part 2, Supplement, June 1968, pp. 88-138; and M.U.P., 1968;
Firth, G. *Rising Prices in Australia*, Committee for Economic Development of Australia, October 1962;
Grant, J. McB. and others, *Economic Institutions and Policy*, Chaps 17 and 18;
Lydall, H. F. 'The Economy as a Whole: Policies for Growth', *Economic Record*, Vol. 42, March 1966, pp. 149-68;

Perkins, J. O. N. *Anti-cyclical Policy in Australia 1960-1966*, M.U.P.,
    1967; *Australia in the World Economy*, Chaps 3 and 4;
    and *International Policy for the World Economy*;
Samuelson, P. A. and others, *Economics: Australian edition*,
    Chaps 15-19 and 37-39;
Snape, R. H. *International Trade and the Australian
    Economy*, Chaps 4 and 5;
Vernon Report, Vol. I, Chap 17; and Vol. II, App. N.

LIST OF TABLES

1 Gross National Product at Factor Cost by Industry of Origin, Australia, Selected Years, 1900–1 to 1967–8, *p. 8*

2 Composition of G.N.P. at Factor Cost by Industry of Origin, Selected Countries, 1950 to 1960, *p. 9*

3 Average Annual Rates of Increase in Real G.N.P., Population, Employment, and Productivity; and Average Annual Capital Inflow and Import Surplus, Australia, Selected Periods, 1861 to 1968–9, *p. 14*

4 Average Annual Rates of Growth in G.N.P., Total Population, and G.N.P. Per Head, Australia, Selected Periods, 1861 to 1968–9, *p. 15*

5 Comparative Growth Performance and G.N.P. Per Head of Population in Selected Countries, *p. 32–3*

6 Population, Urban and Rural, Australia, Censuses 1881–1966, *p. 38*

7 Percentage Distribution of the Australian Population among the States and Territories, Certain Censuses, 1881–1966, *p. 38*

8 Total Population, Masculinity, and Rates of Increase of Population, Australia, 1861–1968, *p. 40*

9 Age Distribution of Population, Australia, Certain Censuses 1881–1966, and of Projected Population, 2001, *p. 44*

10 Average Issue of Existing Marriages, Australia, Censuses 1911–1966, *p. 45*

11 Crude Birth Rates and Fertility Rates: Australia, 1880–2 to 1965–7, *p. 46*

12 Birth Rates, by Age of Mother, Australia, Selected Years, 1921–1968, *p. 48*

13 'Ever Married' Males and Females, Percentages of Total Population of Each Sex, in Age Groups, Australia, Censuses 1891 to 1966, *p. 50*

14 Size and Rates of Growth, Population and Labour Force, Australia, Censuses 1901 to 1966, *p. 53*

15 Labour force Participation Rates, Australia, Censuses, 1911 to 1966, *p. 55*

16 Labour Force Classified by Industry Groups, Numbers, and Percentage Distribution, Australia, Censuses 1901 to 1966, *p. 58–9*

17 Percentage Changes in Numbers Engaged in Various Industries, Australia, Between Certain Censuses, 1947 to 1966, *p. 61*

18 Percentages of Population of Certain Age Groups Engaged in Full-Time Education, Australia, Certain Censuses, 1911 to 1966, *p. 63*

19 Exports of Principal Articles of Australian Produce and Gold Production as a Percentage of Total Home-Produced Merchandise Exports and Gold Production, Selected Periods, 1881 to 1968–9. *p. 68*

20 Proportion of Value of Exports of Australian Produce According to Industrial Groups, Selected Years, 1953–4 to 1967–8, *p. 70*

21 Exports and Investment as Proportions of G.N.P., Australia, Selected Periods, 1881 to 1968–9, *p. 79*

22 Average Annual Rates of Growth of Population, Real Exports and G.N.P., Australia, Selected Periods, 1861 to 1968–9, *p. 84*

23 Shifts in the Directions of Australian Exports, Selected Years, 1899 to 1968–9, *p. 91*

24 Size of Gross Fixed Capital Expenditure and of G.N.P. at Average 1959–60 Prices, Selected Years, Australia, 1948–9 to 1968–9, *p. 99*

25 Average Annual Rates of Increase of Gross Fixed Capital Expenditure, Number in Work, and G.N.P., Australia, Selected Periods 1948–9 to 1968–9, *p. 99*

26 Components of Gross Public Investment, Australia, Selected Years, 1948–9 to 1968–9, *p. 101*

27 Gross Fixed Capital Expenditure, Percentages of Total, Australia, Selected Years, 1948–9 to 1966–7, *p. 104*

28 Source of Savings for Capital Expenditure Australia, Selected Periods, 1950–1 to 1968–9, *p. 107*

29 Net Capital Imports as Percentage of Gross Fixed Capital Expenditure, Australia, Selected Periods 1861 to 1968–9, *p. 108*

30 Annual Inflow of Overseas Investment in Australia, Private Companies and Public, and Gross Private Fixed Capital Expenditure as Percentage of Private Overseas Investment, Selected Periods, 1950–1 to 1968–9, *p. 109*

31 Property Income Payable Overseas as Percentage of Merchandise Exports and G.N.P., Australia, Selected Periods, 1861 to 1968–9, *p. 116*

32 Size of Capital and Consumption Expenditure, and Growth Indicators, Selected Countries, Average 1955 to 1966. *p. 119*

33 Manufacturing: Average Employment and Total Value of Production by Major Industry Groups, Australia, Selected Years, 1903 to 1967–8, *p. 127*

34 Classification of the Major Industry Group: 'Industrial Metals, Machines, Conveyances', Australia, Selected Years, 1948–9 to 1967–8, *p. 131*

35 Average Annual Rates of Growth of Output, Employment, and Productivity in Major Industrial Divisions, Australia, 1949–50 to 1967–8, *p. 134*

36 Relative Distribution of Population and Factory Employment, by States, 1967–8, *p. 140*

37 Proportion of Population and Factory Employment in Metropolitan Areas, by States, 30 June 1961, *p. 140*

38 Imports of Merchandise According to Economic Classes and Merchandise Imports as a Percentage of G.N.P., Australia, Selected Years, 1913 to 1968–9, *p. 152*

39 Shifts in Source of Australian Imports, 1904 to 1968–9, *p. 153*

40 Receipts and Outlay of Commonwealth and State Governments, 1968–9, *p. 163*

41 Commonwealth Payments to the States Per Head of Population and Total for Australia, 1968–9, *p. 164*

42 Public Debt of the Commonwealth and the States, 1950 to 1969, *p. 170*

43 Selected Indicators of Living Standards, Australia, 1938–9 to 1968–9, *p. 202*

44 Average Annual Rates of Increase in Selected Measures of Living Standards and in G.N.P. (at 1959–60 Prices), Australia, Expressed Per Head and Per Person Employed, 1953–4 to 1968–9, *p. 203*

45 Government Expenditure on Goods and Services and Transfer Payments as a Proportion of G.N.P., Australia, Selected Years, 1938–9 to 1968–9, *p. 216–7*

46 Index Numbers of Consumer Prices in Selected Countries, 1951–1969, *p. 224–5*

LIST OF CHARTS

1 Estimates of National Product at Current and Constant Prices, Australia, 1900–1 to 1968–9, *p. 5*

2 Population of Australia, 1788 to 1969, *p. 6*

3 Percentage unemployment, Australia, 1906–1969, *p. 17*

4 Rates of Increase: Births, Deaths, Natural Increase, and Net Migration, Australia, 1860 to 1969, *p. 41*

5 G.N.P. at Current and Constant Prices, Merchandise Exports at Current and Constant Prices, Value of Gold Production, and Export Price Index, 1901–69, *p. 72*

6 Quantity of Exports of Leading Products of Australian Origin, Australia, 1900 to 1968–9, *p. 75*

7 Indexes of Export Prices, Import Prices, and Terms of Trade, Australia, 1901 to 1968–9, *p. 81*

8 Australian Labour Force and Employment, Manufacturing and Total, 1904 to 1968–9, *p. 124*

9 Indexes of Consumer Prices, Average Minimum Weekly Wage Rates, and Average Weekly Earnings, Australia, September Quarter 1947 to March Quarter 1970, *p. 192*

10 Government Expenditure on Goods and Services and Transfer Payments as a Proportion of G.N.P., Australia, 1938–9 and 1948–9 to 1968–9, *p. 219*

11 Relation Between Inflation and Unemployment, Australia, 1956–69, *p. 222*

INDEX

Age and invalid pensions, 51, 56, 162n, 210n, 211, 229n
Agriculture, 10, 70, 86, 89, 157, 172
Andrews, J., 11
Appleyard, R. T., 65
Argentina, 30, 33, 35, 76n, 224, 228
Arndt, H. W., 11, 92n, 173n, 177-9, 182-3, 199, 237
Australian Industry Development Corporation, 113-5
Australian Resources Development Bank, 115, 181-2
Australian The, 167n, 169n

Balance of payments, 21-2, 29, 92, 108, 117-8, 155-7, 192, 214, 221, 228, 230, 237
Banking: bank credit, 171-80 *pass.*; central bank, 173-6, 179, 183, 184, 198, 220-1; Commonwealth Constitution and Legislation, 159, 173-9 *pass.*, 220-1; interest rates, 174, 175n, 176, 179-84 *pass.*; liquidity convention, 176-8, 183-4; non-bank finance companies, 178-80; note issue, 22, 173-4; role of Commonwealth Government, 160, 198; short-term money market, 176, 182-4; special accounts, 174-6; S.R.D. system, 175-8; savings banks, 173, 175, 179-80; trading banks, 173-82 *pass.*; widening range of activities, 176, 179-82, 184; *see also* Monetary policy, Reserve Bank
Belgium, 9, 32, 106n, 119
Blainey, G., 11, 67n, 69n, 73n, 102n
Borrie, W. D., 65
Boxer, A. H., 13n, 24n, 27n, 35, 43n, 65, 198, 210-1, 215n, 218n, 221n
Boyer, R., 156n
Brash, D. T., 121
Brigden, J. B., 148n
B.H.P. Co. Ltd, 136, 140-1, 147n
Bruce, S. M. (Lord), 12
Brunt, Maureen, 11, 135, 138n, 157
Bury, L. H. E., 234n

Bush, M. G., 19, 23n, 35
Bushnell, J. A., 138n
Butlin, N. G., 5, 8, 10n, 15, 73n, 79, 98n, 102n, 108, 116
Butlin, S. J., 21n
Butter, 7, 67-8, 75-7, 81, 89, 144

Canada, 9, 30-5 *pass.*, 57, 62, 76n, 91, 110, 113, 119-25 *pass.*, 153, 160n, 209, 214n, 218n, 224, 233
Capital accumulation, 3, 21, 25, 35, 51, 96-122, 166, 215; *see also* Investment
Capital deepening, 27, 60-1, 96-8, 100, 106, 121, 132-3
Capital, definition and contribution of, 4, 20-1, 96-8, 132-5
Capital formation: *see* Investment
Capital inflow: benefits and costs, 65, 111-5, 129, 145; dependence on, 2, 12, 14, 21-2, 26-9, 76, 89, 106-11, 117-8; policy towards, 113-5, 117, 171, 215; *see also*: Economic growth, Overseas borrowing, Overseas investment
Capital widening, 27, 35, 51, 96-8, 100, 106, 120-1
Cash benefits to persons, 210, 217, 219
Ceylon, 33, 35, 52, 91
Chifley, J. B., 115, 174
China (mainland), 90-2
Clark, C., 5, 15, 124
Closer settlement, 10, 69, 76, 85, 88, 159
Coal, 25, 69, 71, 90, 92, 140-1, 187
Coghlan, T. A., 15
Cohen, A. M., 19, 23n, 35
Commonwealth-State finances: cooperative federalism, 172-3, 198; dominance of Commonwealth, 159-63, 171-3, 198; effects of inflation, 169, 229; Financial Agreement of 1927, 161-2, 172; financial arrangements since 1945, 165-72; Grants Commission, 165-7, 172-3; growth tax, and States' lack of, 169, 171,

229; Loan Council, 161-2, 168-9, 172-3, 220; payments to the States, 164-73, 229; Premiers' and Ministerial Conferences, 166, 172-3; unitary state, 160, 173; *see also* Income tax, Public debt, Taxation
Competition, 135-6, 138, 195, 226, 228
Condliffe, J. B., 233n
Constitution of Australia, 159-62, 165, 174, 179, 186, 188
Consumption expenditure, 105-6, 118-9, 161, 201-4, 208
Coombs, H. C., 177n, 180, 213
Corden, W. M., 143n, 147n, 157, 237
Crawford, J. G. (Sir John), 95
C.S.I.R.O., 85, 87
Curtin, J., 161

Dairy Farming, 69, 70, 77, 85-8, 217; *see also* Butter
Davidson, F. G., 157
Denison, E. F., 34n, 35
Denmark, 9, 32, 34, 106n, 119, 120
Downing, R. I., 4n, 27, 43n, 195n
Drane, N. T., 132n
Droughts, 12, 15, 20, 28, 71, 78, 81, 123, 227n, 237
Drysdale, P., 95
Dunsdorfs, E., 74n

Economic depressions of 1890s and 1930s, 15-28 *pass.*, 42, 47, 49, 51, 56, 78, 80-2, 85, 92, 94, 115-7, 123-4, 128-9, 138, 144-5, 165, 191-2, 203, 214, 220; *see also* Unemployment
Economic growth: and population growth, 3, 25-6, 35, 37, 119-21, 143, 148, 227; importance, 1, 27, 213-5; limitations of size of market, 10, 27, 66, 90, 98, 125, 136-42 *pass.*, 147, 154-7; problems of measuring, 3-4, 98, 118, 203-4; meaning and sources of, 2-3, 25; rate of, 1, 12-36 *pass.*, 52, 65, 82, 113, 119, 128-9, 134, 143, 173, 201-4, 214, 227, 234-7; relationship with immigration and capital inflow, 12, 26-9, 89, 108, 148, 215; trend and cycle, 12-29, 31, 34, 123-4, 215; widespread interest in, 1-2, 23-4, 64, 200-1; *see also* Exports, Immigration, Investment, Technical progress
Economic strategy: and tactics, 213-5, 218, 227-8, 232; co-ordination and overall control, 197-8, 220-1; forecasting and planning, 135, 232-7; price stability, 1, 197, 214, 220, 226-7, 230, 232; steady state growth at full employment, 11, 159, 198,

213-5, 218, 232, 235, 237; *see also* Fiscal policy, Full employment, Inflation, Monetary policy, Tariffs, Wage determination
Economies of scale, 20-1, 27, 51-2, 88, 100, 120-1, 126, 133, 136, 139, 142, 147-8, 155-7
Economist The, 182n
Education: and training, general standard of, 44, 56, 61-5, 97, 103, 121, 129, 137, 206; expenditure on, 51, 62-5, 101, 103, 163, 166, 172, 204-5, 215-9 *pass.*, 236; full-time students, 62-4; human capital, 64-5, 96; school-leaving age, 44, 61-2; *see also* Labour force
Edwards, H. R., 132n
Emery, R. F., 81n, 83
Exports: and economic fluctuations, 20-4, 77-8, 155, 228; composition, 70-8; contribution to growth, 6-7, 25, 78-84, 89-92, 236; dependence on, 6-7, 23, 78-81, 139; destination, 89-92; development of staples, 66-71, 82, 88-9, 92; government promotion, 94, 215, 235; manufactures, 70, 94, 141-2, 155-7, 215, 235; prices, 20-1, 23, 72, 77-8, 80-2, 94, 195, 229; staple theory, backward and forward linkages, 66-9, 80, 90; value and volume, 66-83 *pass.*, 91, 234
External: balance, 214, 218, 221; economies and diseconomies, 20-1, 147-8, 207

Fadden, A. W. (Sir Arthur), 174
Fertilizers, 69, 74, 86, 129
Firth, G. G., 237
Financial Review, The Australian, 156-7, 227n
Fiscal policy, 137, 172, 194, 197-8, 214, 220, 228, 232
Ford, G. W., 199, 231n
Forster, C., 157
France, 9, 32, 57, 76n, 90-1, 106n, 119-20, 153, 218n, 224, 230n, 233
Freeman, R. D., 215n
Full employment: degree of since 1945, 16-7, 23-7, 191-3, 218, 230; objective, 1, 11, 123, 149, 159, 192, 198, 213-5, 220-1, 226-7, 232; policy in other countries, 159, 214n, 221, 226-7; White Paper on, 214, 220

Galbraith, J. K., 213
G.A.T.T., 93-4

Germany, West, 9, 30, 32, 34, 42, 57, 62, 90-1, 118-20, 150, 153-4, 209, 224

Giblin, L. F., 21n, 22n, 173n, 220n

Gilbert, R. S., 152

G.N.P.: fluctuations, 12-6, 21-6, 116; growth, 3-5, 8-9, 12-35 *pass.*, 72, 78-84, 98-9, 201-4

Gold, 7, 39, 49, 67-72, 79-83 *pass*

Gorton, J. G., 113

Government expenditure: relative importance, 98, 173, 198, 216-9, 232; transfer payments, 217, 219-20; *see also* Investment

Government securities, 96, 115, 171, 180, 183-4

Greece, 30, 33, 62

Grant, J. McB., 95, 157, 179n, 198-9, 237

Hagger, A. J., 95

Hancock, K., 11, 191-4 *pass.*, 211, 223n

Harper, R. J. A., 211-2

Harris, C. P., 173n, 177-9, 182-3, 199

Heat, light, and power, 8, 58-9, 101, 132-6 *pass.*, 163, 206

Henderson, R. F., 211n

Hicks, J. R. (Sir John), 19n

Hire purchase, 178-80

Hirst, R. R., 182n, 199

Hocking, A., 95

Housing: expenditure on, 101, 103-4, 120-1, 162; finance, 179; home ownership, 8, 104, 205, 228; quality and quantity, 204-6, 211, 215

Hughes, Helen, 128n, 141n, 147n

Hunter, A., 121, 129n, 143n, 147n, 157

Immigration: and economic growth, 13, 26-9, 42-3, 49-54, 64-5, 89, 103, 129, 211; government policy towards, 26-7, 40-4, 160, 215; influence of trade cycle, 42, 50, 227; nationality, 6, 40-3; passage assistance, 42-3; 'pull' *v.* 'push', 26, 29, 42, 148; rate of, 14, 26-9, 39-44; *see also* Economic growth

Import: replacement, 29, 128, 143, 148, 154-5, 215; restrictions, 145, 150

Imports: and economic fluctuations, 18n, 154, 228; as proportion of G.N.P., 152, 154-5; dependence on, 10, 80, 139; economic classes, 143, 151-2; prices, 81, 82, 195, 228; proportion protected, 142

Income tax, uniform, 141, 161, 169, 172, 229

India, 33, 35, 52, 91, 224

Indonesia, 33, 35, 153, 224, 228

Inflation: and employment, Phillips curve, 222-7; cost, 26, 192-7, 222-3, 230-2; demand, 26, 161, 172, 192-4, 222-3, 230, 232; policy towards, 176-7, 180, 198, 214, 227-32; problem and effects of, 106, 169, 213, 220-32

Innovations: capital-intensive, 31, 60-1, 85, 88, 96-7, 132-3, 135, 228; role of, 2, 100, 137-8, 181

Internal: balance, 214, 218; economies, 20n, 147

International comparisons: consumption ratio, 118-21; education, 62-3, 118; growth rates, 12, 30-5, 118-21, 228; income distribution, 209, indicative planning, 233-4; investment ratio, 118-21; manufacturing industry, 125, 136; population growth, 32-3, 35, 119-21; rate of price inflation, 221-5 *pass.*, 228; size of government sector, 218n; technical progress, 31, 34; women in labour force, 57

Investment: and economic growth, 20 26-9, 34-5, 83-5, 88, 96-122, 143, 147-8, 208, 236; and technical progress, 27, 34, 60-1, 76, 83-9 *pass.*, 97, 100, 143, 215; as proportion of G.N.P., 25, 34, 79-81, 98-100, 118-21; composition of, 100-5; government (public), 21, 40, 69, 76, 98-103, 171, 218-9; instability, 21-2, 80-1; mechanization, 83-5, 96-7; private, 21, 88, 98-100, 103-5, 234; *see also* Capital accumulation, Savings

Iron ore, 25, 39, 71, 73, 90, 92, 140-1, 157

Isaac, J. E., 187-99 *pass.*, 227-8, 231n

Italy, 9, 30, 32, 62, 91, 106n, 119-20, 150, 153, 224

Japan, 9, 30, 32, 34, 57, 73, 90-4, 118-20, 128, 150, 153-4, 224

Johns, B. T., 117n, 121

Karmel, P. H., 11, 62n, 135n, 138n, 157, 213n

Keating, M., 123-4

Kelley, A. C., 65

Keynes, J. M. (Lord), 26, 200, 214

Kuwait, 31n

Labour force: contribution from immigration, 52, 54, 64-5, 129; industrial distribution, 57-61, 123-35; married females, 53, 57; mobility, 191;

participation rate, 54-7; quality, 61-5, 97, 129-30, 133; rate of growth, 14, 16-7, 25-6, 31, 52-7, 98-9, 117, 204; proportion of women in, 53, 56-7; size, 52-7, 96, 124, 218; *see also* Education, Full employment
Lewis, Essington, 140n
Lewis, W. A., 2n, 3n, 200
Linge, G. J. R., 139n
Living standards: distribution of income, 197, 207-10, 229; expectation of life, 205; general measures: real personal income and consumption, 2-3, 34n, 64-5, 90, 96, 103, 105, 108, 148, 201-4, 208, 215; hours of work, 207; level of employment, 207, 209; measurement, 3, 200-4, 208; needs, wants, 200-1, 207, 211; non-material elements, 2, 200, 207-8; policy objective, 1, 26, 29, 117, 129, 198, 200, 215, 218-9; specific measures, 204-7; *see also* Social services, Welfare
Low, A. R., 233n
Lydall, H. F., 132-3, 209, 236n, 237

McCarthy, J. W., 67n, 69n
McColl, G. D., 95
McEwen, J., 113n, 114
McLean, I. W., 116, 152
Maddison, A., 26n, 33
Malaysia, 30, 33, 91
Mallyon, J. S., 35
Manufacturing: concentration and competition, 37, 135-8, 141, 145; development, 7, 16, 22, 37, 57-61, 69, 88, 123-35, 141-3, 179; diversification, 128-9, 144, 147-50; employment, 57-61, 123-5; growth rates, 133-5, 146, 148; industrial classification, 57-61, 126-7; location, 126, 139-42; mergers, 138; overseas ownership and control, 112-3, 138, 145; protection, 22, 125-9 *pass.*, 133, 137, 142-51, 215; relative importance, 7-9, 37, 104, 123-5; technical progress, 132-5; *see also* Economic growth, Exports, Motor vehicles, Tariffs
Marshall, Alfred, 20n
Matthews, R. C. O., 35
Maxwell, J. A., 162n, 166n
Meats, 7, 10, 67-9, 75-7, 81, 87, 89-90
Menzies, R. G. (Sir Robert), 174-5, 234
Metals, non-ferrous, 25, 39, 69, 71, 90, 92, 113, 129, 132, 136-7, 157
Mexico, 33
Mill, J. S., 146
Minerals and mining: growth rates, 134; investment in, 103-4; overseas

ownership and control, 112-3; relative importance and exports, 7-10, 25, 39, 66-74, 89, 134, 182, 215, 234-5
Mishan, E. J., 11n, 200, 212
Miskelly, Judith, 158
Monetary policy, 173, 176, 179, 184, 194, 197-8, 214, 220-1, 228, 232
Motor vehicles: development, 60-1, 102, 128-31, 136, 141, 144, 179; exports, 155; number of, 102, 206-7; overseas ownership and control, 113; protection, 128, 142, 145, 151-4
Myrdal, K. G., 3n

Natural gas, 25, 182
Natural resources, discovery and exploitation of, 6-7, 10, 25, 52, 64, 66, 69, 83, 85, 89, 96, 101-3, 114-5, 138, 140, 181-2, 235
Netherlands, 9, 32, 118-21, 224, 230n
Nevile, J. W., 121, 132n
New Zealand, 32, 35; 90-1, 93, 119, 153, 185, 207, 209, 214n, 224, 233n
Norway, 9, 32, 118-20, 133n

Oil, 25, 70, 136, 172, 182, 217
Ottawa Agreement, 93, 144-5
Overseas borrowing: ownership and control of Australian businesses, 111-5, 182; private, 108-10, 117-8; public, 21-2, 108-10, 117-8, 171; servicing of overseas debt, 115-7, 157; *see also* Capital inflow
Overseas investment: direct, 109-12, 129, 145; portfolio and institutional, 109-13; rate of return on, 117

Pakistan, 33, 52
Pastoral industry, 10, 67-74, 77, 87, 157, 185; *see also* Wool
Paterson, Janet, 211n
Perkins, J. O. N., 95, 122, 157, 214n, 238
Philippines, 33, 35
Phillips, A. W., 222-7 *pass*
Poland, 209
Population: age distribution, 44, 49-51, 204; birth rates, 39-52; death rates, 39-41, 51, 205; distribution, 10, 37-9, 140-1; effects of economic development on growth of, 44-9, 52; expectation of life, 205; family size, 45, 47-8; fertility rates, 45-51; growth, 3, 5-6, 12-5, 26-52 *pass.*, 84, 117, 119, 121, 125, 204, 234; infant mortality rates, 205; marriage patterns, 47-51; masculinity, 39-40, 49; natural increase, 13, 39-42, 48, 51-2; optimum, 52; projected increase,

43-4; rural, 37-8, 45; sex-composition, 39-40, 49-50; slump in births in 1930s, 47-8, 51; urbanization, 37-8, 45; *see also* Immigration, Labour force.
Portus, J. H., 188n
Poverty, 186, 208, 211, 215; *see also* Living standards
Prest, W., 160n, 162n, 165-7, 172n, 198
Prices: consumer, 192, 195, 210n, 222-5, 227n, 230-1; primary products, 149; *see also* Exports, Imports, Inflation, Terms of trade, wheat, wool
Primary industry: employment, 57-61, 88, 103, 134, 148; exports, 6, 70, 77-8; growth, 83-4, 133-5; guaranteed prices, 144; importance, 7-9, 70, 103, 125; investment, 103-4; productivity, 88, 133-4, 148; technological progress, 83-9
Productivity: definition and measurement, 4, 132-5, 196-7; importance of increase in, 29, 64, 196-7, 215; level 85, 96, 118, 120; rate of increase, 14, 26, 86-7, 97, 121, 130, 132-5, 137, 227-8, 230-1
Profits, 27-8, 76, 117-8, 137, 148, 195, 228, 230-1; *see also* Wages: shares of wages and profits
Public debt: burden, 168-71, 217-20 *pass.*, 228; Commonwealth, State, 168-71; overseas, 115, 171

Railways, 69, 100-2, 141, 163
Rattigan, G. A., 150n
Reitsma, A. J., 146n
Research and development, 85-7, 97-8, 137-8
Reserve Bank, 114, 162, 175-84 *pass.*, 199, 220-1; *see also* Banking
Resource allocation: 87-9, 103, 105, 135, 138, 145, 150, 172, 205, 218, 229, 237
Restrictive practices, 137
Robertson, D. H. (Sir Dennis), 19n
Rose, P. J., 182-4

Samuelson, P. A., 11, 35, 65, 95, 157, 198-9, 212, 223n, 227n, 238
Savings: domestic, 12, 26-8, 105-7, 113, 171, 208, 215; overseas, 12, 26-9, 106-11, 117; *see also* Capital inflow, Investment, Taxation
Schedvin, C. B., 21n
Shaw, A. G. L., 11
Sheridan, Kyoko, 136
Ship-building, 130, 141, 217

Sinclair, W. A., 126n
Singapore, 91
Smith, Adam, 1-2
Smithies, A., 213n
Snape, R. H., 73, 82n, 89n, 92n, 95, 110-1, 117n, 122, 145n, 154, 214n, 221n, 238
Social security, 207-8, 215, 218, 227, 237
Social services, 51, 55-6, 160-2, 172, 210-1, 215, 230n
Solow, R. M., 133n, 227n
South Africa, 30, 33
Spencer, Geraldine, 65
Steel industry: development, 69, 128-31 *pass.*, 136-7, 140, 144; exports, 155; location, 140-1; protection, 147n
Stubbs, P., 137n, 145n, 158
Sugar, 66, 89-90, 94, 136
Sweden, 9, 32, 34, 119-20, 209, 218n, 224, 230n, 233
Switzerland, 32, 34, 118-21

Tariffs: and resource allocation, 145, 149-51, 160; benchmark for tariff revision, 149-51; Brigden Committee, 148; British Preferential, 144-5, 154; burden and cost structure, 133, 144-6, 149; case for protection, 146-51; dependence on, 142-3; 'Economic and efficient', 149-50; Greene tariff, 143, 147n; infant industries, 145-8; Japanese Trade Treaty, 145, 154; Lyne tariff, 143; primage, 144; reductions under G.A.T.T., 92-4; Scullin tariff, 144-5; stages in development of, 143-6, 149-51; *see also* Manufacturing; protection
Taxation: depreciation provision, 106, 137; direct and indirect, 126, 160, 195, 210, 220; finance for public works, 171, 220; investment concessions, 137; proportion of G.N.P., 210; *see also* Income tax, Tariffs
Technical progress: and economic growth, 3, 25-34 *pass.*, 44, 52, 60-1, 64-6, 83-9, 97, 100, 108, 132-5, 140, 143, 147, 155-7, 215; measurement, 132-5; *see also* Investment
Terms of trade, 20, 81-2, 89, 117, 204
Tertiary industries: employment, 57-61, 134-5, importance, 7-9, 103-5, 125; productivity, 97, 133-5, 148
Textiles, 60-1, 126-30, 134, 142
Trade, international agreements, 92-4, 144-5, 154
Trade Practices Act, 137, 141

Transport and communications, 58, 61, 69, 100-3, 118, 130-1, 141, 163, 166, 172-3, 205, 216

Trade cycle: before 1914, 17-21, 80; characteristics and duration, 12-24, 214, 223, 229, 236; in 1920s and 1930s, 17-23, 123-4, 203; meaning, 12-3, since 1945, 19, 23-4, 124, 149, 201-3, 221, 229, 237; *see also* Economic depressions, Economic growth, Exports

Trade unions, 17, 62, 185, 188, 190, 235

Underdeveloped countries, 1, 2, 31n, 52, 110, 222, 224

Unemployment: benefit payments, 162n, 211; extent, 16-7, 26, 130, 191-2, 207, 209, 214, 227; in depression of 1930s, 17, 22, 31, 144

U.K., 9-10, 18n, 29-32 *pass.*, 40-3 *pass.*, 57, 62, 73, 77, 90-3, 106n, 110, 115n, 119, 125, 128-9, 136, 150, 153-4, 178, 185, 190, 209, 214n, 218n, 224, 227, 230n, 233

U.S.A., 9, 29-35, 57, 62, 76-7, 90-1, 94, 110, 119, 121, 125, 128-9, 133n, 136, 150, 153-4, 160n, 178, 190, 207, 209, 214n, 218n, 224, 227, 230n

U.S.S.R., 32, 62

Vernon Report, 1-4 *pass.*, 9-12 *pass.*, 17, 20n, 30n, 35, 45, 62n, 65, 89n, 95, 98n, 101, 110-22 *pass.*, 130-3 *pass.*, 137-49, 154, 158, 188-213, *pass.*, 222n, 227n, 232-8 *pass*

Wages: and conditions of employment, 185-8 *pass.*, 207-8; award rates, 188, 192-3, 231-2; basic wage, 188-9, 191, 232; drift, 193, 231; earnings, 192, 196, 230-1; Harvester Standard, 189, 194, Justice Higgins, 189, 194; margins, 189, 191, 231; minimum wage, 189, 231-2; over-awards, 189, 193, 231-2; secondary wage, 189, 191, 232; shares of wages and profits, 195-6, 230; total wage, 189, 191, 232

Wage determination: Arbitration Commission: functions, 186-7, 231, influence, 188, 232, principles for, 190-7, 232; Arbitration Court, 186, 207; balance of payments, 196-7, 230; capacity to pay, 191-2, 195-7, 232; comparative wage justice and egalitarianism, 190-1, 210; cost of living, 194-5; gearing with productivity, 193, 196-7, 226, 228, 230-2; incomes policy, 196, 198, 230-2; Industrial Court, 186-7; inflation and unemployment, 222-7; legislation, 185-7; national cases and policy, 187-8, 190, 194, 231-2; needs, 191, 231n; price changes, 194-7, 230-2; prices plus productivity, 194; role of government, 160, 187, 232; State tribunals, 185-6, 231n; sweating, 185-6; work-value, 190-1; *see also* Inflation

Wallace, R. H., 11, 182n, 199, 223n

War and defence expenditure, 15-6, 23, 161, 216-9 *pass*

Water supply, 10, 103, 166

Watkins, M. H., 66n

Weather, 4, 10, 23-4, 34, 74, 78, 80, 223, 236; *see also* Droughts

Welfare, 11, 27, 138, 200-1, 216, 220, 231, 236

Westerman, W. A. (Sir Alan), 157n

Wheat: area under, 74-6; exports, 67-8, 74-7, 81, 89n, 92; marketing, 76, 94, 172; prices, 74-6; production, 15, 74-7, 88-9; subsidies, 217; yield, 74-6, 86

Wheelwright, E. L., 158

Wilson, R. (Sir Roland), 15, 73n, 79

Wool: exports, 67, 75, 81, 89-90; prices, 73, 80-1, 89n; production, 20, 77; relative importance of exports, 7, 67-8, 71-4, 77-8; synthetics, 73, 92; yield, 86